GREAT RECIPES COLLECTION

Grilling
recipes

GAS OR CHARCOAL

BARNES
& NOBLE

Pictured on front cover:
BLT Steak (*see recipe, page 30*)

Pictured on back cover:
Sweet and Sour Pork Kabobs (*see recipe, page 191*)
Grilled Steak with Martini Twist (*see recipe, page 17*)
Terrific Teriyaki Burgers (*see recipe, page 148*)

Previously published as
Grand Avenue Books *Great Recipes Collection Grilling Gas or Charcoal*

Copyright 2003, 2005 by Meredith Corporation, Des Moines, Iowa. First Edition.

This edition published for Barnes & Noble, Inc., by Meredith Books

Printed in China

ISBN: 0-7607-6959-1

grilling made easy

Brimming with delectable recipes and practical tips, <u>Great Recipes Collection: Grilling</u> brings you the best in grilled meat, poultry, and fish as well as ideas for smoke cooking and sides.

If you find it hard to resist the tantalizing aroma of something savory sizzling on the grill, you'll be delighted with *Great Recipes Collection: Grilling*. This captivating cookbook brings you more than 250 easy-to-use recipes for grilling your favorite foods. Whether it's a quick family supper or a block party barbecue you have in mind, you'll find recipes to fit the occasion. Choose from main dishes that range from steaks, chops, and ribs to poultry and fish and seafood. In addition, there are a bevy of burgers, sandwiches, and pizzas as well as more than 30 kabob ideas.

For those times when you want to grill a favorite cut of meat, poultry, or fish, *Great Recipes Collection: Grilling* has grilling charts at the back of the book. Simply follow these general timings to grill your meal to perfection. What's more, if you enjoy the smoky taste of foods grilled over wood, there's a whole chapter devoted to smoke cooking to tempt you. And to complete your cookout meals, try one of the grilled side dishes or desserts.

In addition to fabulous recipes, you'll find a wealth of advice in *Great Recipes Collection: Grilling*. To help make grilling easy, there's a basics section for quick reference, as well as tips and pointers sprinkled throughout.

So don't wait any longer. Indulge that hankering for a hot-off-the-grill meal. In *Great Recipes Collection: Grilling,* you're sure to discover a mouthwatering recipe that hits the spot.

Grilled Jerk Chicken, page 95

contents

grilling basics

You don't have to be a cookout expert to turn out juicy, tender foods when you fire up the grill. All you need are a few grilling fundamentals to help keep you on track. The basics on the next few pages will explain what you should know.

Lighting the Fire

To build a charcoal fire, spread a single layer of briquettes on the grill's bottom grate over an area that is about 3 inches larger than the food you'll be grilling. If it is humid or windy, add a few more briquettes (too many briquettes are better than not enough). Arrange the briquettes in a mound or put them in a chimney starter. Ignite the briquettes, leaving the grill lid off. Allow the briquettes to heat about 20 minutes or until they have a red glow. Spread the coals in a single layer, and let them burn about 10 minutes more or until they look ash gray during the day or glow red at night. At this point, you're ready to start grilling.

There are several products available to help start a charcoal fire. Instant-lighting briquettes are saturated with a petroleum product that lights easily with a match. In addition there are electric starters, fire-starter gels, and paraffin fire starters to make the job easier. (Another popular option—liquid lighter fluid—has been outlawed in some areas because it emits pollutants.) Remember to wait about a minute after adding a gel or paraffin starter before lighting the coals. Never use gasoline or kerosene as a fire starter.

For gas or electric grills, check your owner's manual for the manufacturer's directions for lighting and preheating the grill.

Direct Versus Indirect Grilling

You can grill foods two ways—directly and indirectly. The method you use will depend on the type of food you want to cook. With the direct grilling technique, the foods are placed directly over the heat source and the fire browns the outside of the food, forming a thin caramelized layer. The food cooks on the inside by heat conducted from the outside. Items grilled directly have a mild smoky flavor because they are on the fire only a short time. Direct grilling works best for small items that are thin and tender. Steaks, thin chops, burgers, kabobs, cooked link sausage, chicken pieces, and fish fillets or steaks are all good candidates.

Most grills can be used for direct cooking, including braziers (a firebox on legs) and hibachis. You can direct grill foods either covered or uncovered. If you choose to cook with the grill cover closed, the grill works like an oven, supplying both direct heat and reflecting the heat off the lid. Closing the lid decreases the supply of oxygen to the coals, lowering the fire's temperature. As a result, foods cook more slowly and have a fuller smoky flavor than foods grilled on an open fire.

To prepare a charcoal grill for direct grilling, light the coals as explained on the opposite page. Using long-handled tongs, arrange the glowing coals in the grill box under the grill rack where the food will cook. There should be enough coals to extend about 3 inches beyond the edge of the food.

For a gas or electric grill, preheat the grill and adjust the heat setting according to the manufacturer's directions.

Indirect grilling involves cooking in a covered grill with the foods positioned adjacent to the heat source rather than directly over it. Indirect grilling cooks foods slowly, resulting in tender foods with a rich smoky flavor. The advantage of indirect grilling is that it allows you to cook foods evenly without turning. This technique is recommended for large or fatty cuts of meat, such as brisket, ribs, and roasts, because with indirect grilling they cook through without burning. It's also ideal for whole birds and whole fish.

A guideline for indirect grilling is don't peek. Every time you lift the cover, heat escapes, adding as much as 15 minutes to the grilling time. For the fastest cooking time, grill food the minimum time specified in a recipe, and then check for doneness.

To grill indirectly on a charcoal grill, light the coals as explained on the opposite page. With long-handled tongs, arrange the glowing coals around the edge of the grill box. After the coals are ash gray and up to temperature, position a drip pan on the bottom grate centered beneath where the food will be placed. The pan will capture drippings from the food and cut down on flare-ups. Besides helping to control flare-ups, a drip pan also can hold liquids, such as juice, beer, or wine, which will form steam and help flavor foods during cooking.

For a gas or electric grill, light and preheat the grill according to the manufacturer's directions. Adjust for indirect cooking over medium or medium-high heat. Check your owner's manual for advice on the use of a drip pan.

Keeping the Coals Hot

Successful grilling depends on maintaining the right temperature consistently throughout the recommended cooking time. For a gas or electric grill, you can control the heat of your grill by the turn of a dial. But with a charcoal grill, controlling the temperature requires a little adjusting. First, you'll need to regulate the airflow in the cooking chamber. Do this by opening or closing the vents in the grill bottom or sides. Closing the vents cuts off airflow and lowers the heat. Opening them increases the heat by promoting airflow. Shut the vents in the grill cover only when you want the fire to die out.

Fire temperature also depends on the readiness and spacing of the briquettes. Briquettes are at cooking temperature about 30 minutes after lighting and when they are ash gray. To gauge the temperature of the coals, hold your hand over the coals (see the tip box on page 9). If the fire is too hot, lower the temperature by positioning the coals in a thin single layer and letting them burn 5 to 10 minutes longer. You also may want to close the air vents halfway. If the fire is too slow, add additional briquettes and don't let them burn down as long before adding more briquettes. To increase the heat from already burning coals, remove excess ash by tapping them with long-handled tongs. You also may want to position the coals closer together and open the vents wider.

If the food you're grilling requires long cooking, you'll need to replenish the coals. Using long-handled tongs, carefully add 8 to 10 fresh briquettes every 30 to 45 minutes. The number of briquettes needed depends on the weather. Strong winds and cold temperatures mean you'll need more coals. If it's difficult to change the temperature of the coals, adjust the heat by changing the level of the grill rack. For more heat, lower the rack; to reduce the heat, raise it.

Grilling Safety

Although grilling is fun, it involves fire, which means it's important to keep an eye out for potential problems. These safety hints will help ensure that your backyard cookouts are safe ones.

- Before you start, check to see that all grill parts are firmly in place and that the grill is level and stable. For gas grills make sure the connectors, regulators, and hoses are in good condition and installed according to the manufacturer's directions. Never move a hot grill.
- Grill in a well-ventilated, open area. Don't grill in a garage or other enclosed area, on a wooden deck, or within 10 feet of combustible materials.
- Make sure the fire starter you use is certified for outdoor grills. Never use gasoline, kerosene, or other flammable nonfood-safe chemicals. Never use any starter on hot—or even warm—coals.
- The best clothing for grilling includes long pants made from lightweight material and a long apron if you have one. (Shorts leave more skin exposed to sparks and splatters.) Avoid flowing or loose clothing.
- Make sure you have heavy-duty, long-handled grill tools, including a fork, a spatula, and tongs. Heavy, fireproof mitts are essential for protecting your hands and forearms.
- Watch the grill continuously while it's in use. Never leave it unattended. Keep children and pets away.
- Be sure the grill is completely cool before putting it away or covering it. The coals and ashes should be completely cool. Never place hot or warm coals from the grill into a trash can. They can easily cause a fire.
- Unplug an electric starter immediately after you use it. Set it on a fireproof surface to cool.
- Position a spray bottle of water nearby to help put out minor flare-ups and keep a box of baking soda handy for grease flare-ups. Also having a fire extinguisher in good working order is a valuable safeguard.

Controlling Flare-Ups

During grilling, small flare-ups caused by dripping fat and meat juices sometimes occur. There are several things you can do to control these small fires: raise the grill rack, cover the grill, or space the coals farther apart. In extreme cases, remove the food from the grill and spritz the fire with water. Once the flame subsides, return the food to the grill rack and continue grilling.

Here's how to avoid flare-ups with gas grills. After each use, cover the grill and turn the heat setting to high for 10 to 15 minutes. Besides cleaning the grill, this procedure also will burn off any residue that's on the lava rock or ceramic briquettes. When the grill rack has cooled, remove baked-on food from the rack with a brass-bristle brush.

Check Your Gas Grill

Before using a gas grill, make sure it's in good working order. This is especially important if it hasn't been used for a while or if you're attaching a new gas cylinder. To check out the grill:

- Review the safety precautions in your owner's manual for the specifics for your unit.
- Test for gas leaks by spraying the joints and fittings with soapy water. If you detect tiny bubbles, there may be a leak. Don't light the grill until you repair the leak.
- See that the hoses are in good condition. Look for cracks, brittle areas, leaks, and blockages. (Spiders can sometimes block hoses.) Make sure there are no sharp bends in the hoses and that they are far away from heat or hot surfaces. You may need to install a shield to protect the hoses from heat.
- Make it a regular practice to clean the tubes that lead to the burners (venturi tubes), following the manufacturer's instructions.
- Keep in mind that if your grill was manufactured some time ago, it may not have several safety features found on current models. One of the most important features is a shut-off mechanism that's used when a hose ruptures or leaks.
- Always follow the safety precautions noted on your gas cylinder. These cylinders usually hold 20 pounds of propane that can leak or explode if the cylinder isn't handled correctly.

Is It Hot Yet?

Knowing when your grill is the right temperature is the secret to cookout success. A grill thermometer will give you a reliable estimate of a fire's temperature, but it can be used only with a covered grill. To determine a fire's temperature without a thermometer, simply count how long you can hold your hand above the heat at cooking level.

Begin by counting "one thousand one," "one thousand two," etc. If you can hold your hand comfortably above the heat for 2 seconds, the fire is hot (400° to 450°). Charcoal coals will be barely covered with gray ash at this stage. Four seconds indicates a medium fire (350° to 375°). Charcoal coals will glow and be covered with a layer of gray ash. A low fire (300° to 350°) equates to 5 seconds. Charcoal coals will have a thick layer of gray ash.

Meats

When it's time for a backyard cookout, rely on
one of these tender beef, veal, pork, or
lamb favorites as your mealtime headliner.
You'll find sizzling ideas for roasts, steaks,
ribs, chops, and more.

Sweet Pepper Steak, page 23

Grilled Beef Tenderloin With Mediterranean Relish

Kalamata olives and balsamic vinegar give this tomato relish a delightful Mediterranean accent.

Prep: 25 minutes **Grill:** 1 hour **Stand:** 15 minutes **Makes:** 10 servings

2 teaspoons dried oregano, crushed

2 teaspoons cracked black pepper

1½ teaspoons finely shredded lemon peel

3 cloves garlic, minced

1 3- to 4-pound center-cut beef tenderloin

2 Japanese eggplants, halved lengthwise

2 red and/or yellow sweet peppers, halved lengthwise and seeded

1 sweet onion (such as Walla Walla or Vidalia), cut into ½-inch-thick slices

2 tablespoons olive oil

2 plum tomatoes, chopped

2 tablespoons chopped, pitted kalamata olives

2 tablespoons snipped fresh basil

1 tablespoon balsamic vinegar

¼ to ½ teaspoon salt

⅛ teaspoon ground black pepper

1. In a small bowl combine oregano, cracked pepper, lemon peel, and 2 cloves of the garlic. Rub the mixture onto all sides of the meat.

2. In a grill with a cover arrange hot coals around a drip pan. Test for medium-hot heat above the pan. Place tenderloin on grill rack over pan. Brush eggplants, sweet peppers, and onion slices with oil. Arrange vegetables on edges of grill rack directly over coals. Cover; grill for 10 to 12 minutes or until vegetables are tender, turning once. Remove vegetables from grill; set aside. Cover grill and continue grilling for 50 to 65 minutes or until medium-rare doneness (135°), turning once halfway through grilling. Cover; let stand for 15 minutes before slicing (the temperature of the beef will rise 10° during standing).

3. Meanwhile, for relish, coarsely chop grilled vegetables. In a medium bowl combine chopped vegetables, the remaining garlic, tomatoes, olives, basil, vinegar, salt, and ground pepper. Serve with tenderloin.

Nutrition Facts per serving: 240 calories, 12 g total fat, 77 mg cholesterol, 133 mg sodium, 6 g carbohydrate, 27 g protein.

Grilled Filet Mignon with Blackened Tomato and Oregano Sauce

The tomatoes are charred for flavor in the broiler and then simmered into a sauce that's seasoned with oregano, sweet peppers, and a pasilla pepper.

Prep: 1 hour **Grill:** 11 minutes **Makes:** 6 servings

1. For the sauce, place the tomatoes on the unheated rack of a broiler pan. Broil 3 to 4 inches from heat for 12 to 14 minutes or until tomato skins are blistered and begin to blacken, turning occasionally. Transfer tomatoes to a bowl. Cool. Coarsely chop unpeeled tomatoes. Set aside.

2. In a medium saucepan cook onion in 2 tablespoons hot butter over medium heat about 5 minutes or until lightly browned. Add the sweet pepper and garlic. Cook about 4 minutes more or until sweet pepper is tender. Stir in the vinegar and wine. Bring to boiling, scraping up any browned bits; reduce heat. Simmer, uncovered, about 5 minutes or until liquid is reduced by half. Stir in tomatoes, broth, and pasilla pepper. Bring to boiling; reduce heat. Simmer, uncovered, about 15 minutes or until reduced to 2⅔ cups. Pour half of the mixture into a blender container or food processor bowl. Cover and blend or process until nearly smooth. Pour into a bowl. Repeat with remaining mixture. Stir in oregano and thyme. Set aside.

3. Season steaks with salt and black pepper. Grill steaks on the rack of an uncovered grill directly over medium coals to desired doneness, turning once halfway through grilling. [Allow 11 to 15 minutes for medium-rare (145°) or 14 to 18 minutes for medium doneness (160°).] Before serving, reheat sauce until bubbly. Remove from heat. Whisk in 2 tablespoons butter. Season to taste with salt and black pepper. Serve with the steaks.

Nutrition Facts per serving: 423 calories, 23 g total fat, 144 mg cholesterol, 410 mg sodium, 6 g carbohydrate, 43˙ g protein.

5 plum tomatoes
  (about 1 pound)
½ of a medium onion,
  finely chopped
2 tablespoons butter
½ of a medium yellow sweet
  pepper, chopped
1 large clove garlic, minced
¼ cup red wine vinegar
¼ cup dry white wine
1 cup chicken broth
1 dried pasilla pepper,
  finely snipped
2 tablespoons snipped
  fresh oregano
1 tablespoon snipped
  fresh thyme
6 7-ounce beef tenderloin
  steaks, cut 1 inch thick
  Salt
  Ground black pepper
2 tablespoons butter

Tri-Tip with Jambalaya Rice

Tri-tip beef roasts are popular on the West coast. If you can't find one in your area, substitute the beef sirloin steak instead.

Prep: 25 minutes **Grill:** 35 minutes **Stand:** 10 minutes **Makes:** 6 servings

¼ cup soy sauce

2 tablespoons finely chopped onion

2 tablespoons granulated sugar

2 tablespoons brown sugar

2 tablespoons lemon juice

1 tablespoon vinegar

½ teaspoon chili powder

1 1½- to 2-pound boneless beef bottom sirloin roast (tri-tip) or boneless beef sirloin steak, cut 1½ to 2 inches thick

4 ounces bulk hot Italian sausage

2 stalks celery, sliced

1 small red sweet pepper, chopped

1 small yellow sweet pepper, chopped

⅓ cup chopped onion

1 clove garlic, minced

¾ cup long grain rice

¼ teaspoon ground red pepper

¼ teaspoon paprika

1 10½-ounce can condensed cream of mushroom or cream of chicken soup

1¼ cups water

1. For brush-on, in a small bowl stir together soy sauce, the 2 tablespoons onion, the granulated sugar, brown sugar, lemon juice, vinegar, and chili powder; set aside.

2. In a grill with a cover arrange medium-hot coals around a drip pan. Test for medium heat above pan. Place roast or steak on grill rack over pan. Cover and grill to desired doneness, turning once halfway through grilling and brushing often with soy sauce mixture during last 10 minutes of grilling. [Allow 35 to 40 minutes for medium-rare (140°) or 40 to 45 minutes for medium doneness (155°).] Remove roast or steak from grill. Cover with foil and let stand 10 minutes before slicing (the temperature of the beef will rise 5° during standing).

3. Meanwhile, in large saucepan cook Italian sausage until browned. Add celery, sweet peppers, the ⅓ cup onion, and the garlic. Cook and stir for 5 minutes. Add uncooked rice, ground red pepper, and paprika; cook and stir for 2 minutes more. Add soup and the water. Bring just to boiling; reduce heat. Cover and simmer for 15 to 20 minutes or until rice is tender, stirring occasionally. To serve, slice roast or steak. Serve rice mixture with meat.

Nutrition Facts per serving: 387 calories, 14 g total fat, 80 mg cholesterol, 1,204 mg sodium, 34 g carbohydrate, 30 g protein.

Herbed Beef Tenderloin

The slow heat of indirect grilling allows this beef tenderloin roast, and other roasts, to cook to juicy perfection.

Prep: 10 minutes **Grill:** 45 minutes **Stand:** 15 minutes **Makes:** 8 servings

1. In small bowl stir together parsley, the 2 tablespoons mustard, the rosemary, thyme, garlic, oil, and the ½ teaspoon pepper. Rub over top and sides of roast.

2. In a grill with a cover arrange hot coals around a drip pan. Test for medium-hot heat above pan. Place tenderloin roast on grill rack over pan. Insert an oven-going meat thermometer into center of roast. Cover and grill about 45 minutes or until meat thermometer registers 135°.

3. Cover roast with foil; let stand for 15 minutes before slicing (the temperature of the roast will rise 10° during standing).

4. Meanwhile, stir together sour cream and the 2 teaspoons mustard. Thinly slice meat. Serve meat with sour cream mixture. If desired, sprinkle with additional black pepper.

Nutrition Facts per serving: 189 calories, 9 g total fat, 66 mg cholesterol, 193 mg sodium, 3 g carbohydrate, 23 g protein.

¼ cup finely snipped
   fresh parsley
2 tablespoons Dijon-style
   mustard
1 tablespoon snipped
   fresh rosemary
2 teaspoons snipped
   fresh thyme
2 cloves garlic, minced
1 teaspoon olive oil or
   cooking oil
½ teaspoon coarsely ground
   black pepper
1 2-pound beef tenderloin roast
½ cup light dairy sour cream
2 teaspoons Dijon-style
   mustard
   Coarsely ground black pepper
   (optional)

Peppercorn Beef

Fresh garlic chives give the marinade a pleasant herb flavor. If you can't find them at a farmer's market or grocery store, use regular chives plus minced garlic.

Prep: 15 minutes **Marinate:** 8 to 12 hours **Grill:** 13 minutes **Makes:** 4 servings

4 beef tenderloin steaks
   (about 1½ pounds total)
   or 1 to 1½ pounds
   boneless beef top loin
   steak, cut 1¼ inches thick
⅓ cup bottled oil and vinegar
   salad dressing
⅓ cup dry red wine
¼ cup snipped fresh garlic
   chives or ¼ cup snipped
   fresh chives plus
   1 teaspoon bottled
   minced garlic
1 teaspoon cracked multicolor
   or black peppercorns

1. Place steaks in a heavy, large self-sealing plastic bag set in a shallow bowl. For marinade, in a small bowl combine salad dressing, dry red wine, garlic chives or chives and garlic, and peppercorns. Pour marinade over steaks. Seal bag; turn to coat steaks. Marinate in the refrigerator for at least 8 hours or up to 12 hours, turning bag occasionally.

2. Drain steaks, reserving marinade. Grill steaks on the rack of an uncovered grill directly over medium coals to desired doneness, turning once halfway through grilling and brushing once with reserved marinade after 8 minutes of grilling. [Allow 13 to 18 minutes for medium-rare (145°) or 16 to 22 minutes for medium doneness (160°).] Discard any remaining marinade. If using top loin steak, cut steak into 4 serving-size pieces.

Nutrition Facts per serving: 287 calories, 16 g total fat, 96 mg cholesterol, 218 mg sodium, 1 g carbohydrate, 32 g protein.

Grilled Steak with Martini Twist

This classy steak boasts many of the elements of a martini—gin, olives, and even a lemon twist.

Prep: 10 minutes **Marinate:** 30 minutes **Grill:** 16 minutes **Makes:** 4 servings

1. Place steaks in a heavy, large self-sealing plastic bag set in a shallow bowl. For marinade, stir together the green onions, gin, oil, and shredded lemon peel. Pour marinade over steaks. Seal bag; turn to coat steaks. Marinate steaks in the refrigerator for 30 minutes. Drain steaks, discarding marinade.

2. Press the crushed peppercorns onto both sides of each steak. In a grill with a cover arrange medium-hot coals around a drip pan. Test for medium heat above pan. Place steaks on the grill rack over pan. Cover and grill to desired doneness, turning once halfway through grilling. [Allow 16 to 20 minutes for medium-rare (145°) or 20 to 24 minutes for medium doneness (160°).] Season to taste with salt. Garnish with sliced olives and lemon peel strips.

Nutrition Facts per serving: 299 calories, 9 g total fat, 107 mg cholesterol, 216 mg sodium, 0 g carbohydrate, 49 g protein.

4 boneless beef top loin
  steaks, cut 1 inch thick
  (about 2 pounds total)
¼ cup finely chopped
  green onions
¼ cup gin
1 tablespoon olive oil
1 teaspoon finely shredded
  lemon peel
1 teaspoon multicolor
  peppercorns, crushed
  Salt
2 tablespoons sliced pimiento-
  stuffed green olives
  Lemon peel strips

Argentinean-Style Steak

Chimichurri—a basting sauce seasoned with parsley and oregano—is a specialty of Argentine steak houses. It's used here on T-bone steaks.

Prep: 30 minutes **Grill:** 16 minutes **Makes:** 4 servings

2 **beef T-bone or porterhouse steaks, cut 1 inch thick**
3 **tablespoons olive oil**
2 **tablespoons snipped fresh flat-leaf parsley**
2 **tablespoons snipped fresh oregano or 1 teaspoon dried oregano, crushed**
2 **or 3 cloves garlic, minced**
¼ **teaspoon salt**
¼ **teaspoon ground red pepper**

1. In a grill with a cover arrange medium-hot coals around a drip pan. Test for medium heat above pan. Place steaks on grill rack directly over pan. Cover and grill steaks to desired doneness, turning once halfway through grilling. [Allow 16 to 20 minutes for medium-rare (145°) or 20 to 24 minutes for medium doneness (160°).]

2. Meanwhile, for the sauce, stir together oil, parsley, oregano, garlic, salt, and red pepper. Spoon the sauce over the steaks during the last 2 minutes of grilling.

Nutrition Facts per serving: 332 calories, 20 g total fat, 75 mg cholesterol, 227 mg sodium, 1 g carbohydrate, 35 g protein.

Steaks with Piquant Sauce

Spanish-style rice makes a colorful side dish for this first-rate steak. Just stir your favorite chunky salsa into hot cooked rice and heat through.

Prep: 15 minutes **Marinate:** 4 to 24 hours **Grill:** 11 minutes **Makes:** 4 servings

1. Cut steaks into 4 serving-size pieces. Place in a heavy, large self-sealing plastic bag set in a shallow bowl. For marinade, in a small bowl stir together the vinegar, soy sauce, and garlic. Pour marinade over steaks. Seal bag; turn to coat steaks. Marinate in the refrigerator for at least 4 hours or up to 24 hours, turning bag occasionally.

2. Drain steaks, discarding marinade. Coat unheated grill rack with nonstick cooking spray. Place steaks on rack. Grill directly over medium coals to desired doneness, turning once halfway through grilling. [Allow 11 to 15 minutes for medium-rare (145°) or 14 to 18 minutes for medium doneness (160°).] Keep warm while preparing sauce.

3. For sauce, in a small saucepan stir together chili sauce, spreadable fruit, orange or apple juice, and mustard. Cook and stir over low heat until heated through and spreadable fruit is melted. Serve over steaks.

Nutrition Facts per serving: **195 calories, 7 g total fat, 64 mg cholesterol, 312 mg sodium, 10 g carbohydrate, 22 g protein.**

2 beef top loin steaks,
  cut 1 inch thick
  (about 1 pound total)
⅓ cup red wine vinegar
2 tablespoons reduced-sodium
  soy sauce
2 cloves garlic, minced
  Nonstick cooking spray
3 tablespoons bottled
  chili sauce
2 tablespoons seedless
  raspberry spreadable fruit
1 tablespoon orange juice
  or apple juice
1½ teaspoons brown mustard
  or spicy brown mustard

Sage-Brushed Cowboy Steak

Using a homemade sage "brush" to slather on the butter mixture adds more fresh sage flavor to the steak.

Prep: 40 minutes **Grill:** 11 minutes **Makes:** 4 servings

3 cups fresh cut corn kernels

1 tablespoon olive oil

¼ teaspoon salt

2 beef T-bone or porterhouse steaks, cut 1 inch thick

Salt (optional)

Ground black pepper (optional)

1 small red or yellow sweet pepper, halved and seeded

¼ cup snipped fresh sage

2 tablespoons butter or margarine, melted

3 or 4 large fresh sage leaves (optional)

⅓ cup crumbled queso fresco or farmer's cheese

1. In a large skillet cook corn in hot oil over medium-high heat about 10 minutes or until corn is tender and golden brown, stirring often. Stir in the ¼ teaspoon salt. Remove from heat. Cover; keep warm.

2. If desired, sprinkle steaks with salt and black pepper. Grill steaks and sweet pepper halves on the rack of an uncovered grill directly over medium coals until steak is desired doneness and sweet peppers are tender, turning once halfway through grilling. [For steaks, allow 11 to 14 minutes for medium-rare (145°) or 13 to 16 minutes for medium doneness (160°). For sweet peppers, allow 8 to 10 minutes; remove when tender.]

3. Meanwhile, stir 2 tablespoons of the snipped fresh sage into the melted butter. If desired, make a sage "brush" by tying the fresh sage leaves together at the base of the leaves; tie again closer to the leaves to make a sturdier brush. After turning steaks, brush with butter mixture using sage brush (or use a pastry brush).

4. Chop grilled sweet peppers. Stir chopped sweet pepper and remaining 2 tablespoons snipped sage into corn. Just before serving, sprinkle corn mixture with crumbled cheese. Serve corn mixture with steaks.

Nutrition Facts per serving: **483 calories, 22 g total fat, 111 mg cholesterol, 317 mg sodium, 29 g carbohydrate, 44 g protein.**

Grilled Steaks with Gorgonzola Butter

To quick-chill the butter mixture, put it in the freezer for about 30 minutes or until firm.

Prep: 15 minutes **Grill:** 11 minutes **Makes:** 8 servings

1. For butter, stir together Gorgonzola cheese or blue cheese, cream cheese, butter, and nuts. Shape into 1-inch-diameter log. Wrap in plastic wrap; refrigerate until firm.

2. Grill steaks on the rack of an uncovered grill directly over medium coals to desired doneness, turning once halfway through grilling. [Allow 11 to 15 minutes for medium-rare (145°) or 14 to 18 minutes for medium doneness (160°).]

3. If desired, season grilled steaks with salt. To serve, cut grilled steaks into 8 serving-size pieces and cut butter mixture into 8 slices. Place 1 slice of the butter mixture on each serving of steak; serve immediately.

Nutrition Facts per serving: 268 calories, 19 g total fat, 82 mg cholesterol, 110 mg sodium, 0 g carbohydrate, 23 g protein.

2 tablespoons crumbled
   Gorgonzola cheese
   or other blue cheese
2 tablespoons soft-style
   cream cheese with onion
   and garlic
1 to 2 tablespoons butter,
   softened
1 tablespoon chopped pine
   nuts or walnuts, toasted
4 boneless beef top loin
   steaks, cut 1 inch thick
   (about 2 pounds total)
Salt (optional)

Jalapeño-Glazed Ribeyes With Corn Relish

If you like a fiery relish, be sure to add the fresh jalapeño pepper.

Prep: 20 minutes **Grill:** 16 minutes **Makes:** 4 servings

¼ cup jalapeño pepper jelly

¼ cup catsup

4 beef ribeye steaks, cut
   1 inch thick (about
   2½ pounds total)

2 tablespoons jalapeño
   pepper jelly

1 tablespoon lime juice

½ teaspoon chili powder

¼ teaspoon ground cumin

1 10-ounce package frozen
   whole kernel corn, thawed
   (2 cups)

¾ cup chopped red
   sweet pepper

¼ cup finely chopped
   green onions

1 fresh jalapeño pepper,
   seeded and finely chopped
   (optional)*
   Salt

1. For glaze, in a small bowl stir together the ¼ cup pepper jelly and the catsup. Set aside.

2. In a grill with a cover arrange medium-hot coals around a drip pan. Test for medium heat above pan. Place steaks on grill rack directly over pan. Cover and grill to desired doneness, turning once halfway through grilling and brushing with the glaze during the last 5 minutes of grilling. [Allow 16 to 20 minutes for medium-rare (145°) or 20 to 24 minutes for medium doneness (160°).]

3. Meanwhile, for corn relish, in a small saucepan stir together the 2 tablespoons pepper jelly, the lime juice, chili powder, and cumin. Cook and stir until jelly is melted and mixture is bubbly. Stir in corn, sweet pepper, green onions, and, if desired, the fresh jalapeño. Cook and stir just until heated through. Season to taste with salt. Serve corn relish with the steaks.

Nutrition Facts per serving: 903 calories, 58 g total fat, 187 mg cholesterol, 473 mg sodium, 42 g carbohydrate, 53 g protein.

__Note:__ Because chile peppers, such as jalapeños, contain volatile oils that can burn your skin and eyes, avoid direct contact with them as much as possible. When working with chile peppers, wear plastic or rubber gloves. If your bare hands do touch the chile peppers, wash your hands and nails well with soap and warm water.

Sweet Pepper Steak

For a less generous serving, use only two steaks and cut each steak in half.

Prep: 15 minutes **Grill:** 11 minutes **Makes:** 4 servings

1. Press cracked pepper into 1 side of each steak, using about ½ teaspoon pepper per steak.

2. Grill steaks on the rack of an uncovered grill directly over medium coals to desired doneness, turning once halfway through grilling. [Allow 11 to 15 minutes for medium-rare (145°) or 14 to 18 minutes for medium doneness (160°).]

3. Meanwhile, in a medium skillet cook sweet pepper strips in hot butter or oil until tender. In a saucepan prepare au jus gravy mix according to package directions.

4. Serve steaks on warm plates; top steaks with pepper strips and au jus gravy.

Nutrition Facts per serving: 535 calories, 30 g total fat, 160 mg cholesterol, 910 mg sodium, 5 g carbohydrate, 58 g protein.

Cracked black pepper
4 12-ounce beef top loin steaks, cut 1 inch thick
½ of a medium red sweet pepper, cut into bite-size strips
½ of a medium yellow sweet pepper, cut into bite-size strips
½ of a medium green sweet pepper, cut into bite-size strips
2 tablespoons butter or cooking oil
1 0.6-ounce envelope au jus gravy mix

Basil-Stuffed Steak

A parsley rub and a basil stuffing make this steak a masterpiece.

Prep: 25 minutes **Grill:** 32 minutes **Stand:** 5 minutes **Makes:** 6 servings

1 2- to 2½-pound boneless
   beef sirloin steak, cut
   about 1½ inches thick
½ teaspoon salt
¼ teaspoon pepper
¼ teaspoon dried parsley
   flakes
1 cup lightly packed fresh
   basil leaves, coarsely
   snipped
¼ cup finely chopped onion
4 cloves garlic, minced
1½ teaspoons finely snipped
   fresh rosemary or
   ½ teaspoon dried
   rosemary, crushed
⅛ teaspoon finely snipped
   fresh thyme or dried thyme,
   crushed
1 teaspoon olive oil
   Fresh basil sprigs (optional)

1. With sharp knife, make 5 lengthwise slits three-quarters of the way through the steak. For rub, in a small bowl combine the salt, pepper, and parsley flakes. Sprinkle rub evenly over steak; rub in with your fingers.

2. In a small bowl combine snipped basil, onion, garlic, rosemary, and thyme. Press basil mixture into slits in steak. Using 100%-cotton kitchen string, tie steak loosely at 2-inch intervals to close the slits and hold in the filling. Drizzle with oil.

3. In a grill with a cover arrange medium-hot coals around a drip pan. Test for medium heat above pan. Place steak on grill rack over pan. Cover and grill to desired doneness, turning once halfway through grilling. [Allow 32 to 36 minutes for medium-rare (145°) or 36 to 40 minutes for medium doneness (160°).]

4. Transfer steak to a carving board; remove strings. Cover with foil; let stand for 5 minutes before carving. Cut into ½-inch-thick slices. If desired, garnish with basil sprigs.

Nutrition Facts per serving: **282 calories, 14 g total fat, 101 mg cholesterol, 253 mg sodium, 2 g carbohydrate, 37 g protein.**

Steak Teriyaki with Grilled Pineapple

To make sure the pineapple you select is at its peak, look for one with deep green leaves and a sweet aroma.

Prep: 25 minutes **Marinate:** 6 to 24 hours **Grill:** 14 minutes **Makes:** 6 servings

1. Place steak in a heavy, large self-sealing plastic bag set in a shallow bowl. For marinade, in a small bowl stir together soy sauce, sherry or orange juice, molasses, ginger, mustard, and garlic. Pour marinade over steak. Seal bag; turn to coat steak. Marinate in the refrigerator for at least 6 hours or up to 24 hours, turning bag occasionally.

2. Meanwhile, use a large sharp knife to cut bottom and top off pineapple. Peel pineapple and remove eyes. Cut into quarters and core. Cut each quarter lengthwise into 3 wedges. Set aside.

3. Drain steak, discarding the marinade. Grill steak on the rack of an uncovered grill directly over medium coals to desired doneness, turning once halfway through grilling. [Allow 14 to 18 minutes for medium-rare (145°) or 18 to 22 minutes for medium doneness (160°).] For the last 5 minutes of grilling, place the pineapple wedges on the grill rack alongside the steak. Grill pineapple until heated through, turning once halfway through grilling.

4. To serve, thinly slice the meat across the grain. Serve with pineapple wedges.

Nutrition Facts per serving: 184 calories, 7 g total fat, 50 mg cholesterol, 382 mg sodium, 12 g carbohydrate, 18 g protein.

1 pound boneless beef top
   sirloin steak, cut 1 inch
   thick
¼ cup soy sauce
2 tablespoons dry sherry
   or orange juice
1 tablespoon molasses
1½ teaspoons grated fresh
   ginger or ½ teaspoon
   ground ginger
1 teaspoon dry mustard
1 clove garlic, minced
1 small fresh pineapple

Grilled Sirloin with Smoky Pepper Sauce

Chipotle peppers are the smoked and dried version of jalapeño peppers. They have all the heat of jalapeños with a slightly sweet, smoky accent to boot.

Prep: 25 minutes **Stand:** 30 minutes **Marinate:** 2 to 8 hours **Grill:** 14 minutes
Makes: 4 servings

12 dried tomato halves
    (not oil packed)
1 to 3 dried chipotle peppers
1 cup boiling water
1 cup dry red or white wine
    or 1 cup water plus
    ½ teaspoon beef bouillon
    granules
½ cup chopped onion
1 tablespoon brown sugar
1 tablespoon lime juice or
    lemon juice
2 cloves garlic, quartered
¼ teaspoon ground black
    pepper
12 ounces boneless beef top
    sirloin steak, cut 1 inch
    thick

1. For marinade, in a medium bowl place tomatoes and chipotles; add the boiling water. Let stand about 30 minutes or until vegetables are softened. Drain, reserving liquid. Cut up tomatoes; place in a food processor bowl. Seed chipotles and cut up.* Add peppers to tomatoes along with ¼ cup of the reserved soaking liquid, the wine or water and bouillon, the onion, brown sugar, juice, garlic, and black pepper. Cover; process until nearly smooth.

2. Place steak in a shallow glass bowl; pour marinade over steak. Cover and marinate in the refrigerator for at least 2 hours or up to 8 hours.

3. Drain, reserving marinade. Grill steak on the rack of an uncovered grill directly over medium coals to desired doneness, turning once halfway through grilling and brushing with reserved marinade during first 8 minutes of grilling. [Allow 14 to 18 minutes for medium-rare (145°) or 18 to 22 minutes for medium doneness (160°).] In a small saucepan heat remaining marinade until bubbly. Thinly slice steak. Serve steak with warmed marinade.

Nutrition Facts per serving: **240 calories, 8 g total fat, 57 mg cholesterol, 105 mg sodium, 12 g carbohydrate, 21 g protein**

Note: Because chile peppers, such as chipotles, contain volatile oils that can burn your skin and eyes, avoid direct contact with them as much as possible. When working with chile peppers, wear plastic or rubber gloves. If your bare hands do touch the peppers, wash your hands and nails well with soap and warm water.

Steak with Roasted Garlic and Herbs

When roasted, garlic turns mild and sweet—ideal for spreading on grilled steak or your favorite bread or crackers.

Prep: 15 minutes **Grill:** 30 minutes **Makes:** 6 servings

1. Remove papery outer layers from garlic bulb(s), leaving individual cloves attached to bulb(s). Cut off about ½ inch from top of bulb(s) and discard. Tear off a 20×10-inch piece of heavy foil. Fold in half to make a double thickness of foil that measures 10×10 inches. Place garlic in center of foil. Bring foil up around garlic to form a shallow bowl. Sprinkle garlic with basil and snipped or dried rosemary; drizzle with oil.

2. Completely enclose garlic in foil, twisting ends of foil on top. Grill foil packet on rack of an uncovered grill directly over medium coals about 30 minutes or until garlic cloves are soft. Remove bulb(s) from foil packet, reserving herb-oil mixture. Let cool slightly.

3. Meanwhile, for rub, in a small bowl combine pepper and salt. Sprinkle rub evenly over both sides of steak; rub in with your fingers. Grill steak alongside the garlic packet to desired doneness, turning steak once halfway through grilling. [For sirloin steak, allow 14 to 18 minutes for medium-rare (145°) or 18 to 22 minutes for medium doneness (160°). For ribeye steaks, allow 11 to 15 minutes for medium-rare (145°) or 14 to 18 minutes for medium doneness (160°).]

4. To serve, cut steak into serving-size pieces. Carefully squeeze the pulp from the garlic cloves onto the steak pieces. Mash pulp slightly with a fork and spread over steak pieces. Drizzle steaks with the reserved herb-oil mixture.

Nutrition Facts per serving: 251 calories, 15 g total fat, 76 mg cholesterol, 235 mg sodium, 2 g carbohydrate, 26 g protein.

- **1 or 2 whole garlic bulb(s)**
- **3 to 4 teaspoons snipped fresh basil or 1 teaspoon dried basil, crushed**
- **1 tablespoon snipped fresh rosemary or 1 teaspoon dried rosemary, crushed**
- **2 tablespoons olive oil or cooking oil**
- **1 to 2 teaspoons cracked black pepper**
- **½ teaspoon salt**
- **1 1½-pound boneless beef top sirloin steak, cut 1 inch thick, or 1½ pounds beef ribeye steaks, cut 1 inch thick**

Tropical Fiesta Steak

Fruit salsa adds an island beat to grilled sirloin.

Prep: 25 minutes **Marinate:** 1 to 24 hours **Grill:** 14 minutes **Makes:** 6 servings

¼ cup frozen orange juice
  concentrate, thawed

3 tablespoons cooking oil

2 tablespoons honey

1 tablespoon spicy brown
  or Dijon-style mustard

3 green onions, sliced
  (about ⅓ cup)

1 teaspoon snipped fresh mint
  or ¼ teaspoon dried mint,
  crushed
  Several dashes bottled
  hot pepper sauce

½ of a medium red sweet
  pepper, chopped

1 small red apple, chopped

1 small pear, chopped

1 small peach, peeled and
  chopped

½ of a stalk celery, chopped

2 teaspoons lemon juice

1½ pounds boneless beef top
  sirloin steak, cut 1 inch
  thick

1. For marinade, in a small bowl combine the orange juice concentrate, oil, honey, mustard, 1 of the green onions, the mint, and hot pepper sauce. Reserve ¼ cup of the marinade for fruit salsa. Set remaining marinade aside.

2. For the fruit salsa, in a medium bowl combine the ¼ cup reserved marinade, the remaining green onions, the sweet pepper, apple, pear, peach, celery, and lemon juice. Cover and chill in the refrigerator until serving time or up to 24 hours.

3. Place steak in a heavy, large self-sealing plastic bag set in a shallow bowl. Pour the remaining marinade over steak. Seal bag; turn to coat steak. Marinate in the refrigerator for at least 1 hour or up to 24 hours, turning bag occasionally.

4. Drain steak, reserving marinade. Grill steak on rack of an uncovered grill directly over medium coals to desired doneness, turning once halfway through grilling and brushing occasionally with reserved marinade during the first 8 minutes of grilling. [Allow 14 to 18 minutes for medium-rare (145°) or 18 to 22 minutes for medium doneness (160°).] Discard any remaining marinade. To serve, top steak with fruit salsa.

Nutrition Facts per serving: 300 calories, 16 g total fat, 76 mg cholesterol, 91 mg sodium, 13 g carbohydrate, 27 g protein.

Fajita-Style Steak

With both a marinade and a glaze, this Southwestern-style steak has double the flavor.

Prep: 15 minutes **Marinate:** 30 minutes to 6 hours **Grill:** 14 minutes
Makes: 4 servings

1. Sprinkle steaks with salt and black pepper. Place in a heavy, large self-sealing plastic bag set in a shallow bowl. For marinade, in a small bowl stir together lime juice, oil, cinnamon, and 2 cloves garlic. Pour over steak. Seal bag; turn to coat steak. Marinate in the refrigerator for at least 30 minutes or up to 6 hours.

2. For glaze, in a small saucepan stir together red sweet peppers, honey, mustard, and the 2 or 3 cloves garlic. Bring to boiling; reduce heat. Simmer, uncovered, for 5 to 7 minutes or until glaze is slightly thickened and reduced to ¾ cup. Remove from the heat; set aside. Drain the steaks, discarding marinade.

3. Grill steaks on the rack of an uncovered grill directly over medium coals to desired doneness, turning once halfway through grilling and brushing several times with glaze during the last 5 minutes of grilling. [Allow 14 to 18 minutes for medium-rare (145°) or 18 to 22 minutes for medium doneness (160°).] Reheat any remaining glaze until bubbly; serve with the steaks.

Nutrition Facts per serving: **561 calories, 29 g total fat, 151 mg cholesterol, 188 mg sodium, 20 g carbohydrate, 52 g protein.**

4 boneless beef top sirloin
   steaks, cut 1 inch thick
   (about 2 pounds total)
   Salt
   Ground black pepper
⅓ cup lime juice
¼ cup cooking oil
2 teaspoons ground cinnamon
2 cloves garlic, minced
½ of a 7-ounce jar roasted
   red sweet peppers (about
   ½ cup), finely chopped
¼ cup honey
¼ cup Dijon-style mustard
2 or 3 cloves garlic, minced

BLT Steak

The makings of the classic summer sandwich deliciously top this belt-busting steak.

Prep: 15 minutes   **Grill:** 12 minutes   **Makes:** 4 servings

2 12-ounce beef top loin steaks, cut 1¼ inches thick
8 slices bacon
½ cup bottled balsamic vinaigrette salad dressing
12 red and/or yellow tomato slices
2 cups torn mixed salad greens

1. Grill steaks on the rack of an uncovered grill directly over medium coals to desired doneness, turning once halfway through grilling. [Allow 12 to 18 minutes for medium-rare (145°) or 16 to 22 minutes for medium doneness (160°).]

2. Meanwhile, in a skillet cook bacon until crisp. Drain bacon on paper towels, reserving 1 tablespoon drippings in skillet. Add balsamic vinaigrette salad dressing to the drippings in skillet. Cook and stir for 1 minute, scraping up any browned bits. Halve the steaks. Top steaks with tomato slices, bacon, mixed greens, and dressing mixture.

Nutrition Facts per serving: **556 calories, 42 g total fat, 122 mg cholesterol, 636 mg sodium, 5 g carbohydrate, 38 g protein.**

Beef with Mushroom-Tomato Sauce

For a more sophisticated mushroom sauce, substitute ⅓ cup dry red wine plus ⅓ cup water for the vegetable juice.

Prep: 20 minutes **Grill:** 8 minutes **Makes:** 4 servings

1. Rub pepper over steaks. Grill steaks on the rack of an uncovered grill directly over medium coals until desired doneness, turning once halfway through grilling. [Allow 8 to 9 minutes for medium-rare doneness (145°) for ¾-inch-thick steaks or 16 to 18 minutes for medium-rare doneness (145°) for 1-inch-thick steaks.]

2. Meanwhile, in a saucepan cook mushrooms, green onions, and garlic in hot margarine or butter until vegetables are tender. Stir in cornstarch. Add vegetable juice and beef bouillon granules. Cook and stir until thickened and bubbly. Cook and stir for 2 minutes more. Keep warm. Serve sauce with steaks.

Nutrition Facts per serving: **173 calories, 8 g total fat, 58 mg cholesterol, 172 mg sodium, 5 g carbohydrate, 20 g protein.**

⅛ teaspoon pepper
4 3-ounce beef eye of round steaks, cut ¾ to 1 inch thick
1 cup sliced fresh mushrooms
½ cup sliced green onions
2 cloves garlic, minced
2 teaspoons margarine or butter
2 teaspoons cornstarch
⅔ cup no-salt-added vegetable juice
½ teaspoon instant beef bouillon granules

Asian Family Steak

The ginger, soy sauce, garlic, and sherry marinade gives these thin steak slices wonderful flavor.

Prep: 15 minutes   **Marinate:** 8 to 24 hours   **Grill:** 16 minutes   **Stand:** 5 minutes
Makes: 6 to 8 servings

⅓ cup soy sauce
⅓ cup dry sherry
2 green onions, thinly sliced
1 tablespoon brown sugar
½ teaspoon dry mustard
⅛ teaspoon ground ginger
1 clove garlic, minced
1 1½- to 2-pound boneless
   beef top round steak,
   cut 1 inch thick
Soy sauce (optional)

1. For marinade, in a small bowl combine the ⅓ cup soy sauce, the sherry, green onions, brown sugar, mustard, ginger, and garlic. Place steak in a heavy, large self-sealing plastic bag set in a shallow bowl. Pour marinade over steak. Seal bag; turn to coat steak. Marinate in the refrigerator for at least 8 hours or up to 24 hours, turning bag occasionally.

2. Drain steak, reserving marinade. Grill the steak on the rack of an uncovered grill directly over medium coals for 16 to 18 minutes or until medium-rare doneness (145°), turning once halfway through grilling and brushing occasionally with reserved marinade during the first 10 minutes of grilling. Discard any remaining marinade. Remove steak from grill. Cover steak with foil; let stand for 5 minutes. To serve, thinly slice steak. If desired, serve with additional soy sauce.

Nutrition Facts per serving: **185 calories, 5 g total fat, 72 mg cholesterol, 512 mg sodium, 3 g carbohydrate, 28 g protein.**

Jerk London Broil

A Scotch bonnet pepper adds extra sizzle to this jerk-marinated steak.

Prep: 10 minutes   **Marinate:** 4 to 24 hours   **Grill:** 17 minutes   **Makes:** 6 servings

1. For jerk marinade, in a blender container combine green onions, lime juice, ginger, Scotch bonnet pepper (if desired), oil, garlic, and jerk seasoning; cover and blend until smooth. Score both sides of the steak in a diamond pattern by making shallow diagonal cuts at 1-inch intervals. Place the steak in a glass dish; spread the marinade over the steak. Cover with plastic wrap and marinate in the refrigerator for at least 4 hours or up to 24 hours.

2. Drain steak, discarding marinade. Grill the steak on the rack of an uncovered grill directly over medium coals for 17 to 21 minutes or until medium doneness (160°), turning once halfway through grilling. Transfer to a cutting board; cut across the grain into ⅛- to ¼-inch-thick slices.

Nutrition Facts per serving: **187 calories, 11 g total fat, 44 mg cholesterol, 117 mg sodium, 2 g carbohydrate, 18 g protein.**

Note: Because chile peppers, such as Scotch bonnets, contain volatile oils that can burn your skin and eyes, avoid direct contact with them as much as possible. When working with chile peppers, wear plastic or rubber gloves. If your bare hands do touch the chile peppers, wash your hands and nails well with soap and warm water.

4 green onions
¼ cup lime juice
1 1-inch piece fresh ginger, sliced
1 Scotch bonnet pepper, seeded and finely chopped (optional)*
2 tablespoons cooking oil
3 cloves garlic
2 teaspoons Jamaican jerk seasoning
1 1¼- to 1½-pound beef flank steak

Flank Steak with Bean Relish

This Tex-Mex topper turns grilled flank steak into a south-of-the-border sensation.

Prep: 10 minutes **Chill:** 30 minutes to 4 hours **Grill:** 17 minutes **Makes:** 4 servings

½ of a 15-ounce can (¾ cup) black beans, rinsed and drained
⅔ cup corn relish
¼ cup halved and thinly sliced radishes
1 small fresh jalapeño pepper, seeded and finely chopped*
2 teaspoons lime juice
¼ teaspoon ground cumin
1 12-ounce beef flank steak
  Salt
  Ground black pepper
  Fresh rosemary sprigs (optional)

1. For relish, in a small bowl combine black beans, corn relish, radishes, jalapeño pepper, lime juice, and cumin. Cover; chill in the refrigerator for at least 30 minutes or up to 4 hours.

2. Score both sides of steak in a diamond pattern by making shallow diagonal cuts at 1-inch intervals. Sprinkle with salt and black pepper. Grill steak on the rack of an uncovered grill directly over medium coals for 17 to 21 minutes or until medium doneness (160°), turning once halfway through grilling.

3. To serve, thinly slice steak diagonally across the grain. Serve with relish. If desired, garnish with rosemary sprigs.

Nutrition Facts per serving: 221 calories, 6 g total fat, 40 mg cholesterol, 488 mg sodium, 22 g carbohydrate, 20 g protein.

Note: Because chile peppers, such as jalapeños, contain volatile oils that can burn your skin and eyes, avoid direct contact with them as much as possible. When working with chile peppers, wear plastic or rubber gloves. If your bare hands do touch the chile peppers, wash your hands and nails well with soap and warm water.

Flank Steak Salad with Cantaloupe

Because you tuck the flank steak in the refrigerator to marinate at least 12 hours ahead of time, there's less last-minute work in the kitchen.

Prep: 20 minutes   **Marinate:** 12 to 24 hours   **Grill:** 17 minutes   **Makes:** 6 servings

1. In a small bowl combine dressing and lemon peel. Sprinkle both sides of steak with lemon-pepper seasoning. Place steak in a heavy, large self-sealing plastic bag set in a shallow bowl. Pour ¾ cup of the dressing mixture over steak. Seal bag; turn to coat steak. Marinate in the refrigerator for at least 12 hours or up to 24 hours, turning bag occasionally. Chill remaining dressing mixture in refrigerator until serving time.

2. Drain steak, discarding marinade. Grill steak on rack of an uncovered grill directly over medium coals for 17 to 21 minutes or until medium doneness (160°), turning steak once halfway through grilling.

3. Meanwhile, in a covered medium saucepan cook beans in a small amount of boiling water about 2 minutes or until crisp-tender. Drain; rinse in cold water. Set aside. In a large bowl toss beans with lettuce and watercress or arugula. Arrange greens mixture on a serving platter. Thinly slice flank steak across grain. Arrange steak slices on top of greens. Serve with cantaloupe wedges. If desired, garnish with tomatoes. Drizzle salad with chilled dressing mixture.

Nutrition Facts per serving: 248 calories, 15 g total fat, 35 mg cholesterol, 245 mg sodium, 12 g carbohydrate, 16 g protein.

1 8-ounce bottle Italian salad dressing
2 teaspoons finely shredded lemon peel
1 pound beef flank steak
   Lemon-pepper seasoning
8 ounces fresh haricots vert or other young, tender green beans, trimmed
5 cups torn leaf lettuce
3 cups watercress or arugula
1 medium cantaloupe, cut into wedges
   Baby pear-shaped tomatoes (optional)

Grilled Flank Steak With Chili Sauce

A touch of honey mellows the tomatoey sauce.

Prep: 20 minutes **Grill:** 17 minutes **Makes:** 6 servings

1 cup chopped onion
4 cloves garlic, minced
2 teaspoons chili powder
½ cup water
1 8-ounce can low-sodium
   tomato sauce
⅓ cup vinegar
2 tablespoons honey
½ teaspoon salt
¼ teaspoon pepper
1¼ pounds beef flank steak

1. For sauce, in a medium saucepan cook onion, garlic, and chili powder in the water until tender. Stir in tomato sauce, vinegar, honey, salt, and pepper. Bring to boiling, stirring constantly. Boil about 5 minutes or until slightly thickened.

2. Meanwhile, score both sides of steak in a diamond pattern by making shallow diagonal cuts at 1-inch intervals. Brush lightly with sauce. Grill steak on the rack of an uncovered grill directly over medium coals for 17 to 21 minutes or until medium doneness (160°), turning once halfway through grilling and brushing with the sauce during the last 5 minutes of grilling.

3. In a small saucepan reheat remaining sauce until bubbly. To serve, thinly slice steak across grain. Pass warmed sauce.

Nutrition Facts per serving: **189 calories, 7 g total fat, 44 mg cholesterol, 254 mg sodium, 13 g carbohydrate, 19 g protein.**

Lemony Flank Steak

Grilled or steamed asparagus is a delectable accompaniment to this lean flank steak bathed in a lemon marinade.

Prep: 15 minutes **Marinate:** 2 to 24 hours **Grill:** 17 minutes **Makes:** 3 servings

1. Score both sides of steak in a diamond pattern by making shallow diagonal cuts at 1-inch intervals. Place steak in a heavy, large self-sealing plastic bag set in a shallow bowl. For marinade, in a small bowl combine the lemon peel, lemon juice, sugar, soy sauce, snipped or dried oregano, and pepper. Pour over steak. Seal bag; turn to coat steak. Marinate in the refrigerator for at least 2 hours or up to 24 hours, turning bag occasionally.

2. Drain steak, reserving marinade. Grill steak on the rack of an uncovered grill directly over medium coals for 17 to 21 minutes or until medium doneness (160°), turning once halfway through grilling and brushing once with reserved marinade after 8 minutes of grilling. Discard any remaining marinade.

3. To serve, thinly slice steak diagonally across the grain. If desired, garnish with lemon slices and oregano leaves.

Nutrition Facts per serving: **267 calories, 12 g total fat, 80 mg cholesterol, 357 mg sodium, 5 g carbohydrate, 33 g protein.**

Note: For grilled asparagus, precook asparagus spears in a small amount of boiling water in a saucepan for 3 minutes. Drain the spears well and brush them with olive oil, butter, or margarine to prevent the asparagus from sticking to the grill rack. Thread the spears onto metal skewers as shown in the photo at top right. (Or use green onion tops to tie spears into serving-size bundles.) Place the asparagus directly over medium coals, laying them perpendicular to the wires on the rack. Grill, uncovered, for 3 to 5 minutes or until crisp-tender, turning occasionally.

- 1 1½-pound beef flank steak or boneless beef top sirloin steak
- 1 teaspoon finely shredded lemon peel
- ½ cup lemon juice
- 2 tablespoons sugar
- 2 tablespoons soy sauce
- 2 teaspoons snipped fresh oregano or ½ teaspoon dried oregano, crushed
- ⅛ teaspoon pepper
  Lemon slices (optional)
  Fresh oregano leaves (optional)

Pepper-Marinated Flank Steak

Three types of pepper—crushed red, coarsely ground black, and crushed green peppercorns—blend with red wine to make a dynamite marinade for beef.

Prep: 10 minutes **Marinate:** 6 to 24 hours **Grill:** 17 minutes **Makes:** 4 to 6 servings

1 1- to 1½-pound beef flank
  steak
½ cup dry red wine
⅓ cup finely chopped onion
2 tablespoons lime juice
1 tablespoon reduced-sodium
  soy sauce
1 tablespoon cooking oil
1 teaspoon crushed
  red pepper
½ teaspoon coarsely ground
  black pepper
½ teaspoon dried whole green
  peppercorns, crushed
3 cloves garlic, minced
1 tablespoon snipped fresh
  parsley

1. Score both sides of steak in a diamond pattern by making shallow diagonal cuts at 1-inch intervals. Place steak in a heavy, large self-sealing plastic bag set in a shallow bowl.

2. For marinade, in a medium bowl stir together wine, onion, lime juice, soy sauce, oil, red pepper, black pepper, green peppercorns, and garlic. Pour over steak in bag. Seal bag; turn to coat steak. Marinate in the refrigerator for at least 6 hours or up to 24 hours, turning bag occasionally.

3. Drain steak, reserving marinade. Grill steak on the rack of an uncovered grill directly over medium coals for 17 to 21 minutes or until medium doneness (160°), turning once halfway through grilling and brushing once with reserved marinade after 8 minutes of grilling. Discard any remaining marinade.

4. To serve, thinly slice steak diagonally across the grain. Sprinkle with parsley.

Nutrition Facts per serving: 232 calories, 12 g total fat, 53 mg cholesterol, 224 mg sodium, 4 g carbohydrate, 23 g protein.

Molasses and Mustard Barbecued Short Ribs

Ordinary bottled barbecue sauce gets a flavor boost from molasses, mustard, balsamic vinegar, and hot pepper sauce in this family-pleasing recipe.

Prep: 15 minutes **Bake:** 1½ hours **Chill:** 4 to 24 hours **Grill:** 10 minutes
Makes: 6 servings

1. Trim fat from short ribs. For rub, in a small bowl stir together the ground peppercorns, garlic, and thyme. Sprinkle rub evenly over short ribs; rub in with your fingers.

2. In an ovenproof Dutch oven or kettle combine beer, onion, and bay leaves. Add short ribs. Cover and bake in a 350° oven about 1½ hours or until meat is very tender.

3. Remove from oven; cool slightly. Remove short ribs from cooking liquid. Place ribs and cooking liquid in separate storage containers; cover and store in the refrigerator for at least 4 hours or up to 24 hours.

4. Spoon fat from surface of cooking liquid; discard fat. Reserve 1 cup of the cooking liquid; discard remaining cooking liquid and bay leaves. In a medium bowl stir together reserved cooking liquid, barbecue sauce, mustard, molasses, vinegar, and hot pepper sauce.

5. Grill ribs, bone sides down, on the rack of an uncovered grill directly over medium coals about 10 minutes or until crisp and heated through, turning and basting frequently with the molasses mixture.

6. In a small saucepan heat remaining molasses mixture until bubbly. Pass warmed molasses mixture with ribs.

Nutrition Facts per serving: **428 calories, 19 g total fat, 88 mg cholesterol, 833 mg sodium, 30 g carbohydrate, 34 g protein.**

- **5 pounds beef chuck short ribs**
- **2 tablespoons freshly ground multicolor peppercorns or regular peppercorns**
- **2 tablespoons bottled minced garlic (about 12 cloves)**
- **2 teaspoons dried thyme, crushed**
- **1 12-ounce bottle dark beer**
- **1 medium onion, coarsely chopped**
- **3 bay leaves**
- **1 cup bottled barbecue sauce**
- **¼ cup stone-ground mustard**
- **¼ cup molasses**
- **2 tablespoons balsamic vinegar or cider vinegar**
- **2 teaspoons bottled hot pepper sauce**

Veal Chops with Pesto-Stuffed Mushrooms

For maximum flavor, marinate the chops in the white wine and sage mixture for 24 hours.

Prep: 10 minutes **Marinate:** 30 minutes to 24 hours **Grill:** 10 minutes
Makes: 4 servings

¼ cup dry white wine

3 large cloves garlic, minced

1 tablespoon snipped fresh
   sage or snipped fresh
   thyme

1 tablespoon white wine
   Worcestershire sauce

1 tablespoon olive oil

4 veal loin chops, cut ¾ inch
   thick (about 1¼ pounds
   total)
   Pepper

8 large fresh mushrooms (2 to
   2½ inches in diameter)

2 to 3 tablespoons purchased
   pesto
   Hot cooked rice (optional)
   Steamed baby carrots with
   tops (optional)

1. For marinade, in a small bowl combine wine, garlic, the sage or thyme, the Worcestershire sauce, and oil. Place chops in a heavy, large self-sealing plastic bag set in a shallow bowl. Pour marinade over chops. Seal bag; turn to coat chops. Marinate in refrigerator for at least 30 minutes or up to 24 hours, turning bag occasionally.

2. Drain chops, reserving marinade. Sprinkle chops with pepper. Grill chops on the rack of an uncovered grill directly over medium coals for 10 to 14 minutes or until medium doneness (160°), turning once halfway through grilling and brushing with reserved marinade during first 5 minutes of grilling.

3. Meanwhile, carefully remove stems from mushrooms; chop stems for another use or discard. Brush mushroom caps with reserved marinade. Discard any remaining marinade. Place mushrooms, stem sides down, on grill rack. Grill for 4 minutes. Turn stem sides up; spoon some pesto into each. Grill about 4 minutes more or until heated through. Serve mushrooms with chops. If desired, serve with hot cooked rice and carrots.

Nutrition Facts per serving: 285 calories, 16 g total fat, 100 mg cholesterol, 157 mg sodium, 4 g carbohydrate, 28 g protein.

Grilled Mustard-Glazed Pork

Start the tenderloins marinating; then put your feet up and relax until it's time to grill.

Prep: 10 minutes **Marinate:** 30 minutes **Grill:** 40 minutes **Makes:** 6 servings

1. Place tenderloins in a heavy, large self-sealing plastic bag set in a shallow bowl. For marinade, in a small bowl combine the apple juice, shallots, vinegar, mustard, oil, brown sugar, soy sauce, and pepper. Pour over tenderloins. Seal bag; turn to coat tenderloins. Marinate in the refrigerator for 30 minutes, turning bag occasionally. Drain meat, reserving marinade.

2. In a grill with a cover arrange hot coals around a drip pan. Test for medium-hot heat above pan. Place tenderloins on grill rack over pan. Cover and grill for 40 to 50 minutes or until juices run clear (160°), turning once halfway through grilling.

3. Meanwhile, for sauce, pour reserved marinade into a medium saucepan. Bring to boiling; reduce heat. Simmer, uncovered, about 8 minutes or until reduced to ⅔ cup. Slice tenderloins across the grain. Serve with the sauce. If desired, sprinkle with chives.

Nutrition Facts per serving: 215 calories, 9 g total fat, 81 mg cholesterol, 280 mg sodium, 7 g carbohydrate, 26 g protein.

- 2 pork tenderloins (about 1½ pounds total)
- ½ cup apple juice or apple cider
- 2 large shallots, minced
- ¼ cup cider vinegar
- ¼ cup coarse-grain brown mustard
- 2 tablespoons olive oil
- 1 tablespoon brown sugar
- 1½ teaspoons soy sauce
  Dash pepper
  Snipped fresh chives (optional)

Temperature-Taking Hint

Using a regular liquid-filled meat thermometer to check the internal temperature of chops or steaks doesn't work because these cuts are too thin. The best way to check the doneness of thin cuts is to use an instant-read thermometer. Insert the thermometer into the side of the cooked chop or steak to a depth of 2 to 3 inches, being careful not to touch bone. Wait a few seconds for the reading. If the chop or steak is done, the temperature should read 160° for medium. If the meat is not done, remove the thermometer, continue grilling for a few more minutes, and then check the internal temperature again.

Pork Barbecue with Melon-Berry Salsa

A medley of summer fruits stars in this quick-as-a-wink salsa.

Prep: 25 minutes **Grill:** 40 minutes **Makes:** 6 servings

1½ cups chopped honeydew
  melon
1½ cups chopped cantaloupe
 1 cup sliced strawberries
 1 tablespoon snipped fresh
  mint
 1 tablespoon lemon juice
 1 tablespoon honey
 4 teaspoons Jamaican jerk
  seasoning
 2 pork tenderloins
  (about 1½ pounds total)

1. For salsa, in a medium bowl combine honeydew melon, cantaloupe, strawberries, mint, lemon juice, and honey. Cover and chill in the refrigerator until serving time or up to 1 hour.

2. Sprinkle Jamaican jerk seasoning evenly over tenderloins, pressing onto surface. In a grill with a cover arrange hot coals around a drip pan. Test for medium-hot heat above the pan. Place tenderloins on grill rack over pan. Cover and grill for 40 to 50 minutes or until juices run clear (160°), turning once halfway through grilling. Slice and serve with salsa.

Nutrition Facts per serving: 198 calories, 5 g total fat, 81 mg cholesterol, 189 mg sodium, 13 g carbohydrate, 26 g protein.

Pork Spirals with Red Pepper Sauce

The easy red pepper sauce featured here on pork tastes equally delicious with grilled or broiled beef, chicken, or fish.

Prep: 30 minutes   **Grill:** 40 minutes   **Stand:** 10 minutes   **Makes:** 4 servings

1. Using a sharp knife, make a lengthwise cut along the center of the tenderloin cutting to, but not through, the opposite side. Spread tenderloin open. Place between 2 pieces of plastic wrap. Using flat side of a meat mallet, pound tenderloin into an 11×7-inch rectangle, working from center to edges. Remove plastic wrap. Fold in narrow ends to make an even rectangle.

2. Stack spinach leaves on top of each other; slice crosswise into thin strips. In a medium bowl stir together spinach, mushrooms, basil, egg white, bread crumbs, and Parmesan cheese. Spread evenly over tenderloin. Starting at 1 of the short sides, roll up into a spiral. Tie with 100%-cotton kitchen string at 1½-inch intervals. Brush surface of meat with 1 teaspoon of the oil; sprinkle with black pepper.

3. In a grill with a cover arrange hot coals around a drip pan. Test for medium-hot heat above pan. Place tenderloin on grill rack over pan. Cover and grill for 40 to 50 minutes or until juices run clear (160°), turning once halfway through grilling. Remove from grill. Cover with foil; let stand for 10 minutes before slicing.

4. Meanwhile, for sauce, in a food processor bowl combine the remaining oil, the roasted peppers, wine vinegar, garlic, and salt. Cover; process until smooth. Transfer sauce to a small saucepan; cook over medium heat until heated through. To serve, remove strings from pork. Slice pork; serve with sauce.

Nutrition Facts per serving: 176 calories, 7 g total fat, 62 mg cholesterol, 146 mg sodium, 6 g carbohydrate, 22 g protein.

- 1 **12-ounce pork tenderloin**
- 1 **cup loosely packed fresh spinach leaves, stems removed**
- ⅓ **cup finely chopped fresh mushrooms**
- ¼ **cup snipped fresh basil**
- 1 **slightly beaten egg white**
- 2 **tablespoons fine dry bread crumbs**
- 1 **tablespoon finely shredded Parmesan cheese**
- 1 **tablespoon olive oil Ground black pepper**
- ½ **of a 7-ounce jar roasted red sweet peppers, drained**
- 1 **teaspoon red or white wine vinegar**
- 1 **clove garlic Dash salt**

Spicy Maple-Glazed Pork

Beer, peanut butter, chipotle peppers, and maple-flavored syrup blend to make a fabulous brush-on for pork. Try it on poultry too.

Prep: 35 minutes   **Grill:** 2 hours   **Stand:** 10 minutes   **Makes:** 8 servings

¾ cup beer (half of a
    12-ounce can)
¼ cup maple-flavored syrup
    or mild-flavored molasses
1 to 2 canned chipotle
    peppers in adobo sauce,
    finely chopped
2 cloves garlic, minced
2 tablespoons creamy
    peanut butter
1 tablespoon Worcestershire
    sauce
2 teaspoons Dijon-style
    mustard
½ teaspoon ground cinnamon
1 4- to 5-pound pork loin
    center rib roast (backbone
    loosened*)
¼ teaspoon salt
¼ teaspoon ground black
    pepper

1. For glaze, in a medium saucepan combine beer, maple syrup or molasses, chipotle peppers, garlic, peanut butter, Worcestershire sauce, mustard, and cinnamon. Bring to boiling; reduce heat. Simmer, uncovered, for 20 to 30 minutes or until of desired consistency, stirring occasionally. Set aside.

2. Meanwhile, sprinkle roast with the salt and black pepper. Insert an oven-going meat thermometer into center of roast, making sure bulb does not touch bone.

3. In a grill with a cover arrange medium coals around edge of grill. Test for medium-low heat in center of grill (not over coals). Place roast on a rack in a roasting pan. Place pan on grill rack in center of grill. Cover and grill for 2 to 2½ hours or until thermometer registers 155°, brushing with glaze during the last 20 minutes of grilling. Add additional coals as needed.

4. Remove roast from grill. Cover with foil; let stand for 10 minutes before slicing (the temperature of the pork will rise 5° during standing). Slice roast. Reheat any remaining glaze until bubbly; pass with meat.

Nutrition Facts per serving: 378 calories, 13 g total fat, 142 mg cholesterol, 264 mg sodium, 10 g carbohydrate, 51 g protein.

Note: Ask your butcher to loosen the backbone for you.

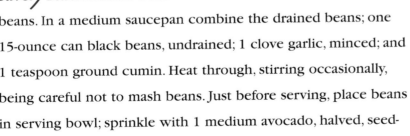

Herb-Cured Pork Platter

Black beans and pineapple add tropical flair to this herbed pork.

Prep: 15 minutes **Chill:** 24 hours **Grill:** 1 hour **Stand:** 15 minutes
Makes: 6 to 8 servings

1. For rub, in a small bowl combine thyme, sage, rosemary, garlic, black pepper, salt, and red pepper. Sprinkle rub evenly over roast; rub in with your fingers. Place roast in baking dish. Cover tightly with plastic wrap; chill in refrigerator for 24 hours.

2. In a grill with a cover arrange medium coals around a drip pan. Test for medium-low heat above pan. Insert an oven-going meat thermometer into center of roast. Place roast on grill rack over pan. Cover and grill 1 to 1½ hours or until thermometer registers 155°. Add additional coals as needed. Cover; let stand 15 minutes before slicing (the temperature of the pork will rise 5° during standing).

3. To prepare pineapple, cut pineapple lengthwise into 6 to 8 wedges, leaving leaves on fruit. Cut away center core. Brush pineapple with oil. Grill directly over coals for the last 15 minutes of grilling roast, turning occasionally. Serve pork with pineapple and Savory Black Beans.

Savory Black Beans: Drain and rinse one 15-ounce can black beans. In a medium saucepan combine the drained beans; one 15-ounce can black beans, undrained; 1 clove garlic, minced; and 1 teaspoon ground cumin. Heat through, stirring occasionally, being careful not to mash beans. Just before serving, place beans in serving bowl; sprinkle with 1 medium avocado, halved, seeded, peeled, and cubed; ½ cup crumbled feta cheese or shredded Monterey Jack cheese; and 1 small tomato, seeded and chopped.

Nutrition Facts per serving: 407 calories, 21 g total fat, 76 mg cholesterol, 646 mg sodium, 32 g carbohydrate, 30 g protein.

1 tablespoon snipped fresh
   thyme or ¾ teaspoon
   dried thyme, crushed
1 tablespoon snipped fresh
   sage or ¾ teaspoon
   dried sage, crushed
1 tablespoon snipped fresh
   rosemary or ¾ teaspoon
   dried rosemary, crushed
2 cloves garlic, minced
1½ teaspoons coarsely ground
   black pepper
1 to 1½ teaspoons coarse salt
½ teaspoon crushed red pepper
1 2- to 3-pound boneless pork
   top loin roast (single loin)
1 large fresh pineapple
1 tablespoon cooking oil
1 recipe Savory Black Beans

Mushroom-Stuffed Pork Chops

The ginger jelly glaze reinforces the hint of ginger in the mushroom and spinach stuffing.

Prep: 25 minutes   **Grill:** 35 minutes   **Makes:** 4 servings

½ cup coarsely chopped fresh
mushrooms (such as
button, chanterelle, or
shiitake)
¼ cup chopped onion
1 tablespoon margarine
or butter
1 teaspoon grated fresh
ginger
¼ teaspoon salt
¼ teaspoon pepper
1 cup coarsely chopped
fresh spinach leaves
¼ cup soft sourdough or
white bread crumbs
4 pork loin or rib chops,
cut 1¼ inches thick
(about 3 pounds total)
Salt
Pepper
¼ cup ginger jelly, ginger
preserves, or orange
marmalade
12 green onions
2 teaspoons olive oil

1. In a small bowl soak 8 wooden picks in water for 10 minutes. Meanwhile, for stuffing, in a saucepan cook mushrooms and onion in hot margarine or butter until onion is tender. Remove from heat. Stir in grated ginger, the ¼ teaspoon salt, and the ¼ teaspoon pepper. Add spinach and bread crumbs, tossing gently to combine.

2. Make a pocket in each chop by cutting horizontally from the outside edge almost to the bone. Spoon one-quarter of the stuffing into each pocket. Secure openings with water-soaked wooden picks. Sprinkle chops with salt and pepper.

3. In a grill with a cover arrange medium-hot coals around a drip pan. Test for medium heat above the pan. Place chops on grill rack over pan. Cover and grill for 35 to 40 minutes or until juices run clear (160°), turning once halfway through grilling and brushing occasionally with ginger jelly during the last 5 minutes of grilling. Remove wooden picks before serving.

4. Meanwhile, trim roots and tops of the green onions. In a medium skillet cook green onions in hot oil for 1 to 3 minutes or until slightly softened. Serve green onions with chops.

Nutrition Facts per serving: 442 calories, 17 g total fat, 132 mg cholesterol, 355 mg sodium, 19 g carbohydrate, 50 g protein.

Apple and Walnut-Stuffed Pork Chops

If you like, make the stuffing ahead and refrigerate it. Stuff the chops just before grilling.

Prep: 30 minutes **Grill:** 35 minutes **Makes:** 4 servings

1. In a small bowl soak 8 wooden picks in water for 10 minutes. Meanwhile, for stuffing, in a small bowl toss together stuffing mix, apple, walnuts, and, if desired, apple juice or water. Set aside.

2. Make a pocket in each chop by cutting horizontally from the outside edge almost to the bone. Spoon one-quarter of the stuffing into each pocket. Secure openings with water-soaked wooden picks.

3. In a grill with a cover arrange medium-hot coals around a drip pan. Test for medium heat above the pan. Place chops on grill rack over pan. Cover and grill for 35 to 40 minutes or until juices run clear (160°), turning once halfway through grilling and brushing occasionally with apple jelly during last 5 minutes of grilling. Remove wooden picks before serving.

Nutrition Facts per serving: 464 calories, 22 g total fat, 128 mg cholesterol, 239 mg sodium, 23 g carbohydrate, 42 g protein.

½ cup herb-seasoned stuffing
   mix
¼ cup coarsely shredded apple
 3 tablespoons chopped
   walnuts, toasted
 1 tablespoon apple juice
   or water (optional)
 4 pork loin or rib chops, cut
   1¼ inches thick (about
   2½ pounds total)
¼ cup apple jelly, melted

Plum-Good Pork Chops

These plum-good chops are plum easy too.

Prep: 15 minutes **Grill:** 18 minutes **Makes:** 4 servings

3 tablespoons plum preserves
1 green onion, thinly sliced
1 tablespoon soy sauce
2 teaspoons lemon juice
⅛ teaspoon curry powder
   Dash ground cinnamon
   Dash ground red pepper
4 pork loin or rib chops,
   cut 1¼ inches thick
   (about 2 pounds total)
1 clove garlic, split
   Plum wedges (optional)

1. For sauce, in a small saucepan heat and stir preserves, green onion, soy sauce, lemon juice, curry powder, cinnamon, and red pepper over medium heat until bubbly. Set aside. Rub both sides of each chop with cut side of garlic.

2. Grill chops on the rack of an uncovered grill directly over medium coals for 18 to 22 minutes or until juices run clear (160°), turning once halfway through grilling and brushing frequently with sauce during last 5 minutes of grilling. Discard any remaining sauce. If desired, garnish with plum wedges.

Nutrition Facts per serving: **224 calories, 11 g total fat, 66 mg cholesterol, 283 mg sodium, 11 g carbohydrate, 20 g protein.**

Pork Chops with Mushroom Stuffing

For a richer mushroom flavor, use crimini mushrooms in this captivating mushroom stuffing.

Prep: 15 minutes **Grill:** 12 minutes **Makes:** 4 servings

1. In a small bowl soak 8 wooden picks in water for 10 minutes. Meanwhile, for stuffing, in a large skillet cook green onion in hot oil for 1 minute. Stir in mushrooms, rosemary or oregano, the $\frac{1}{8}$ teaspoon salt, and the $\frac{1}{8}$ teaspoon pepper. Cook and stir for 2 to 3 minutes more or until mushrooms are tender. Remove from heat.

2. Make a pocket in each chop by cutting horizontally from the outside edge almost to, but not through, the opposite side. Spoon one-quarter of the stuffing into each pocket. Secure openings with water-soaked wooden picks.

3. Brush chops with Worcestershire sauce. Season chops lightly with salt and pepper. Grill chops on the rack of an uncovered grill directly over medium coals for 12 to 15 minutes or until juices run clear (160°), turning once halfway through grilling. Remove wooden picks before serving.

Nutrition Facts per serving: 241 calories, 14 g total fat, 77 mg cholesterol, 218 mg sodium, 4 g carbohydrate, 25 g protein.

2 tablespoons thinly sliced green onion

2 teaspoons olive oil

1 8-ounce package fresh mushrooms, coarsely chopped

2 teaspoons snipped fresh rosemary or oregano

$\frac{1}{8}$ teaspoon salt

$\frac{1}{8}$ teaspoon pepper

4 boneless pork top loin chops, cut 1 inch thick

2 teaspoons Worcestershire sauce

Salt

Pepper

Cranberry-Chipotle Pork Chops

This colorful sauce with pizzazz is equally delicious teamed with chicken or fish.

Prep: 10 minutes   **Grill:** 35 minutes   **Makes:** 4 servings

4 pork loin or rib chops,
   cut 1¼ inches thick
   (about 3 pounds total)
1 8-ounce can jellied
   cranberry sauce
⅓ cup apricot or peach
   preserves or apricot or
   peach spreadable fruit
¼ cup chopped onion
1 tablespoon lemon juice
   or cider vinegar
1 drained canned chipotle
   pepper in adobo sauce
   or 1 fresh jalapeño pepper,
   seeded and chopped*

1. In a grill with a cover arrange medium-hot coals around a drip pan. Test for medium heat above pan. Place chops on grill rack over pan. Cover and grill for 35 to 40 minutes or until juices run clear (160°), turning once halfway through grilling.

2. Meanwhile, for sauce, in a small saucepan combine the cranberry sauce, preserves or spreadable fruit, onion, lemon juice or vinegar, and drained chipotle or jalapeño pepper. Bring to boiling, stirring constantly; reduce heat. Simmer, uncovered, for 5 minutes, stirring occasionally.

3. To serve, brush grilled chops with some of the sauce. Pass remaining sauce.

Nutrition Facts per serving: 449 calories, 14 g total fat, 116 mg cholesterol, 187 mg sodium, 42 g carbohydrate, 36 g protein.

Note: Because chile peppers, such as jalapeños, contain volatile oils that can burn your skin and eyes, avoid direct contact with them as much as possible. When working with chile peppers, wear plastic or rubber gloves. If your bare hands do touch the chile peppers, wash your hands and nails well with soap and warm water.

Corn Bread-Stuffed Chops

A jazzed-up corn bread stuffing with sausage and cranberries makes these thick-cut chops a real stick-to-the-ribs meal.

Prep: 25 minutes   **Grill:** 35 minutes   **Makes:** 4 servings

1. In a small bowl soak 8 wooden picks in water for 10 minutes. For rub, stir together black pepper, celery seed, onion or garlic salt, cloves, and, if desired, red pepper. Set aside.

2. For stuffing, in a small saucepan cook the sausage and onion until sausage is browned and onion is tender. Drain off fat. Stir in the stuffing mix, cranberries, chili peppers, and parsley Toss in enough of the apple juice, broth, or water to just moisten the stuffing mix.

3. Make a pocket in each chop by cutting horizontally from the outside edge almost to the bone. Spoon one-quarter of the stuffing into each pocket. Secure openings with water-soaked wooden picks. Sprinkle the rub evenly over both sides of chops; rub in with your fingers.

4. In a grill with a cover arrange medium-hot coals around a drip pan. Test for medium heat above the pan. Place chops on grill rack directly over pan. Cover and grill for 35 to 40 minutes or until the juices run clear (160°), turning once halfway through grilling. Remove wooden picks before serving.

Nutrition Facts per serving: **384 calories, 11 g total fat, 129 mg cholesterol, 458 mg sodium, 17 g carbohydrate, 48 g protein.**

¼ teaspoon ground black pepper
⅛ teaspoon celery seed
⅛ teaspoon onion salt or garlic salt
Dash ground cloves
Dash ground red pepper (optional)
4 ounces bulk pork sausage or bulk turkey sausage
¼ cup chopped onion
½ cup corn bread stuffing mix
¼ cup dried cranberries
½ of a 4-ounce can diced green chili peppers, drained
2 tablespoons snipped fresh parsley
1 to 2 tablespoons apple juice, chicken broth, or water
4 pork loin rib chops, cut 1½ inches thick (about 3 pounds total)

Southwest Pork Chops With Corn Salsa

Summer's sweet corn and juicy tomatoes will make this chunky salsa especially fresh-tasting.

Prep: 20 minutes **Grill:** 12 minutes **Makes:** 4 servings

1 cup fresh or frozen whole
    kernel corn
¼ cup white wine vinegar
3 tablespoons snipped fresh
    cilantro
1 teaspoon olive oil
3 plum-shaped tomatoes,
    chopped
½ cup thinly sliced green
    onions
1 small fresh jalapeño pepper,
    seeded and finely chopped*
4 center-cut pork loin chops,
    cut ¾ inch thick
    Cactus leaves (optional)
    Fresh cilantro sprigs
    (optional)

1. Thaw corn, if frozen. For sauce, in a small bowl combine 3 tablespoons of the vinegar, 1 tablespoon of the snipped cilantro, and the oil. For salsa, in a medium bowl combine corn, tomatoes, green onions, jalapeño pepper, the remaining vinegar, and the remaining snipped cilantro. Set aside.

2. Grill chops on rack of an uncovered grill directly over medium coals for 12 to 15 minutes or until juices run clear (160°), turning once halfway through grilling and brushing occasionally with sauce during first 6 minutes of grilling. Discard any remaining sauce. If desired, serve pork chops on cactus leaves and garnish with cilantro sprigs. Serve with salsa.

Nutrition Facts per serving: 201 calories, 9 g total fat, 51 mg cholesterol, 51 mg sodium, 14 g carbohydrate, 18 g protein.

Note: Because chile peppers, such as jalapeños, contain volatile oils that can burn your skin and eyes, avoid direct contact with them as much as possible. When working with chile peppers, wear plastic or rubber gloves. If your bare hands do touch the chile peppers, wash your hands and nails well with soap and warm water.

Grilled Apricot-Stuffed Pork Chops

Cut into these juicy, flavorful pork chops and you'll find a thyme-flecked rice stuffing studded with dried apricots.

Prep: 25 minutes **Grill:** 22 minutes **Makes:** 4 servings

1. In a small bowl soak 8 wooden picks in water for 10 minutes. Meanwhile, for stuffing, in a medium bowl stir together the rice, apricots, onion, the 1 tablespoon apricot spread, the thyme, and pepper. Make a pocket in each chop by cutting horizontally from the outside edge almost to the bone. Spoon one-quarter of the stuffing into each pocket. Secure the openings with water-soaked wooden picks.

2. In a grill with a cover arrange medium-hot coals around a drip pan. Test for medium heat above pan. Place chops on grill rack over pan. Cover and grill for 22 to 25 minutes or until juices run clear (160°), turning once halfway through grilling.

3. Meanwhile, in a saucepan heat the ¼ cup apricot spread until melted. Brush over pork chops during the last 5 minutes of grilling.

Nutrition Facts per serving: **208 calories, 7 g total fat, 48 mg cholesterol, 59 mg sodium, 19 g carbohydrate, 16 g protein.**

½ cup cooked brown rice
   or long grain rice
¼ cup snipped dried apricots
¼ cup finely chopped onion
1 tablespoon reduced-calorie
   apricot spread
¼ teaspoon dried thyme,
   crushed
¼ teaspoon pepper
4 center-cut pork loin chops,
   cut 1 inch thick
¼ cup reduced-calorie apricot
   spread

Pork Chops with Onion-Raisin Chutney

The sweet-sour fusion of raisins, onion, sweet pepper, and vinegar in this relish is sure to please.

Prep: 25 minutes **Marinate:** 2 to 24 hours **Grill:** 12 minutes **Stand:** 10 minutes
Makes: 4 servings

---

4 boneless pork top loin
   chops, cut ¾ inch thick
   (about 1 pound total)
½ of a 12-ounce bottle lemon-
   pepper marinade or herb
   and garlic marinade
½ cup finely chopped onion
½ cup finely chopped
   red sweet pepper
¼ cup raisins
¼ teaspoon ground cloves
1 tablespoon margarine
   or butter
¼ cup red wine vinegar
2 tablespoons brown sugar
2 tablespoons finely chopped
   toasted walnuts
   Fresh sage sprigs (optional)

1. Place chops in a heavy, large self-sealing plastic bag set in a shallow bowl. Pour marinade over chops. Seal bag; turn to coat chops. Marinate in the refrigerator for at least 2 hours or up to 24 hours, turning bag occasionally.

2. Drain chops, discarding marinade. Grill chops on rack of an uncovered grill directly over medium coals for 12 to 15 minutes or until juices run clear (160°), turning once halfway through grilling.

3. Meanwhile, for chutney, in a medium skillet cook and stir onion, sweet pepper, raisins, and cloves in hot margarine or butter about 4 minutes or until onion is tender. Add vinegar and brown sugar; reduce heat. Simmer, uncovered, about 5 minutes or until liquid is nearly evaporated. Stir in nuts. Remove from heat; cover and let stand for 10 minutes.

4. Spoon some of the chutney over chops. If desired, garnish with sage sprigs. Pass remaining chutney.

Nutrition Facts per serving: **273 calories, 14 g total fat, 59 mg cholesterol, 1,270 mg sodium, 20 g carbohydrate, 18 g protein.**

Jamaican Pork Chops With Melon Salsa

You'll find jerk seasoning in the seasoning aisle of the supermarket or in food specialty shops.

Prep: 15 minutes **Grill:** 12 minutes **Makes:** 4 servings

1. For salsa, in a medium bowl combine honeydew, cantaloupe, the snipped mint, and the honey. Cover and refrigerate until ready to serve.

2. Sprinkle both sides of chops evenly with Jamaican jerk seasoning; rub in with your fingers. Grill chops on the rack of an uncovered grill directly over medium coals for 12 to 15 minutes or until juices run clear (160°), turning once halfway through grilling. Serve salsa with chops. If desired, garnish with star anise and/or mint sprigs.

Nutrition Facts per serving: **189 calories, 8 g total fat, 51 mg cholesterol, 231 mg sodium, 13 g carbohydrate, 17 g protein.**

1 cup chopped honeydew
   melon
1 cup chopped cantaloupe
1 tablespoon snipped fresh
   mint
1 tablespoon honey
4 boneless pork top loin chops,
   cut ¾ to 1 inch thick
4 teaspoons Jamaican jerk
   seasoning
   Star anise (optional)
   Fresh mint sprigs (optional)

Lemon and Herb-Rubbed Pork Chops

A flavorful coating of garlic, lemon peel, rosemary, and sage seasons the chops as they grill.

Prep: 10 minutes **Grill:** 30 minutes **Makes:** 4 servings

 4 teaspoons bottled minced
  garlic (about 8 cloves)
1½ teaspoons finely shredded
  lemon peel
 1 teaspoon dried rosemary,
  crushed
 ½ teaspoon salt
 ½ teaspoon dried sage,
  crushed
 ½ teaspoon pepper
 4 boneless pork top loin
  chops, cut 1¼ inches thick
  Fresh sage sprigs (optional)

1. For rub, in a small bowl combine the garlic, lemon peel, rosemary, salt, dried sage, and pepper. Sprinkle rub evenly onto all sides of chops; rub in with your fingers.

2. In a grill with a cover arrange medium-hot coals around a drip pan. Test for medium heat above pan. Place chops on grill rack over pan. Cover and grill for 30 to 35 minutes or until juices run clear (160°), turning once halfway through grilling. If desired, garnish with sage sprigs.

Nutrition Facts per serving: **351 calories, 19 g total fat, 116 mg cholesterol, 374 mg sodium, 3 g carbohydrate, 41 g protein.**

Curried Mustard Pork Chops

Team these spunky chops with hot cooked brown rice, fresh fruit, and steamed pea pods.

Prep: 10 minutes **Marinate:** 6 to 24 hours **Grill:** 20 minutes **Makes:** 4 servings

1. For marinade, in a small bowl stir together brown mustard, wine, curry powder, oil, red pepper, green onion, and garlic.

2. Place chops in a heavy, large self-sealing plastic bag set in a shallow bowl. Pour marinade over chops in bag. Seal bag; turn to coat chops. Marinate in the refrigerator for at least 6 hours or up to 24 hours, turning bag occasionally.

3. Drain chops, reserving marinade. In a grill with a cover arrange medium-hot coals around a drip pan. Test for medium heat above the pan. Place chops on grill rack over pan. Cover and grill for 20 to 24 minutes or until juices run clear (160°), turning once halfway through grilling and brushing with reserved marinade during first 15 minutes of grilling. Discard any remaining marinade. If desired, serve with fruit. If desired, garnish with oregano.

Nutrition Facts per serving: **191 calories, 12 g total fat, 51 mg cholesterol, 343 mg sodium, 2 g carbohydrate, 18 g protein.**

½ cup spicy brown mustard
¼ cup dry white wine
1 tablespoon curry powder
1 tablespoon olive oil
¼ to ½ teaspoon crushed
   red pepper
1 green onion, sliced
1 clove garlic, minced
4 boneless pork top loin chops,
   cut 1 inch thick
   (about 1 pound total)
   Papaya, mango, and/or
   carambola (star fruit) slices
   (optional)
   Fresh oregano sprigs
   (optional)

Lime Salsa Chops

Put together a Southwestern meal by serving Mexican-style rice and warm tortillas with these zesty chops.

Prep: 15 minutes **Marinate:** 2 to 4 hours **Grill:** 12 minutes **Makes:** 6 servings

¼ cup finely chopped red onion
¼ cup lime juice
2 fresh serrano or jalapeño peppers, seeded and finely chopped (see note on page 52)
1 tablespoon toasted sesame oil
1 teaspoon cumin seed, crushed
6 boneless pork top loin chops, cut ¾ inch thick
4 plum tomatoes, chopped
1 small cucumber, seeded and chopped
2 green onions, sliced
2 tablespoons snipped fresh cilantro
1 tablespoon honey
3 tablespoons jalapeño pepper jelly
Lime peel strips (optional)

1. For marinade, in a small bowl combine red onion, lime juice, serrano or jalapeño peppers, oil, and cumin seed. Reserve 2 tablespoons of the marinade for the salsa. Place chops in a heavy, large self-sealing plastic bag set in a shallow bowl. Pour remaining marinade over chops. Seal bag; turn to coat chops. Marinate in the refrigerator for at least 2 hours or up to 4 hours, turning bag occasionally.

2. For salsa, in a medium bowl combine reserved marinade, tomatoes, cucumber, green onions, cilantro, and honey. Cover and chill until serving time.

3. Drain chops, reserving marinade. Transfer reserved marinade to a small saucepan. Stir jalapeño pepper jelly into reserved marinade; cook and stir until mixture boils. Remove from heat; set aside.

4. Grill chops on the rack of an uncovered grill directly over medium coals for 12 to 15 minutes or until juices run clear (160°), turning once halfway through grilling and brushing with jelly mixture during the last 5 minutes of grilling. Discard any remaining jelly mixture. If desired, garnish with lime peel strips. Serve chops with salsa.

Nutrition Facts per serving: 211 calories, 10 g total fat, 51 mg cholesterol, 46 mg sodium, 14 g carbohydrate, 17 g protein.

Plum-Sauced Spareribs

A homemade plum sauce and sesame seeds add an Asian touch to these ribs.

Prep: 30 minutes **Grill:** 1½ hours **Makes:** 6 servings

1. For sauce, drain plums, reserving liquid. Pit plums. In a food processor bowl or blender container combine the pitted plums, reserved plum liquid, the orange juice concentrate, hoisin sauce, soy sauce, ginger, and the ¼ teaspoon pepper. Cover and process or blend until mixture is almost smooth. Transfer the mixture to a saucepan. Bring to boiling; reduce heat. Simmer, uncovered, about 15 minutes or until slightly thickened. Stir in sesame seeds.

2. Trim fat from ribs. Sprinkle ribs with salt and additional pepper. In a grill with a cover arrange medium-hot coals around a drip pan. Test for medium heat above the pan. Place the ribs, bone sides down, on the grill over the pan. (Or place ribs in a rib rack; place on grill rack.) Cover and grill for 1½ to 1¾ hours or until ribs are tender, brushing with sauce during the last 10 minutes of grilling. Add additional coals as needed. Reheat any remaining sauce until bubbly and pass with the ribs.

Nutrition Facts per serving: 589 calories, 40 g total fat, 141 mg cholesterol, 486 mg sodium, 18 g carbohydrate, 33 g protein.

1 16-ounce can whole unpitted purple plums
2 tablespoons frozen orange juice concentrate, thawed
2 tablespoons hoisin sauce
1 tablespoon soy sauce
1 teaspoon grated fresh ginger
¼ teaspoon pepper
2 tablespoons sesame seeds, toasted
4 pounds pork spareribs, cut into serving-size pieces
Salt
Pepper

Chutney Spareribs

Traditional barbecue fixin's—such as potato salad, coleslaw, and grilled corn on the cob—go great with these saucy ribs.

Prep: 35 minutes   **Cook:** 1 hour   **Grill:** 15 minutes   **Makes:** 6 servings

3 to 4 pounds meaty pork
   spareribs or loin back ribs
   Salt
1 cup mango chutney
¼ cup bottled chili sauce
2 tablespoons vinegar
1 tablespoon Worcestershire
   sauce
1 tablespoon water
1 teaspoon dry mustard
½ teaspoon onion powder
   Several dashes bottled
   hot pepper sauce
   Fresh thyme sprigs
   (optional)

1. Cut ribs into serving-size pieces. Place ribs in a large Dutch oven. Add enough water to cover ribs. Bring to boiling; reduce heat. Cover and simmer about 1 hour or until ribs are tender. Drain ribs; sprinkle lightly with salt.

2. Meanwhile, for sauce, chop any large pieces of chutney. In a medium saucepan combine chutney, chili sauce, vinegar, Worcestershire sauce, the water, dry mustard, onion powder, and hot pepper sauce. Cook and stir over medium heat until heated through.

3. Place ribs, meaty sides down, on the rack of an uncovered grill directly over medium coals. (Or place ribs in a rib rack; place on grill rack.) Grill for 10 minutes. Turn ribs; brush with sauce. Grill for 5 minutes more.

4. To serve, reheat any remaining sauce; serve with ribs. If desired, garnish ribs with thyme sprigs.

Nutrition Facts per serving: **421 calories, 23 g total fat, 70 mg cholesterol, 297 mg sodium, 29 g carbohydrate, 23 g protein.**

Down-Home Ribs

Set out plenty of extra napkins—they'll come in handy for these finger lickin' ribs.

Prep: 15 minutes **Grill:** 1½ hours **Makes:** 6 servings

1. For sauce, in a medium skillet cook onion in hot oil over medium heat about 4 minutes or until onion is tender. Stir in catsup, orange juice, brown sugar, chili powder, and ginger. Cook about 5 minutes more or until sauce is slightly thickened.

2. Cut ribs into serving-size pieces. In a grill with a cover arrange medium-hot coals around a drip pan. Test for medium heat above the pan. Place the ribs, bone sides down, on grill rack over drip pan. (Or place ribs in a rib rack; place on grill rack.) Cover and grill for 1½ to 1¾ hours or until ribs are tender, brushing occasionally with sauce during the last 10 minutes of grilling. Add additional coals as needed. Reheat any remaining sauce until bubbly; serve with ribs.

Nutrition Facts per serving: **313 calories, 22 g total fat, 79 mg cholesterol, 245 mg sodium, 8 g carbohydrate, 19 g protein.**

- 1 medium onion, chopped
- 1 tablespoon cooking oil
- ⅓ cup catsup
- 2 tablespoons orange juice
- 1 tablespoon brown sugar
- 1 teaspoon chili powder
- ½ teaspoon grated fresh ginger
- 4 pounds pork loin back ribs or meaty spareribs

Sweet and Spicy BBQ Ribs

Catsup and brown sugar make this sauce sweet while curry powder makes it spicy.

Prep: 35 minutes **Chill:** 30 minutes **Grill:** 1½ hours **Makes:** 8 servings

---

1½ cups catsup

¾ cup white wine vinegar

½ cup packed brown sugar

2 tablespoons curry powder

1 tablespoon Worcestershire sauce

1 teaspoon hickory-flavored salt

1 teaspoon pepper

2 or 3 cloves garlic, minced

3½ to 4 pounds pork loin back ribs

1. For sauce, in a large bowl combine the catsup, vinegar, brown sugar, curry powder, Worcestershire sauce, hickory-flavored salt, pepper, and garlic. Cover; refrigerate for at least 30 minutes (sauce can be stored in refrigerator for up to 5 days).

2. In a grill with a cover arrange medium-hot coals around a drip pan. Test for medium heat above the pan. Place ribs, bone sides down, on the grill rack over the pan. (Or place ribs in a rib rack; place on grill rack.) Cover and grill for 1½ to 1¾ hours or until ribs are tender, brushing generously with sauce during the last 15 minutes of grilling. Add additional coals as needed. Reheat any remaining sauce until bubbly; serve with the ribs.

Nutrition Facts per serving: 295 calories, 8 g total fat, 54 mg cholesterol, 894 mg sodium, 27 g carbohydrate, 26 g protein.

Molasses-Rum Baby Back Ribs

It will take about 1 pound of pork loin back ribs to feed each person at your dinner table.

Prep: 30 minutes **Chill:** 2 to 24 hours **Grill:** 1½ hours **Makes:** 4 servings

1. For rub, in a small bowl combine brown sugar, paprika, garlic powder, pepper, salt, and cumin. Sprinkle rub evenly over ribs; rub in with your fingers. Cover and chill in the refrigerator for at least 2 hours or up to 24 hours.

2. In a grill with a cover arrange medium-hot coals around a drip pan. Test for medium heat above pan. Place ribs, bone sides down, on grill rack over pan. (Or place ribs in a rib rack; place on grill rack.) Cover and grill for 1½ to 1¾ hours or until ribs are tender. Add additional coals as needed.

3. Meanwhile, for sauce, in a medium saucepan cook onion and garlic in hot oil until tender. Remove from heat. Stir in tomato sauce, rum or juice, honey and/or molasses, Worcestershire sauce, vinegar, dry mustard, and chili powder. Bring to boiling; reduce heat. Simmer, uncovered, about 20 minutes or until thickened and reduced to 1½ cups; stir occasionally.

4. To serve, cut ribs into serving-size pieces. Spoon some of the sauce over ribs; pass remaining sauce.

Nutrition Facts per serving: **701 calories, 31 g total fat, 126 mg cholesterol, 1,356 mg sodium, 38 g carbohydrate, 54 g protein.**

- 2 tablespoons brown sugar
- 1 to 2 tablespoons paprika
- 1 tablespoon garlic powder
- 3 to 4 teaspoons coarsely ground black pepper
- 1½ teaspoons salt
- ½ teaspoon ground cumin
- 3¾ to 4 pounds pork loin back ribs
- ½ cup chopped onion
- 1 clove garlic, minced
- 1 tablespoon cooking oil
- 1 8-ounce can tomato sauce
- ⅓ cup pineapple rum, light rum, or pineapple juice
- ⅓ cup honey and/or light-flavored molasses
- 2 tablespoons Worcestershire sauce
- 2 tablespoons vinegar
- 2 teaspoons dry mustard
- 2 teaspoons chili powder

Pork Ribs with Chipotle Barbecue Sauce

Pork loin back ribs offer lots of meat to sop up the smoky sauce.

Prep: 15 minutes **Grill:** 1½ hours **Makes:** 4 servings

1 tablespoon cumin seeds,
  slightly crushed
2 tablespoons brown sugar
1 tablespoon chili powder
1 teaspoon paprika
½ teaspoon ground red pepper
¼ teaspoon cracked black
  pepper
3 to 4 pounds pork loin back
  ribs or meaty spareribs
1½ cups bottled barbecue
  sauce
¼ cup finely chopped onion
3 cloves garlic, minced
½ to 1 teaspoon finely
  chopped canned chipotle
  pepper in adobo sauce

1. For rub, in a small skillet heat cumin seeds over low heat about 3 minutes or until toasted and fragrant, shaking skillet occasionally. Remove from heat; transfer to a small bowl. Stir in brown sugar, chili powder, paprika, red pepper, and black pepper. Sprinkle rub evenly over both sides of ribs; rub in with your fingers.

2. In a grill with a cover arrange medium-hot coals around a drip pan. Test for medium heat above the pan. Place ribs, bone sides down, on grill rack over pan. (Or place ribs in a rib rack; place on grill rack.) Cover and grill for 1¼ hours. Add additional coals as necessary.

3. Meanwhile, for sauce, in a medium saucepan combine barbecue sauce, onion, garlic, and chipotle pepper in adobo sauce. Bring to boiling; reduce heat. Cover and simmer for 10 minutes.

4. Continue grilling ribs for 15 to 30 minutes more or until ribs are tender, brushing frequently with sauce. Reheat any remaining sauce until bubbly; pass with ribs.

Nutrition Facts per serving: 446 calories, 17 g total fat, 99 mg cholesterol, 883 mg sodium, 23 g carbohydrate, 49 g protein.

Strawberry-Jalapeño Barbecue Ribs

Pork loin back ribs slathered with this fruity-jalapeño sauce are a palate-pleasing sensation.

Prep: 20 minutes **Grill:** 1½ hours **Makes:** 6 servings

1. For sauce, in a small saucepan cook onion and garlic in hot oil until tender. Stir in the catsup, strawberry preserves or jam, vinegar or beer, jalapeño peppers, steak sauce, and chili powder. Bring just to boiling; reduce heat. Simmer, uncovered, about 10 minutes or until slightly thickened, stirring occasionally. Set aside.

2. For rub, in a small bowl stir together the cumin, garlic salt, and ground red pepper. Sprinkle rub evenly over both sides of ribs; rub in with your fingers. Cut ribs into serving-size pieces.

3. In a grill with a cover arrange medium-hot coals around a drip pan. Test for medium heat above the pan. Place ribs, bone sides down, on grill rack over pan. (Or place ribs in a rib rack; place on grill rack.) Cover and grill for 1½ to 1¾ hours or until the ribs are tender, brushing occasionally with the sauce during the last 10 minutes of grilling. Add additional coals as needed. Reheat any remaining sauce until bubbly; serve with the ribs.

Nutrition Facts per serving: 329 calories, 11 g total fat, 62 mg cholesterol, 404 mg sodium, 26 g carbohydrate, 29 g protein.

Note: Because chile peppers, such as jalapeños, contain volatile oils that can burn your skin and eyes, avoid direct contact with them as much as possible. When working with chile peppers, wear plastic or rubber gloves. If your bare hands do touch the chile peppers, wash your hands and nails well with soap and warm water.

- ¼ cup chopped onion
- 1 clove garlic, minced
- 1 tablespoon cooking oil
- ½ cup catsup
- ½ cup strawberry preserves or strawberry jam
- ¼ cup cider vinegar or beer
- 1 to 2 fresh jalapeño peppers, seeded and finely chopped*
- 1 tablespoon bottled steak sauce
- 1 teaspoon chili powder
- ½ teaspoon ground cumin
- ¼ teaspoon garlic salt
- ⅛ to ¼ teaspoon ground red pepper
- 3 pounds pork loin back ribs

Thai-Coconut Ribs

Look for canned coconut milk in the Asian food section of your supermarket or at an Asian specialty store.

Prep: 15 minutes   **Marinate:** 8 to 24 hours   **Grill:** 1½ hours   **Makes:** 6 servings

4 **pounds pork loin back ribs**
1 **cup purchased unsweetened coconut milk**
3 **tablespoons brown sugar**
3 **tablespoons soy sauce**
1 **tablespoon grated fresh ginger**
1 **teaspoon finely shredded lime peel**
1 **tablespoon lime juice**
4 **cloves garlic, minced**
1 **teaspoon crushed red pepper**

1. Trim fat from ribs. Cut into serving-size pieces. Place ribs in a self-sealing plastic bag set in a shallow dish. For marinade, in a small bowl combine coconut milk, brown sugar, soy sauce, ginger, lime peel, lime juice, garlic, and red pepper. Pour over ribs; seal bag. Marinate in the refrigerator for at least 8 hours or up to 24 hours, turning bag occasionally. Drain ribs, reserving the marinade.

2. In a grill with a cover arrange medium-hot coals around a drip pan. Test for medium heat above the pan. Place the ribs, bone sides down, on grill rack over pan. (Or place ribs in a rib rack; place on grill rack.) Cover and grill for 1½ to 1¾ hours or until ribs are tender, brushing frequently with reserved marinade during the first hour of grilling. Add additional coals as needed. Discard any remaining marinade.

Nutrition Facts per serving: 431 calories, 32 g total fat, 99 mg cholesterol, 607 mg sodium, 9 g carbohydrate, 25 g protein.

Grilled Italian Sausage with Sweet and Sour Peppers

If you like, serve the sausages with purchased polenta that you sliced and heated on the grill.

Prep: 20 minutes **Grill:** 20 minutes **Makes:** 6 servings

1. In a small nonstick skillet cook and stir almonds for 1 to 2 minutes or until golden brown. Stir in raisins. Remove skillet from heat. Let stand for 1 minute. Carefully stir in vinegar, sugar, salt, and black pepper. Cook and stir just until the sugar dissolves. Set aside.

2. Drizzle oil over sweet pepper strips and onion slices. Prick sausages several times with a fork. In a grill with a cover arrange medium-hot coals around a drip pan. Test for medium heat above pan. Place sausages on grill rack over pan. Cover and grill for 10 minutes. Turn sausages. Place vegetables on rack alongside sausages. Cover and grill for 10 to 20 minutes more or until sausages are cooked through (an instant-read thermometer inserted from an end into the center of sausage should register 160°) and vegetables are tender, turning vegetables once halfway through grilling. Remove vegetables when done.

3. In a large bowl toss the vegetables with the almond mixture; spoon onto a serving platter. Top with sausages.

Nutrition Facts per serving: 276 calories, 19 g total fat, 59 mg cholesterol, 604 mg sodium, 15 g carbohydrate, 13 g protein.

- 3 tablespoons slivered almonds
- ¼ cup raisins
- 3 tablespoons red wine vinegar
- 2 tablespoons sugar
- ¼ teaspoon salt
- ⅛ teaspoon ground black pepper
- 1 tablespoon olive oil
- 2 green sweet peppers, cut into 1-inch-wide strips
- 2 red sweet peppers, cut into 1-inch-wide strips
- 1 medium red onion, thickly sliced
- 6 uncooked sweet (mild) Italian sausage links

Sausage Safety

Because fresh sausage is often seasoned with ingredients that change the color of the meat, the internal color of a sausage link or patty is not a reliable indicator of doneness. To make sure sausage is thoroughly cooked, check its internal temperature with an instant-read thermometer. A fresh pork sausage link or patty cooked to 160°, regardless of color, is safe. To measure the doneness of a link, insert the instant-read thermometer from one end into the center. To measure the doneness of a patty, insert the thermometer into the side to a depth of 2 to 3 inches.

Grilled Ham with Fruit Salsa

Smoky ham paired with a refreshing mango-apple salsa is hard to resist.

Prep: 10 minutes   **Chill:** 30 minutes to 24 hours   **Grill:** 10 minutes   **Makes:** 4 servings

1 mango, peeled and diced
½ of a Granny Smith apple,
   cored and diced
1 tablespoon snipped
   fresh cilantro
2 teaspoons lime juice
1 teaspoon sugar
   Dash salt
½ teaspoon cumin
½ teaspoon sugar
½ teaspoon olive oil
¼ teaspoon pepper
1¾ pounds bone-in ham steak,
   cut ½ inch thick
   Cooked rice (optional)
   Fresh cilantro sprigs
   (optional)

1. For salsa, in a medium bowl combine mango, apple, snipped cilantro, lime juice, the 1 teaspoon sugar, and the salt. Cover and chill in the refrigerator for at least 30 minutes or up to 24 hours.

2. For brush-on, in a small bowl combine cumin, the ½ teaspoon sugar, the oil, and pepper. Brush on both sides of ham. Grill on the rack of an uncovered grill directly over medium coals for 10 to 12 minutes or until heated through, turning once halfway through grilling.

3. Top with salsa. If desired, serve with cooked rice. If desired, garnish with cilantro sprigs.

Nutrition Facts per serving: 280 calories, 12 g total fat, 74 mg cholesterol, 1,909 mg sodium, 13 g carbohydrate, 29 g protein.

Herbed Lamb with Apples

Leaving the apples unpeeled helps the rings maintain their shape.

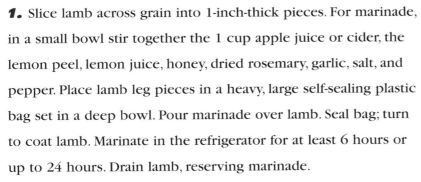

Prep: 20 minutes **Marinate:** 6 to 24 hours **Grill:** 16 minutes **Makes:** 8 servings

1. Slice lamb across grain into 1-inch-thick pieces. For marinade, in a small bowl stir together the 1 cup apple juice or cider, the lemon peel, lemon juice, honey, dried rosemary, garlic, salt, and pepper. Place lamb leg pieces in a heavy, large self-sealing plastic bag set in a deep bowl. Pour marinade over lamb. Seal bag; turn to coat lamb. Marinate in the refrigerator for at least 6 hours or up to 24 hours. Drain lamb, reserving marinade.

2. Place apple rings on an 18×18-inch piece of heavy foil. Sprinkle with the 3 tablespoons apple juice or cider. Bring up 2 opposite edges of the foil; seal edges with a double fold. Fold remaining edges to enclose apples, leaving space for steam to build.

3. In a grill with a cover arrange medium-hot coals around a drip pan. Test for medium heat above pan. Place lamb and the apple packet on the grill rack over pan. Cover and grill lamb to desired doneness, turning once halfway through grilling and brushing occasionally with reserved marinade during first 10 minutes of grilling. [Allow 16 to 18 minutes for medium-rare (145°) or 18 to 20 minutes for medium doneness (160°).] Discard any remaining marinade. Grill apple rings for 16 to 18 minutes or just until tender, turning packet often; remove packet when apples are tender. Serve apple rings with lamb. If desired, garnish with fresh rosemary and lemon peel strips.

Nutrition Facts per serving: 175 calories, 5 g total fat, 57 mg cholesterol, 212 mg sodium, 13 g carbohydrate, 18 g protein.

- 2 **pounds boneless leg of lamb**
- 1 **cup apple juice or apple cider**
- ¼ **teaspoon finely shredded lemon peel**
- 2 **tablespoons lemon juice**
- 1 **tablespoon honey**
- 1 **teaspoon dried rosemary, crushed**
- 1 **clove garlic, minced**
- ½ **teaspoon salt**
- ¼ **teaspoon pepper**
- 4 **small red and/or yellow apples, cored and sliced crosswise into ½-inch-thick rings**
- 3 **tablespoons apple juice or apple cider**
  Fresh rosemary sprigs tied with lemon peel strips (optional)

Tandoori-Style Lamb Chops

Squash, pita bread, and a cooling yogurt-mint mixture complement these chutney-topped chops.

Prep: 20 minutes **Grill:** 12 minutes **Makes:** 4 servings

2 tablespoons cooking oil

6 cloves garlic, minced

2 teaspoons grated fresh ginger

1 tablespoon garam masala*

½ teaspoon salt

8 lamb loin chops, cut 1 inch thick

2 medium yellow summer squash and/or zucchini, halved lengthwise

4 pita bread rounds

½ cup plain low-fat yogurt

1 tablespoon snipped fresh mint

¼ cup chutney or hot chutney

1. In a small bowl combine oil, garlic, ginger, garam masala, and salt. Brush oil mixture onto all sides of lamb chops and squash.

2. Grill chops and squash on the rack of an uncovered grill directly over medium coals until chops are desired doneness and squash is tender, turning once halfway through grilling. [Allow 12 to 14 minutes for medium-rare (145°) or 15 to 17 minutes for medium doneness (160°).] For the last 2 minutes of grilling, place pita rounds on grill rack to heat.

3. Meanwhile, in a small bowl combine yogurt and mint. Transfer squash to a cutting board; cool slightly and slice diagonally into ½-inch-thick pieces. Serve squash, yogurt mixture, pita bread, sand chutney with chops.

Nutrition Facts per serving: 615 calories, 22 g total fat, 135 mg cholesterol, 735 mg sodium, 51 g carbohydrate, 51 g protein.

Note: Look for garam masala at Indian food markets or in the specialty foods section of larger supermarkets. If it's not available locally, make your own blend by combining 1 teaspoon ground cumin, 1 teaspoon ground coriander, ½ teaspoon pepper, ½ teaspoon ground cardamom, ¼ teaspoon ground cinnamon, and ¼ teaspoon ground cloves. Store the mixture in a cool dry place.

Garlic and Rosemary Grilled Lamb Chops

Garlic, rosemary, and thyme are the perfect seasoning counterpoints to succulent lamb.

Prep: 10 minutes **Grill:** 16 minutes **Makes:** 4 servings

1. Spread both sides of lamb chops with mustard. In a small bowl stir together garlic, rosemary, thyme, and pepper. Press mixture evenly onto both sides of each lamb chop.

2. In a grill with a cover arrange medium-hot coals around a drip pan. Test for medium heat above the pan. Place lamb chops on grill rack over pan. Cover and grill to desired doneness, turning once halfway through grilling. [Allow 16 to 18 minutes for medium-rare (145°) or 18 to 20 minutes for medium doneness (160°).]

Nutrition Facts per serving: **211 calories, 11 g total fat, 80 mg cholesterol, 177 mg sodium, 1 g carbohydrate, 25 g protein.**

- 8 lamb rib or loin chops, cut 1 inch thick
- 2 tablespoons coarse-grain brown mustard
- 2 cloves garlic, minced
- 1 tablespoon snipped fresh rosemary or 1 teaspoon dried rosemary, crushed
- 1½ teaspoons snipped fresh thyme or ½ teaspoon dried thyme, crushed
- ½ teaspoon cracked black pepper

Apple-Glazed Lamb Chops

Having friends over for dinner? Serve these curry-spiked chops with couscous as a side dish and sorbet for dessert.

Prep: 15 minutes   **Grill:** 12 minutes   **Makes:** 4 servings

3 tablespoons apple jelly
1 green onion, thinly sliced
1 tablespoon soy sauce
2 teaspoons lemon juice
⅛ teaspoon curry powder
   Dash ground cinnamon
   Dash ground red pepper
2 small red and/or green
   apples, cut crosswise
   into ¼-inch-thick slices
   Lemon juice
8 lamb loin chops,
   cut 1 inch thick
   Hot cooked couscous
   (optional)
1 tablespoon snipped
   fresh mint

1. For glaze, in a small saucepan heat and stir apple jelly, green onion, soy sauce, lemon juice, curry powder, cinnamon, and red pepper over medium heat until bubbly. Remove from heat. Remove seeds from apple slices. Brush apples with lemon juice. Set aside.

2. Grill chops on the rack of an uncovered grill directly over medium coals until desired doneness, turning once halfway through grilling and brushing once with glaze during last 5 minutes of grilling. [Allow 12 to 14 minutes for medium-rare (145°) or 15 to 17 minutes for medium doneness (160°).] Place apples on grill rack next to chops during the last 5 minutes of grilling, turning and brushing once with glaze. If desired, serve with couscous. Sprinkle chops with mint.

Nutrition Facts per serving: 385 calories, 14 g total fat, 133 mg cholesterol, 378 mg sodium, 20 g carbohydrate, 43 g protein.

Mongolian-Style Lamb Chops

A soy sauce, ginger, and sesame oil marinade makes these chops far-from-middling.

Prep: 15 minutes **Marinate:** 2 to 3 hours **Grill:** 12 minutes **Makes:** 4 to 6 servings

1. Place chops in a heavy, large self-sealing plastic bag set in a shallow bowl. For marinade, in a small bowl stir together the soy sauce, brown sugar, garlic, ginger, and sesame oil. Pour marinade over chops. Seal bag; turn to coat chops. Marinate in the refrigerator for at least 2 hours or up to 3 hours, turning bag occasionally.

2. Drain chops, discarding marinade. Grill chops on the rack of an uncovered grill directly over medium coals until desired doneness, turning once halfway through grilling. [Allow 12 to 14 minutes for medium-rare (145°) or 15 to 17 minutes for medium doneness (160°).] If desired, garnish with cilantro and lemon wedges.

Nutrition Facts per serving: 225 calories, 10 g total fat, 83 mg cholesterol, 579 mg sodium, 5 g carbohydrate, 26 g protein.

4 to 6 lamb loin chops,
    cut 1 inch thick
2 tablespoons soy sauce
1 tablespoon brown sugar
6 cloves garlic, minced
1½ teaspoons grated
    fresh ginger
1 teaspoon toasted sesame oil
    Fresh cilantro (optional)
    Lemon wedges (optional)

Poultry

Build a reputation as a cookout master with any one of these succulent chicken, duck, or turkey tempters. Choose from ideas for whole birds or chicken, duck, or turkey pieces.

Chicken with Garden Salsa, page 79

Garlicky Grilled Chickens

Garlic and coffee are an unusual duo, but they work together beautifully in this recipe.

Prep: 15 minutes **Grill:** 1 hour **Stand:** 10 minutes **Makes:** 8 servings

2 tablespoons cooking oil

4 cloves garlic, minced

2 2½- to 3-pound whole
   broiler-fryer chickens

2 teaspoons dark roast
   ground coffee

Salt

Freshly ground black pepper

1. In a small bowl combine oil and garlic. Brush chickens with garlic mixture. Sprinkle with coffee, salt, and pepper. Skewer neck skin to backs. Tie legs to tails. Twist wing tips under backs.

2. In a grill with a cover arrange medium-hot coals around a drip pan. Test for medium heat above pan. Place whole chickens, breast sides up, on grill rack over pan. Cover and grill for 1 to 1¼ hours or until an instant-read thermometer inserted in center of an inside thigh muscle (make sure bulb does not touch bone) registers 180°. At this time, drumsticks move easily in their sockets and chickens are no longer pink.

3. Remove chickens from grill. Cover with foil; let stand 10 minutes before carving.

Nutrition Facts per serving: 200 calories, 12 g total fat, 66 mg cholesterol, 110 mg sodium, 0 g carbohydrate, 20 g protein.

Spice-Grilled Chicken

Jasmine rice studded with snipped dried apricots is a flavorful partner for the spicy chicken.

Prep: 20 minutes **Grill:** 1 hour **Stand:** 10 minutes **Makes:** 4 to 6 servings

1. In a small bowl combine brown sugar, cinnamon, paprika, salt, pepper, and allspice. Set aside 1½ teaspoons of the mixture. Skewer chicken neck skin to back. Twist wing tips under back. Brush whole chicken or drumsticks with oil; gently rub remaining cinnamon mixture onto chicken. Tie legs to tail.

2. In a grill with a cover arrange medium-hot coals around a drip pan. Test for medium heat above pan. Place whole chicken, breast side up, on the grill rack over pan. Cover and grill 1 to 1¼ hours or until an instant-read thermometer inserted in center of an inside thigh muscle (make sure bulb does not touch bone) registers 180°. At this time, drumsticks move easily in their sockets and chicken is no longer pink. (Or grill drumsticks on grill rack over pan for 50 to 60 minutes or until chicken is tender and no longer pink.)

3. Meanwhile, in medium saucepan combine the 1½ teaspoons reserved cinnamon mixture, the uncooked rice, and broth. Bring to boiling; reduce heat. Cover and simmer for 15 minutes. Remove from heat. Stir in dried apricots and raisins. Cover and let stand for 5 minutes before serving.

4. Remove chicken from grill. Cover with foil; let stand 10 minutes before carving. Spoon rice onto platter; top with chicken. If desired, serve with lemon wedges and Swiss chard. Carve the whole chicken or cut it into 4 to 6 pieces using kitchen shears. Pass chopped peanuts.

Nutrition Facts per serving: 646 calories, 23 g total fat, 207 mg cholesterol, 1,012 mg sodium, 54 g carbohydrate, 58 g protein.

- **2 teaspoons brown sugar**
- **1½ teaspoons ground cinnamon**
- **1 teaspoon smoked paprika or paprika**
- **½ teaspoon salt**
- **½ teaspoon pepper**
- **½ teaspoon ground allspice**
- **1 3-pound whole broiler-fryer chicken or 12 chicken drumsticks**
- **4 teaspoons cooking oil**
- **1 cup jasmine or long grain rice**
- **2 cups chicken broth**
- **¼ cup snipped dried apricots**
- **¼ cup golden raisins**
- **4 lemon wedges (optional) Swiss chard (optional)**
- **2 tablespoons chopped peanuts**

Herb-Rubbed Grilled Chicken

No fresh herbs on hand? Try this rub that uses three different dried herbs.

Prep: 10 minutes **Grill:** 35 minutes **Makes:** 6 servings

½ teaspoon salt

½ teaspoon dried thyme, crushed

½ teaspoon dried rosemary, crushed

½ teaspoon dried savory, crushed

¼ teaspoon pepper

2½ to 3 pounds meaty chicken pieces (breasts, thighs, and drumsticks)

Fresh rosemary sprigs (optional)

1. For rub, in a small bowl combine salt, thyme, dried rosemary, savory, and pepper. Sprinkle rub evenly over chicken; rub in with your fingers.

2. Lightly grease the rack of an uncovered grill. Place chicken, bone sides up, on rack. Grill directly over medium coals for 35 to 45 minutes or until chicken is tender and no longer pink, turning once halfway through grilling. If desired, garnish with fresh rosemary sprigs.

Nutrition Facts per serving: **113 calories, 2 g total fat, 50 mg cholesterol, 312 mg sodium, 0 g carbohydrate, 21 g protein.**

Is It Cooked?

Judging poultry doneness can sometimes be tricky. To make sure the poultry you serve is completely cooked, grill it until the meat is tender and no longer pink around the bone and the juices run clear. It is easy to judge the doneness of chicken breasts and other individual pieces this way. Or insert an instant-read thermometer into the thickest part of each cooked piece, making sure the bulb does not touch bone. If you use a thermometer, chicken breasts should register 170° and chicken thighs or drumsticks 180°.

For whole birds and poultry portions, the most accurate way to determine doneness is to use an oven-going meat thermometer and insert it prior to cooking. For whole birds, insert the thermometer into the center of an inside thigh muscle, making sure the bulb does not touch bone. For turkey breast portions, insert the thermometer into the thickest part, making sure not to touch the bone. For chicken halves, quarters, and other smaller portions, use an instant-read thermometer, inserting it into the center of the cooked piece, being careful not to touch bone. The poultry is cooked when the thermometer registers 180°, except in the breast portion where it should register 170°.

Chicken with Garden Salsa

If you make this recipe with chicken quarters, break the wing, hip, and drumstick joints so the quarters will lie flat on the grill. Also, twist wing tips under the backs.

Prep: 10 minutes **Grill:** 50 minutes **Makes:** 4 servings

1. Sprinkle chicken lightly with salt and black pepper. In a grill with a cover arrange medium-hot coals around drip pan. Test for medium heat above the pan. Place chicken, bone sides up, on the grill rack over the pan. Cover and grill for 50 to 60 minutes or until an instant-read thermometer inserted in center of breast (make sure bulb does not touch bone) registers 170° or inserted in center of an inside thigh muscle (make sure bulb does not touch bone) registers 180°. Turn once halfway through grilling.

2. Meanwhile, in a small bowl combine salsa and lime juice. Set aside ½ cup of the salsa-lime mixture. Brush chicken occasionally with the remaining salsa-lime mixture during the last 10 to 15 minutes of grilling. Discard remainder of salsa-lime mixture used for brush-on.

3. For sauce, in a small saucepan combine the reserved salsa-lime mixture, the cucumber, sweet pepper, and cilantro. Bring just to boiling. Remove from heat. Serve the cucumber mixture with chicken.

Nutrition Facts per serving: **348 calories, 17 g total fat, 130 mg cholesterol, 370 mg sodium, 6 g carbohydrate, 43 g protein.**

2½ pounds chicken quarters
   or meaty chicken pieces
   (breasts, thighs, and
   drumsticks)
   Salt
   Ground black pepper
1 cup bottled salsa
1 tablespoon lime juice
½ cup finely chopped, seeded
   cucumber
¼ cup chopped green sweet
   pepper
1 tablespoon snipped fresh
   cilantro

Cranberry-Maple Chicken

Brushing on the sweet cranberry sauce during the last few minutes of grilling allows the sauce to flavor the chicken without burning.

Prep: 10 minutes **Grill:** 1 hour **Makes:** 4 to 6 servings

½ cup whole cranberry sauce

¼ cup maple syrup

3 tablespoons catsup

2 tablespoons cider vinegar

½ teaspoon onion powder

1 3- to 3½-pound broiler-fryer chicken, halved

1. For sauce, in a small saucepan combine cranberry sauce, maple syrup, catsup, cider vinegar, and onion powder. Bring to boiling; reduce heat. Simmer, uncovered, for 5 minutes, stirring occasionally.

2. In a grill with a cover arrange medium-hot coals around a drip pan. Test for medium heat above the pan. Place chicken, bone sides up, on grill rack over pan. Cover and grill for 1 to 1¼ hours or until an instant-read thermometer inserted in center of an inside thigh muscle (make sure bulb does not touch bone) registers 180°, brushing occasionally with sauce during the last 10 minutes of grilling.

3. To serve, cut each chicken half into 2 or 3 pieces. Reheat remaining sauce until bubbly; serve with chicken.

Nutrition Facts per serving: 438 calories, 18 g total fat, 118 mg cholesterol, 274 mg sodium, 31 g carbohydrate, 37 g protein.

Texas-Style Barbecued Chicken Legs

If you like, serve this stick-to-the-ribs chicken with grilled

sweet pepper strips.

Prep: 20 minutes **Grill:** 40 minutes **Makes:** 6 servings

1. For sauce, in a medium saucepan cook and stir onion, garlic, chili powder, and sage in hot margarine or butter until onion is tender. Stir in catsup, the water, vinegar, sugar, lemon juice, Worcestershire sauce, salt, bottled hot pepper sauce, and black pepper. Bring to boiling; reduce heat. Simmer, uncovered, for 5 minutes, stirring occasionally.

2. Grill chicken, bone sides up, on the rack of an uncovered grill directly over medium coals for 40 to 50 minutes or until chicken is tender and no longer pink, turning once halfway through grilling and brushing with sauce during the last 10 minutes of grilling.

3. To serve, reheat remaining sauce until bubbly; pass with chicken.

Nutrition Facts per serving: 276 calories, 15 g total fat, 86 mg cholesterol, 596 mg sodium, 11 g carbohydrate, 25 g protein.

- **1 medium onion, finely chopped**
- **2 cloves garlic, minced**
- **1 teaspoon chili powder**
- **¼ teaspoon ground sage**
- **1 tablespoon margarine or butter**
- **½ cup catsup**
- **2 tablespoons water**
- **2 tablespoons vinegar**
- **1 tablespoon sugar**
- **1 tablespoon lemon juice**
- **1 tablespoon Worcestershire sauce**
- **½ teaspoon salt**
- **½ teaspoon bottled hot pepper sauce**
- **¼ teaspoon cracked black pepper**
- **6 chicken legs (thigh-drumstick pieces) (3 to 3½ pounds total)**

Grilled Provençal Chicken

Indirect grilling helps assure that the herb-seasoned chicken doesn't burn.

Prep: 15 minutes **Chill:** 8 to 24 hours **Grill:** 50 minutes **Stand:** 10 minutes
Makes: 4 servings

5 teaspoons snipped fresh
   rosemary or 1½ teaspoons
   dried rosemary, crushed
1 tablespoon snipped fresh
   thyme or 1 teaspoon
   dried thyme, crushed
1 tablespoon olive oil
2 teaspoons grated orange
   peel
½ teaspoon salt
½ teaspoon pepper
1 3- to 3½-pound broiler-fryer
   chicken, cut up
   Orange slices, halved
   (optional)
   Fresh herb sprigs (optional)

1. For rub, in a small bowl combine rosemary, thyme, oil, orange peel, salt, and pepper. Sprinkle rub evenly over chicken pieces; rub in with your fingers. Cover and chill in the refrigerator for at least 8 hours or up to 24 hours.

2. In a grill with a cover arrange medium-hot coals around a drip pan. Test for medium heat above pan. Place chicken on grill rack over pan. Cover and grill for 50 to 60 minutes or until chicken is tender and no longer pink, turning once halfway through grilling. If desired, garnish with orange slices and fresh herb sprigs.

Nutrition Facts per serving: 450 calories, 27 g total fat, 154 mg cholesterol, 417 mg sodium, 1 g carbohydrate, 48 g protein.

Beer-Grilled Chicken

The marinade for this delectable chicken gets its pizzazz from beer, soy sauce, ginger, and caraway seed.

Prep: 10 minutes **Marinate:** 4 to 24 hours **Grill:** 35 minutes **Makes:** 4 servings

1. Skin chicken. Place chicken in a heavy, large self-sealing plastic bag set into a deep bowl. For marinade, in a medium bowl stir together beer, soy sauce, brown sugar, ginger, and caraway seeds. Pour marinade over chicken. Seal bag; turn to coat chicken. Marinate in the refrigerator for at least 4 hours or up to 24 hours, turning bag occasionally.

2. Drain chicken, reserving marinade. Grill chicken, bone sides up, on the rack of an uncovered grill directly over medium coals for 35 to 45 minutes or until tender and no longer pink, turning once halfway through grilling and brushing occasionally with reserved marinade during the first 25 minutes of grilling. Discard any remaining marinade.

Nutrition Facts per serving: **165 calories, 5 g total fat, 62 mg cholesterol, 287 mg sodium, 6 g carbohydrate, 21 g protein.**

- 1¼ to 1½ **pounds meaty chicken pieces (breasts, thighs, and drumsticks)**
- 1 **12-ounce can beer (at room temperature)**
- 3 **tablespoons reduced-sodium soy sauce**
- 2 **tablespoons brown sugar**
- 1 **tablespoon grated fresh ginger**
- 1 **teaspoon caraway seeds**

Skinning Chicken

Many recipes call for chicken to be skinned. Why? Removing the skin and underlying fat helps lower calories and fat in chicken dishes. Skinning chicken also allows marinades or brush-ons to penetrate more deeply, resulting in a fuller flavor. To skin chicken, place each piece, skin side up, on a cutting board. Starting on one edge of the piece, work your fingers under the skin and pull it away from the meat. Although skinning is easiest with breasts and thighs, you also can skin drumsticks and wings. But they will involve more work because the skin is attached in more places.

Ruby-Glazed Chicken Breasts

A luscious currant jelly and apple juice glaze makes these chicken breast halves low in fat but high in flavor.

Prep: 10 minutes   **Grill:** 35 minutes   **Makes:** 6 servings

⅓ cup apple juice or apple
   cider
3 tablespoons currant jelly
1 teaspoon cornstarch
¼ teaspoon salt
⅛ teaspoon dried marjoram,
   crushed
6 small chicken breast halves
   (about 2¼ pounds total)

1. For sauce, in a small saucepan combine apple juice or apple cider, currant jelly, cornstarch, and salt. Cook and stir until thickened and bubbly. Cook and stir 2 minutes more. Remove from heat. Stir in marjoram. Set aside.

2. If desired, skin chicken. Grill chicken, bone sides up, on the rack of an uncovered grill directly over medium coals for 35 to 45 minutes or until chicken is tender and no longer pink, turning once halfway through grilling and brushing with sauce during the last 10 minutes of grilling.

3. To serve, reheat any remaining sauce until bubbly; brush onto grilled chicken.

Nutrition Facts per serving: 167 calories, 3 g total fat, 69 mg cholesterol, 150 mg sodium, 9 g carbohydrate, 25 g protein.

Honey-Barbecued Broilers

Chicken quarters with an herb rub and a honey brush-on make for some mighty fine barbecue.

Prep: 15 minutes **Chill:** 2 to 24 hours **Grill:** 50 minutes **Makes:** 4 servings

1. If desired, skin chicken. For rub, in a small bowl combine garlic, marjoram, mustard, salt, and pepper. Sprinkle rub evenly over chicken; rub in with your fingers. In a small bowl combine honey and vinegar; lightly brush over entire surface of chicken pieces. Cover and chill in the refrigerator for at least 2 hours or up to 24 hours.

2. In a grill with a cover arrange medium-hot coals around a drip pan. Test for medium heat above pan. Place chicken pieces, bone sides up, on grill rack over pan. Cover and grill for 50 to 60 minutes or until chicken is tender and no longer pink, turning once halfway through grilling. If desired, serve chicken over torn mixed greens. If desired, garnish with edible flowers.

Nutrition Facts per serving: 316 calories, 15 g total fat, 99 mg cholesterol, 227 mg sodium, 12 g carbohydrate, 31 g protein.

1 2½- to 3-pound broiler-fryer chicken, quartered
4 cloves garlic, minced
1½ teaspoons dried marjoram, crushed
1 teaspoon dry mustard
¼ teaspoon salt
¼ teaspoon pepper
2 tablespoons honey
2 tablespoons balsamic vinegar
   Torn mixed salad greens (optional)
   Edible flowers (optional)

Peach-Glazed BBQ Chicken

Just about any flavor of spreadable fruit will work for this grilled chicken.

Prep: 15 minutes   **Grill:** 50 minutes   **Makes:** 4 servings

½ cup peach spreadable fruit
3 tablespoons vinegar
2 teaspoons Worcestershire
   sauce
¼ teaspoon ground cinnamon
⅛ teaspoon ground allspice
2 to 2½ pounds meaty
   chicken pieces (breasts,
   thighs, and drumsticks)

1. For glaze, in a small saucepan combine the spreadable fruit, vinegar, Worcestershire sauce, cinnamon, and allspice. Heat and stir just until the spreadable fruit melts.

2. Skin chicken. In a grill with a cover arrange medium-hot coals around drip pan. Test for medium heat above pan. Place chicken, bone sides up, on grill rack over pan. Cover and grill for 50 to 60 minutes or until chicken is tender and no longer pink, turning once halfway through grilling and brushing the chicken occasionally with the glaze during the last 10 minutes of grilling. To serve, reheat any remaining glaze until bubbly; spoon over the chicken.

Nutrition Facts per serving: 304 calories, 7 g total fat, 92 mg cholesterol, 112 mg sodium, 29 g carbohydrate, 30 g protein.

Drip Pan Advice

When you're grilling foods indirectly, recipes often call for a drip pan. Usually made from foil and positioned underneath the food, a drip pan helps prevent flare-ups by capturing any fat that drips from the meat, poultry, or fish. Drip pans also can be used to hold liquids, such as water seasoned with herbs, fruit juice, beer, or wine. These liquids create steam when heated and help flavor food during long, slow grilling. Commercial drip pans are available where grilling supplies are sold, but you can substitute a disposable foil roasting pan or shape your own pan using heavy foil.

Italian-Seasoned Chicken

A marinade made with wine, olive oil, Italian seasoning, and garlic—now that's Italian!

Prep: 10 minutes **Marinate:** 8 to 24 hours **Grill:** 50 minutes **Makes:** 4 to 6 servings

1. If desired, skin chicken. Put chicken in a heavy, large self-sealing plastic bag set in a shallow bowl.

2. For marinade, in a small bowl combine wine, olive oil, Italian seasoning, and garlic. Pour marinade over chicken. Seal bag; turn to coat chicken. Marinate in the refrigerator for at least 8 hours or up to 24 hours, turning bag occasionally.

3. Drain chicken, reserving marinade. In a grill with a cover arrange medium-hot coals around a drip pan. Test for medium heat above the pan. Place chicken, bone sides up, on grill rack over pan. Cover and grill for 50 to 60 minutes or until chicken is tender and no longer pink, turning once and brushing once with reserved marinade halfway through grilling. Discard any remaining marinade. If desired, garnish with fresh herbs.

Nutrition Facts per serving: 388 calories, 26 g total fat, 90 mg cholesterol, 74 mg sodium, 1 g carbohydrate, 38 g protein.

4 to 6 medium chicken breast halves (2 to 3 pounds total)
1½ cups dry white wine
½ cup olive oil
1 tablespoon dried Italian seasoning, crushed
2 teaspoons bottled minced garlic
Fresh herb sprigs (optional)

Chicken Breasts with Hotter-Than-Heck Barbecue Sauce

Chipotle peppers in adobo sauce are dried, smoked jalapeño peppers in a dark spicy sauce.

Prep: 25 minutes **Grill:** 12 minutes **Makes:** 6 servings

¼ cup canned chipotle
    peppers in adobo sauce
    Nonstick cooking spray
⅓ cup finely chopped onion
3 cloves garlic, minced
1 cup catsup
3 tablespoons white wine
    vinegar
3 tablespoons molasses
    or sorghum
1 tablespoon Worcestershire
    sauce
6 medium skinless, boneless
    chicken breast halves
    (about 1½ pounds total)

1. For the sauce, remove any stems from chipotle peppers. Place peppers and adobo sauce in a blender container. Cover and blend until smooth. Set aside.

2. Coat an unheated medium saucepan with nonstick cooking spray. Preheat saucepan over medium heat. Add onion and garlic; cook until tender. Stir in chipotle peppers, catsup, vinegar, molasses or sorghum, and Worcestershire sauce. Bring to boiling; reduce heat. Simmer, uncovered, about 10 minutes or until slightly thickened.

3. Grill chicken on the rack of an uncovered grill directly over medium coals for 12 to 15 minutes or until chicken is tender and no longer pink, turning once halfway through grilling and brushing with sauce during the last 5 minutes of grilling.

4. To serve, reheat remaining sauce until bubbly; pass with the chicken.

Nutrition Facts per serving: **291 calories, 6 g total fat, 59 mg cholesterol, 1,399 mg sodium, 36 g carbohydrate, 23 g protein.**

Chicken Teriyaki with Summer Fruit

The orange-marmalade and teriyaki sauce brush-on for the chicken plays well against the citrus-spiked fruit.

Prep: 20 minutes **Grill:** 12 minutes **Makes:** 4 servings

1. In a small bowl combine the fruit, the 2 tablespoons marmalade, the lemon or lime juice, ginger, sesame oil, and hot pepper sauce. Set aside.

2. In a small bowl stir together the 1 tablespoon orange marmalade and the teriyaki sauce; brush over chicken breasts. Grill chicken on the rack of an uncovered grill directly over medium coals for 12 to 15 minutes or until chicken is tender and no longer pink, turning once halfway through grilling. Serve with the fruit mixture. If desired, serve with hot cooked rice sprinkled with parsley. If desired, garnish with strawberries and kale.

Nutrition Facts per serving: 200 calories, 4 g total fat, 59 mg cholesterol, 136 mg sodium, 20 g carbohydrate, 22 g protein.

2 cups finely chopped
   nectarines, finely chopped
   plums, and/or blueberries
2 tablespoons orange
   marmalade, melted
1 tablespoon lemon juice
   or lime juice
½ teaspoon grated fresh ginger
¼ teaspoon toasted sesame oil
   Few dashes bottled hot
   pepper sauce
1 tablespoon orange
   marmalade
1 tablespoon reduced-sodium
   teriyaki sauce
4 medium skinless, boneless
   chicken breast halves
   (about 1 pound total)
   Hot cooked rice (optional)
   Snipped fresh parsley
   (optional)
   Fresh strawberries (optional)
   Flowering kale (optional)

Grilled Chicken with Black Bean Salsa

This Tex-Mex salsa also works well with grilled meats or fish— or serve it as a snack with chips.

Prep: 10 minutes   **Chill:** 30 minutes   **Grill:** 12 minutes   **Makes:** 4 servings

3 tablespoons lime juice

1 tablespoon honey

1 teaspoon paprika

½ teaspoon ground turmeric

⅛ teaspoon garlic powder

  Dash salt

  Dash ground red pepper

4 small skinless, boneless chicken breast halves (about 12 ounces total)

1 15-ounce can black beans, rinsed and drained

½ cup frozen whole kernel corn, cooked and drained

1 small tomato, chopped

2 tablespoons snipped fresh cilantro

1 fresh jalapeño pepper, seeded and finely chopped*

  Tomato wedges (optional)

1. In a small bowl combine 1 tablespoon of the lime juice, the honey, paprika, turmeric, garlic powder, salt, and red pepper. Brush over both sides of chicken breasts. Cover and chill in the refrigerator for 30 minutes.

2. Grill chicken on the rack of an uncovered grill directly over medium coals for 12 to 15 minutes or until chicken is tender and no longer pink, turning once halfway through grilling.

3. Meanwhile, for salsa, in a medium bowl combine black beans, corn, chopped tomato, cilantro, jalapeño pepper, and the remaining lime juice. Serve salsa with the chicken. If desired, garnish with tomato wedges.

Nutrition Facts per serving: 202 calories, 3 g total fat, 45 mg cholesterol, 340 mg sodium, 25 g carbohydrate, 24 g protein.

Note: Because chile peppers, such as jalapeños, contain volatile oils that can burn your skin and eyes, avoid direct contact with them as much as possible. When working with chile peppers, wear plastic or rubber gloves. If your bare hands do touch the chile peppers, wash your hands and nails well with soap and warm water.

Grilled Chicken Salad

Serve this hearty salad with your favorite muffins and tall glasses of iced tea.

Prep: 30 minutes **Marinate:** 6 to 24 hours **Grill:** 12 minutes **Makes:** 4 servings

1. Place chicken in a heavy, large self-sealing plastic bag set in a shallow bowl. For marinade, in a small bowl combine the ¼ cup orange juice concentrate, the lemon peel, lemon juice, oil, and garlic. Pour over chicken. Seal bag; turn to coat chicken. Marinate in the refrigerator for at least 6 hours or up to 24 hours, turning bag occasionally.

2. For dressing, in a bowl stir together mayonnaise dressing or salad dressing, milk, the 1 tablespoon orange juice concentrate, the mustard, and pepper. Cover; refrigerate until serving time.

3. Drain chicken, discarding marinade. Grill chicken on the rack of an uncovered grill directly over medium coals for 12 to 15 minutes or until chicken is tender and no longer pink, turning once halfway through grilling.

4. To serve, arrange greens and apple slices on 4 dinner plates. Slice chicken breast halves. Arrange chicken slices on top of the greens; drizzle with dressing. If desired, sprinkle with the toasted walnuts.

Nutrition Facts per serving: **202 calories, 4 g total fat, 45 mg cholesterol, 502 mg sodium, 23 g carbohydrate, 19 g protein.**

- 4 small skinless, boneless chicken breast halves (about 12 ounces total)
- ¼ cup frozen orange juice concentrate, thawed
- 2 teaspoons finely shredded lemon peel
- 2 tablespoons lemon juice
- 2 teaspoons olive oil
- 2 cloves garlic, minced
- ½ cup fat-free mayonnaise dressing or salad dressing
- 2 tablespoons milk
- 1 tablespoon frozen orange juice concentrate, thawed
- 1 tablespoon coarse-grain brown mustard
- ¼ teaspoon pepper
- 6 cups torn mixed salad greens
- 2 medium apples, cored and thinly sliced
- 1 tablespoon broken walnuts, toasted (optional)

Vietnamese-Style Chicken Breasts

Serve these flavorful Asian-accented chicken breasts with your favorite rice pilaf, sautéed yellow summer squash and zucchini, and orange slices.

Prep: 10 minutes **Marinate:** 30 minutes **Grill:** 12 minutes **Makes:** 4 servings

4 small skinless, boneless chicken breast halves (about 12 ounces total)

2 tablespoons fish sauce or soy sauce

2 tablespoons lime juice

1 tablespoon brown sugar

2 cloves garlic, minced

1 teaspoon finely grated fresh ginger

½ teaspoon crushed red pepper

½ teaspoon finely shredded lime peel (optional)

1. Place chicken in a heavy, large self-sealing plastic bag set in a shallow bowl. For marinade, in a small bowl combine fish sauce or soy sauce, lime juice, brown sugar, garlic, ginger, and crushed red pepper. Pour marinade over chicken. Seal bag; turn to coat chicken. Marinate in refrigerator for 30 minutes.

2. Drain chicken, reserving marinade. Grill chicken on the rack of an uncovered grill directly over medium coals for 12 to 15 minutes or until chicken is tender and no longer pink, turning once halfway through grilling.

3. For sauce, bring reserved marinade to boiling; boil for 1 minute. Strain, if desired. To serve, slice chicken; drizzle with sauce. If desired, garnish with lime peel.

Nutrition Facts per serving: **113 calories, 2 g total fat, 47 mg cholesterol, 322 mg sodium, 5 g carbohydrate, 17 g protein.**

Grilled Citrus Chicken And Vegetables

Ease the last-minute rush for dinner by marinating these chicken breasts a day ahead.

Prep: 15 minutes   **Marinate:** 6 to 24 hours   **Grill:** 12 minutes   **Makes:** 4 servings

1. Place chicken in a heavy, large self-sealing plastic bag set in a shallow bowl. Pour 1 cup of the Citrus-Spice Marinade over chicken; add orange slices. Refrigerate remaining marinade. Seal bag; turn to coat chicken. Marinate in the refrigerator for at least 6 hours or up to 24 hours, turning bag occasionally.

2. Drain chicken, discarding marinade and orange slices. Place chicken and vegetables on the rack of an uncovered grill directly over medium coals. Grill vegetables for 8 to 10 minutes or until tender, brushing occasionally with the refrigerated marinade. Grill chicken for 12 to 15 minutes or until chicken is tender and no longer pink, turning once halfway through grilling and brushing with refrigerated marinade during the last 5 minutes of grilling. Discard any remaining marinade. If desired, season chicken with salt and black pepper.

Citrus-Spice Marinade: In a screw-top jar combine ¾ cup orange juice; ¼ cup lemon juice; 3 tablespoons cooking oil; 2 tablespoons Worcestershire sauce; 2 cloves garlic, minced; ¾ teaspoon ground cumin; ½ teaspoon onion powder; ¼ teaspoon salt; and ¼ teaspoon ground black pepper. Cover and shake well to mix. Makes about 1⅓ cups.

Nutrition Facts per serving: 304 calories, 14 g total fat, 59 mg cholesterol, 268 mg sodium, 22 g carbohydrate, 24 g protein.

4 medium skinless, boneless chicken breast halves (about 1 pound total)
1 recipe Citrus-Spice Marinade
1 medium orange, sliced
1 small sweet onion, cut into ½-inch-thick slices
1 small eggplant, cut crosswise into 1-inch-thick slices
1 large red sweet pepper, cut into 1-inch-wide strips
1 medium zucchini or yellow summer squash, quartered lengthwise
Salt (optional)
Ground black pepper (optional)

Southwest Chicken Breasts

Another time, create a salad by slicing the chicken and combining it with torn salad greens. Use the avocado mixture as a dressing and sprinkle on your favorite shredded cheese.

Prep: 20 minutes **Marinate:** 2 to 24 hours **Grill:** 12 minutes **Makes:** 6 servings

¼ cup dry white wine

2 tablespoons olive oil
   or cooking oil

2 teaspoons snipped fresh
   tarragon or ¼ teaspoon
   dried tarragon, crushed

¼ teaspoon salt

6 medium skinless, boneless
   chicken breast halves
   (about 1½ pounds total)

2 avocados, pitted, peeled,
   and chopped

1 tomato, chopped

1 clove garlic, minced

2 tablespoons finely chopped,
   seeded fresh green chile
   peppers (such as jalapeño,
   serrano, or Anaheim)*

2 green onions, finely chopped

1 tablespoon snipped fresh
   cilantro

1 tablespoon honey

1 tablespoon lemon juice
   Lettuce leaves (optional)
   Sliced fresh red chile
   peppers (optional)*

1. For marinade, in a small bowl combine wine, oil, tarragon, and salt. Place chicken in a heavy, large self-sealing plastic bag set into a shallow bowl. Pour marinade over chicken. Seal bag; turn to coat chicken. Marinate in the refrigerator for at least 2 hours or up to 24 hours, turning bag occasionally.

2. In a medium a bowl combine avocados, tomato, garlic, chopped chile peppers, green onions, cilantro, honey, and lemon juice. Toss well to mix. Cover and chill in the refrigerator for up to 2 hours.

3. Drain chicken, reserving marinade. Grill chicken on the rack of an uncovered grill directly over medium coals for 12 to 15 minutes or until chicken is tender and no longer pink, turning once halfway through grilling and brushing once with reserved marinade after 6 minutes of grilling. Discard any remaining marinade. Serve with avocado mixture. If desired, serve on lettuce leaves. If desired, garnish with sliced red chile peppers.

Nutrition Facts per serving: 295 calories, 16 g total fat, 66 mg cholesterol, 169 mg sodium, 9 g carbohydrate, 28 g protein.

*__Note:__ Because chile peppers, such as jalapeños, serranos, or Anaheims, contain volatile oils that can burn your skin and eyes, avoid direct contact with them as much as possible. When working with chile peppers, wear plastic or rubber gloves. If your bare hands do touch the chile peppers, wash your hands and nails well with soap and warm water.

Grilled Jerk Chicken

You can buy Jamaican jerk seasoning or make it from scratch. In this recipe, jalapeños, thyme, and spices are blended with orange juice for a homemade version.

Prep: 15 minutes **Marinate:** 4 to 24 hours **Grill:** 12 minutes **Makes:** 4 servings

1. Place chicken in a heavy, large self-sealing plastic bag set in a shallow bowl. For marinade, in a food processor bowl or blender container combine onion, jalapeño peppers, thyme, allspice, salt, nutmeg, and cloves. Cover; process or blend until almost smooth. With food processor or blender running, add the ¼ cup orange juice. Process or blend until almost smooth. Pour over chicken. Seal bag; turn to coat chicken. Marinate in the refrigerator for at least 4 hours or up to 24 hours, turning bag occasionally.

2. Drain chicken, discarding marinade. Grill chicken on the rack of an uncovered grill directly over medium coals for 12 to 15 minutes or until chicken is tender and no longer pink, turning once halfway through grilling. If desired, arrange greens on 4 dinner plates with pineapple wedges and orange slices. Top with chicken. If desired, drizzle with additional orange juice.

Nutrition Facts per serving: 144 calories, 3 g total fat, 59 mg cholesterol, 189 mg sodium, 5 g carbohydrate, 22 g protein.

Note: Because chile peppers, such as jalapeños, contain volatile oils that can burn your skin and eyes, avoid direct contact with them as much as possible. When working with chile peppers, wear plastic or rubber gloves. If your bare hands do touch the chile peppers, wash your hands and nails well with soap and warm water.

4 medium skinless, boneless
  chicken breast halves
  (about 1 pound total)
1 large onion, quartered
1 to 2 fresh jalapeño peppers,
  seeded and cut up*
1 tablespoon snipped fresh
  thyme or 1 teaspoon
  dried thyme, crushed
½ teaspoon ground allspice
¼ teaspoon salt
¼ teaspoon ground nutmeg
  Dash ground cloves
¼ cup orange juice
  Torn mixed salad greens
  (optional)
  Fresh pineapple wedges
  (optional)
  Orange slices, quartered
  (optional)
  Orange juice (optional)

Chicken and Pears with Pecan Goat Cheese

The distinctive tang of goat cheese complements the flavors of the chicken, pears, and mesclun.

Prep: 15 minutes   **Grill:** 12 minutes   **Makes:** 4 servings

8 ounces skinless, boneless chicken breasts

¼ cup olive oil or salad oil

2 tablespoons balsamic vinegar

1 clove garlic, minced

¼ teaspoon salt

¼ teaspoon pepper

¼ cup finely chopped pecans, toasted

1 4-ounce log semisoft goat cheese (chèvre), cut into ¼-inch-thick slices

8 cups mesclun or torn mixed salad greens

2 medium pears or apples, thinly sliced

1. Grill chicken on the rack of an uncovered grill directly over medium coals for 12 to 15 minutes or until chicken is tender and no longer pink, turning once halfway through grilling. Remove from grill; cool slightly. Cut chicken breasts diagonally into thin slices.

2. Meanwhile, for dressing, in a screw-top jar combine oil, vinegar, garlic, salt, and pepper. Cover and shake well; set aside. Press toasted pecans onto 1 side of each cheese slice.

3. Divide mesclun or salad greens among 4 dinner plates. Arrange chicken, pears or apples, and cheese slices over mesclun. Drizzle with dressing.

Nutrition Facts per serving: 389 calories, 28 g total fat, 55 mg cholesterol, 337 mg sodium, 18 g carbohydrate, 18 g protein.

Grilled Chicken-Spinach Salad

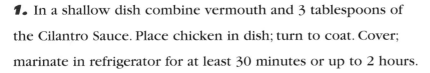

The rich-tasting Cilantro Sauce adds full-bodied flavor to both the marinade and the dressing for this salad.

Prep: 1 hour **Marinate:** 30 minutes to 2 hours **Grill:** 12 minutes **Makes:** 6 servings

1. In a shallow dish combine vermouth and 3 tablespoons of the Cilantro Sauce. Place chicken in dish; turn to coat. Cover; marinate in refrigerator for at least 30 minutes or up to 2 hours.

2. Remove chicken from marinade; reserve marinade. Grill chicken on the rack of an uncovered grill directly over medium coals for 12 to 15 minutes or until chicken is tender and no longer pink, turning once halfway through grilling and brushing once with reserved marinade during first 5 minutes of grilling. Discard any remaining marinade. Lightly brush peppers with oil. Place peppers on the grill rack next to the chicken and grill for 8 to 10 minutes or until tender, turning occasionally. Remove peppers and chicken from grill as done; transfer to cutting board. Slice peppers and chicken breasts into ½-inch-wide strips.

3. To serve, arrange spinach, chicken, peppers, pinto beans, and corn around rice on 6 dinner plates. In a small bowl combine remainder of the ⅓ cup Cilantro Sauce, the sour cream, and milk. Drizzle over salads. Sprinkle with green onions.

Cilantro Sauce: In a blender container or food processor bowl combine 2 cups packed fresh cilantro leaves, 3 tablespoons olive oil or cooking oil, 1 tablespoon lime juice, 1 tablespoon ground cumin, 1 tablespoon grated fresh ginger, 1 tablespoon crushed garlic, ¼ teaspoon ground red pepper, and ¼ teaspoon salt. Cover and blend or process until nearly smooth. Store in the refrigerator for up to 5 days. Makes ⅔ cup.

Nutrition Facts per serving: 416 calories, 11 g total fat, 59 mg cholesterol, 499 mg sodium, 44 g carbohydrate, 31 g protein.

½ cup dry vermouth

⅓ cup Cilantro Sauce

6 medium skinless, boneless chicken breast halves (about 1½ pounds total)

1 medium red sweet pepper, quartered

1 medium green sweet pepper, quartered

1 medium yellow or orange sweet pepper, quartered

1 tablespoon olive oil or cooking oil

4 cups spinach, cleaned, stemmed, and cut into ¼-inch-wide strips

1 15-ounce can pinto beans, rinsed and drained

½ cup frozen whole kernel corn, cooked and drained

1 cup brown basmati rice, cooked according to package directions

½ cup fat-free dairy sour cream

2 teaspoons fat-free milk

4 green onions, sliced

Peach Grove Salad with Poppy Seed Vinaigrette

Fresh peaches or nectarines make this easy salad something to look forward to each summer.

Prep: 20 minutes **Grill:** 12 minutes **Makes:** 4 servings

⅓ cup orange juice

2 tablespoons red wine vinegar

2 tablespoons salad oil

2 teaspoons Dijon-style mustard

1½ teaspoons poppy seed

1 or 2 dashes bottled hot pepper sauce

4 small skinless, boneless chicken breast halves (about 12 ounces total)

5 cups torn mixed salad greens

2 cups torn fresh spinach

2 medium peaches or nectarines, peeled, if desired; pitted; and sliced (2 cups)

Edible flowers (optional)

1. For vinaigrette, in a small bowl combine orange juice, vinegar, oil, mustard, poppy seed, and hot pepper sauce.

2. Grill chicken on the rack of an uncovered grill directly over medium coals for 12 to 15 minutes or until chicken is tender and no longer pink, turning once halfway through grilling. Cool chicken slightly; slice diagonally into ¼-inch-wide strips.

3. In a large bowl combine salad greens and spinach. Drizzle about half of the vinaigrette over spinach mixture; toss to coat. To serve, place spinach mixture on 4 dinner plates. Arrange peach or nectarine slices and sliced chicken on top. Drizzle with remaining vinaigrette. If desired, garnish with edible flowers.

Nutrition Facts per serving: **221 calories, 10 g total fat, 45 mg cholesterol, 132 mg sodium, 15 g carbohydrate, 19 g protein.**

Provençal Grilled Chicken And Herbed Penne

Fines herbes or herbes de Provence, olive oil, and grilled fresh vegetables make this pasta recipe seem like it's straight from the South of France.

Prep: 25 minutes **Grill:** 12 minutes **Makes:** 4 servings

1. Cook pasta according to package directions; drain. Return pasta to hot pan.

2. Meanwhile, brush chicken, zucchini, and asparagus with 1 tablespoon of the oil. Sprinkle all sides of chicken and vegetables with fines herbes or herbes de Provence and salt.

3. Lightly grease the rack of an uncovered grill. Place chicken in center of rack; arrange zucchini and asparagus around chicken. Grill directly over medium coals for 12 to 15 minutes or until chicken is tender and no longer pink and vegetables are tender, turning once halfway through grilling.

4. Transfer chicken and vegetables to cutting board; cool slightly. Cut chicken and zucchini into 1-inch cubes; slice asparagus into 1-inch-long pieces. Add chicken, vegetables, remaining oil, and thyme to pasta; toss to coat.

5. To serve, divide among 4 dinner plates. If desired, top with cheese. Season to taste with pepper.

Nutrition Facts per serving: 441 calories, 14 g total fat, 59 mg cholesterol, 324 mg sodium, 46 g carbohydrate, 30 g protein.

8 ounces dried tomato or garlic and herb-flavored penne pasta or plain penne pasta

4 medium skinless, boneless chicken breast halves (about 1 pound total)

1 medium zucchini, halved lengthwise

8 thick fresh asparagus spears (8 to 10 ounces total), trimmed

3 tablespoons olive oil

1 tablespoon fines herbes or herbes de Provence, crushed

½ teaspoon salt

1 tablespoon snipped fresh thyme

½ cup finely shredded Asiago cheese (optional)

Pepper

To Grease or Not to Grease

Greasing the rack on your grill isn't necessary for every type of food, but it does help with ones that tend to stick or fall apart easily. It works especially well when you're grilling delicate fish and vegetables or meat and poultry that has a high-sugar marinade, rub, brush-on, or sauce. To be safe, always start with an unheated grill rack. Grease the rack by rubbing it with a paper towel moistened with cooking oil or coating it with nonstick cooking spray. Brushing on shortening with a basting brush also works well.

Raspberry Chicken With Plantains

Cousins of bananas, plantains must be cooked before eating. Here a brown sugar glaze adds a touch of sweetness to the plantain slices.

Prep: 20 minutes **Grill:** 12 minutes **Makes:** 4 servings

1 cup fresh raspberries or one 10-ounce package frozen lightly sweetened raspberries
2 tablespoons granulated sugar
1 teaspoon margarine or butter
2 ripe plantains or firm bananas, sliced
2 tablespoons brown sugar
2 tablespoons white wine vinegar
2 green onions, thinly sliced
1 small fresh jalapeño pepper, seeded and finely chopped (see note on page 95)
4 medium skinless, boneless chicken breast halves (about 1 pound total)
Salt
Ground black pepper
Ti leaves (optional)*

1. For sauce, in a small saucepan combine raspberries and granulated sugar. Heat over low heat about 3 minutes or until the berries are softened. Press berries through a fine-mesh sieve; discard seeds.

2. In a large nonstick skillet melt margarine or butter over medium heat. Add the plantains (if using); cook and stir about 2 minutes or until plantains are lightly browned and slightly softened. Stir in brown sugar and vinegar; heat through. Remove from heat; stir in green onions and jalapeño pepper. (Or if using bananas, melt margarine or butter. Stir in bananas, brown sugar, and vinegar; heat through. Remove from heat; stir in green onions and jalapeño pepper.)

3. Sprinkle chicken with salt and black pepper. Grill chicken on the rack of an uncovered grill directly over medium coals for 12 to 15 minutes or until chicken is tender and no longer pink, turning once halfway through grilling. If desired, place each chicken breast on a ti leaf. Spoon sauce over chicken. Serve with plantain or banana mixture.

Nutrition Facts per serving: 300 calories, 5 g total fat, 59 mg cholesterol, 103 mg sodium, 45 g carbohydrate, 23 g protein.

***Note:** If using ti leaves, be sure they have not been sprayed or treated in a way that would make them unsafe for contact with food. Wash them thoroughly before using. Although they are not toxic, they should not be eaten.

Spicy Chicken and Carambola

Here's fusion cooking at its best. This easy chicken is part Italian, part East Indian.

Prep: 15 minutes **Soak:** 30 minutes **Grill:** 12 minutes **Makes:** 4 servings

1. Soak wooden skewers in enough water to cover for 30 minutes; drain. Meanwhile, in a small bowl combine vinegar, oil, rosemary, cumin, coriander, black pepper, and ground red pepper. Alternately thread carambola slices and onions on water-soaked wooden skewers. Set aside.

2. Grill chicken on the rack of an uncovered grill directly over medium coals for 12 to 15 minutes or until chicken is tender and no longer pink, turning once halfway through grilling and brushing once with vinegar mixture after 6 minutes of grilling. During the last 5 minutes of grilling, place kabobs on grill rack next to chicken; brush with vinegar mixture. Turn after 3 minutes of grilling. Discard any remaining vinegar mixture.

3. Serve chicken and kabobs over rice. If desired, drizzle with melted preserves.

Nutrition Facts per serving: 286 calories, 7 g total fat, 59 mg cholesterol, 57 mg sodium, 30 g carbohydrate, 24 g protein.

- 8 6-inch wooden skewers
- 2 tablespoons balsamic vinegar or red wine vinegar
- 1 tablespoon olive oil
- ½ teaspoon dried rosemary, crushed
- ¼ teaspoon ground cumin
- ⅛ teaspoon ground coriander
- ⅛ teaspoon ground black pepper
  Dash ground red pepper
- 2 carambola (star fruit), sliced
- 8 green onions, cut into 2-inch-long pieces, and/or 4 small purple boiling onions, cut into wedges
- 4 medium skinless, boneless chicken breast halves (about 1 pound total)
  Hot cooked rice
- 2 tablespoons peach or apricot preserves, melted (optional)

Mustard Chicken Barbecue

This simple mustard marinade tastes equally terrific on chicken legs or breasts.

Prep: 20 minutes **Marinate:** 4 to 24 hours **Grill:** 50 minutes **Makes:** 4 servings

4 chicken legs (thigh-
drumstick pieces) or
4 each chicken drumsticks
and thighs (about 3 pounds
total) or 4 medium chicken
breast halves (about
2 pounds total)

½ cup Dijon-style mustard

3 tablespoons vinegar

4 teaspoons Worcestershire
sauce

1 teaspoon snipped fresh
thyme or ⅛ teaspoon
dried thyme, crushed

2 tablespoons light-flavored
molasses

1. If desired, skin chicken. Place chicken in a heavy, large self-sealing plastic bag set in a shallow bowl. For marinade, in a small bowl combine mustard, vinegar, Worcestershire sauce, and thyme. Pour marinade over chicken. Seal bag; turn to coat chicken. Marinate in the refrigerator for at least 4 hours or up to 24 hours, turning bag occasionally.

2. Drain chicken, reserving marinade. Set aside ⅓ cup of the reserved marinade for the sauce. In a grill with a cover arrange medium-hot coals around a drip pan. Test for medium heat above pan. Place the chicken pieces, bone sides up, on grill rack over pan. Cover and grill for 50 to 60 minutes or until chicken is tender and no longer pink, brushing occasionally with reserved marinade during the first 40 minutes of grilling. Discard the remainder of the reserved marinade used as brush-on.

3. Meanwhile, for sauce, in a small saucepan combine the ⅓ cup reserved marinade and the molasses. Bring to boiling; reduce heat. Cover and simmer for 5 minutes. Pass sauce with the chicken.

Nutrition Facts per serving: 327 calories, 17 g total fat, 103 mg cholesterol, 904 mg sodium, 10 g carbohydrate, 31 g protein.

Sesame-Ginger Barbecued Chicken

Oriental chili sauce makes this robust barbecue sauce downright awesome.

Prep: 10 minutes **Grill:** 12 minutes **Makes:** 6 servings

1. For sauce, in a small saucepan combine plum sauce or sweet-sour sauce, the water, hoisin sauce, sesame seeds, garlic, ginger, and chili sauce or pepper sauce. Bring to boiling over medium heat, stirring frequently; reduce heat. Cover and simmer for 3 minutes. Set aside.

2. Lightly grease the rack of an uncovered grill. Place chicken on rack. Grill directly over medium coals for 12 to 15 minutes or until chicken is tender and no longer pink, turning once halfway through grilling and brushing with sauce once or twice during the last 5 minutes of grilling.

3. To serve, reheat the remaining sauce until bubbly; pass with chicken.

Nutrition Facts per serving: **166 calories, 4 g total fat, 59 mg cholesterol, 216 mg sodium, 9 g carbohydrate, 22 g protein.**

⅓ **cup bottled plum sauce or sweet-sour sauce**
¼ **cup water**
3 **tablespoons hoisin sauce**
1½ **teaspoons sesame seeds (toasted, if desired)**
1 **clove garlic, minced**
1 **teaspoon grated fresh ginger or ¼ teaspoon ground ginger**
¼ **to ½ teaspoon Oriental chili sauce or several dashes bottled hot pepper sauce**
6 **medium skinless, boneless chicken breast halves and/or thighs (about 1½ pounds total)**

Rosemary Chicken

Serve the chicken with sides of mashed potatoes and a medley of steamed vegetables.

Prep: 15 minutes   **Marinate:** 6 to 24 hours   **Grill:** 35 minutes   **Makes:** 6 servings

2 to 2½ pounds meaty
   chicken pieces (breasts,
   thighs, and drumsticks)
   or chicken legs (thigh-
   drumstick pieces)
½ cup dry white wine
2 tablespoons olive oil
4 cloves garlic, minced
4 teaspoons snipped fresh
   rosemary
1 tablespoon finely shredded
   lemon peel
¼ teaspoon salt
¼ teaspoon pepper
   Fresh rosemary sprigs
   (optional)

1. If desired, skin chicken. Place chicken in a heavy, large self-sealing plastic bag set in a shallow bowl. For marinade, in a blender container or food processor bowl combine the white wine, oil, garlic, snipped rosemary, lemon peel, salt, and pepper. Cover and blend or process about 15 seconds or until well mixed. Pour marinade over chicken. Seal bag; turn to coat chicken. Marinate in the refrigerator for at least 6 hours or up to 24 hours, turning bag occasionally.

2. Drain chicken, reserving marinade. Grill chicken, bone sides up, on the rack of an uncovered grill directly over medium coals for 35 to 50 minutes or until chicken is tender and no longer pink, turning once halfway through grilling and brushing once with reserved marinade after 20 minutes of grilling. Discard any remaining marinade. If desired, garnish chicken with fresh rosemary sprigs.

Nutrition Facts per serving: **192 calories, 10 g total fat, 69 mg cholesterol, 93 mg sodium, 0 g carbohydrate, 22 g protein.**

Note: An assortment of summer vegetables makes a delicious no-fuss side dish to serve with Rosemary Chicken. To prepare the mixture shown in the photo at top left, start with cooked bite-size strips of carrot and half-slices of zucchini and/or yellow summer squash, and toss them with a dressing of equal parts lemon juice, olive oil, and snipped fresh dill.

Peanut-Ginger Chicken With Cucumber Salsa

A fruit salsa and a sesame oil-seasoned slaw are the ideal serve-alongs for this peanutty chicken.

Prep: 30 minutes **Marinate:** 12 to 24 hours **Grill:** 50 minutes **Makes:** 6 servings

1. Place chicken in a heavy, large self-sealing plastic bag set in a shallow bowl. For marinade, in a medium bowl gradually stir boiling water into peanut butter. (The mixture will stiffen at first.) Stir in chili sauce, soy sauce, the 2 tablespoons oil, the 2 tablespoons vinegar, the garlic, ginger, and red pepper. Pour over chicken. Seal bag; turn to coat chicken. Marinate in refrigerator at least 12 hours or up to 24 hours; turn occasionally.

2. For salsa, in a medium bowl combine chopped fruit, cucumber, green onion, sugar, the 1 tablespoon oil, and the 1 tablespoon vinegar. Cover and chill in the refrigerator for at least 1 hour or up to 2 hours.

3. In a grill with a cover arrange medium-hot coals around drip pan. Test for medium heat above pan. Drain chicken, discarding marinade. Place chicken on grill rack over pan. Cover and grill for 50 to 60 minutes or until chicken is tender and no longer pink, turning once halfway through grilling.

4. Serve chicken with salsa. If desired, serve with Napa Cabbage Slaw. If desired, garnish with fruit wedges.

Nutrition Facts per serving: 455 calories, 30 g total fat, 103 mg cholesterol, 715 mg sodium, 12 g carbohydrate, 34 g protein.

Napa Cabbage Slaw: In a large bowl combine 3 cups finely shredded napa cabbage, 1 cup finely shredded bok choy, and 2 to 3 tablespoons very thin red sweet pepper strips. In a small bowl stir together ¼ cup seasoned rice vinegar or white vinegar and 1 tablespoon toasted sesame oil. Drizzle vinegar mixture over cabbage mixture; toss to coat. Makes 6 servings.

---

12 **chicken thighs (about 3 pounds)**
½ **cup boiling water**
½ **cup creamy peanut butter**
¼ **cup bottled chili sauce**
¼ **cup soy sauce**
2 **tablespoons salad oil**
2 **tablespoons vinegar**
4 **cloves garlic, minced**
1 **tablespoon grated fresh ginger or ¾ teaspoon ground ginger**
¼ to ½ **teaspoon ground red pepper**
1 **cup chopped fresh fruit (such as peaches, nectarines, pears, or plums)**
1 **cup chopped, seeded cucumber**
2 **tablespoons thinly sliced green onion**
1 **tablespoon sugar**
1 **tablespoon salad oil**
1 **tablespoon vinegar**
1 **recipe Napa Cabbage Slaw (optional)**
Fresh plum, peach, nectarine, or pear wedges (optional)

Buffalo Chicken Wings

Although these zesty wings make a great appetizer, you also can serve them as a main dish for four.

Prep: 15 minutes   **Chill:** 1 hour   **Grill:** 18 minutes   **Makes:** 32 appetizer servings

16 chicken wings (about
    3 pounds total)
2 tablespoons butter
    or margarine
1 2-ounce bottle hot pepper
    sauce (¼ cup)
1 recipe Blue Cheese Dip
    Celery sticks

1. Cut off and discard wing tips. Bend the 2 larger sections of each wing back and forth, breaking the cartilage connecting them. Use a knife or cleaver to cut through the cartilage and skin, cutting each wing into 2 sections.

2. In a small saucepan melt butter or margarine. Stir in hot pepper sauce. Brush some of the butter mixture over the wing pieces.

3. Grill wing pieces on the rack of an uncovered grill directly over medium coals for 18 to 20 minutes or until chicken is tender and no longer pink, turning once halfway through grilling and brushing occasionally with remaining butter mixture during first 10 minutes of grilling. Discard any remaining butter mixture. Serve wing pieces with Blue Cheese Dip and celery.

Blue Cheese Dip: In a blender container or food processor bowl combine ½ cup dairy sour cream; ½ cup crumbled blue cheese; ¼ cup mayonnaise or salad dressing; 2 cloves garlic, minced; 2 tablespoons lemon juice; 2 tablespoons thinly sliced green onion; and 1 tablespoon milk. Cover and blend or process just until combined. Transfer to a small bowl; cover and chill in refrigerator for 1 hour. Makes about 1¼ cups.

Nutrition Facts per appetizer serving: **71 calories, 6 g total fat, 19 mg cholesterol, 55 mg sodium, 0 g carbohydrate, 4 g protein.**

Duck Breast with Lime Sauce

When company's coming, serve these elegant grilled duck breast halves with the currant-wine sauce.

Prep: 20 minutes **Grill:** 10 minutes **Makes:** 4 servings

1. For sauce, in a small saucepan combine jelly, wine, vinegar, lime peel, lime juice, ginger, salt, and pepper. Bring just to boiling; reduce heat. Simmer, uncovered, about 12 minutes or until sauce is slightly thickened and reduced to ½ cup. Remove from heat; stir in margarine or butter. Set aside ¼ cup of the sauce. Keep remaining sauce warm until serving time.

2. Brush oil over both sides of duck or chicken pieces. Lightly grease the rack of an uncovered grill. Place duck or chicken on rack. Grill directly over medium coals until duck or chicken is tender and no longer pink, turning once halfway through grilling and brushing with the ¼ cup sauce during the last 2 to 3 minutes of grilling. (Allow 10 to 12 minutes for duck or 12 to 15 minutes for chicken.) Discard any of the ¼ cup sauce that remains. Serve duck or chicken with warm sauce. If desired, garnish with raspberries.

Nutrition Facts per serving: 336 calories, 14 g total fat, 116 mg cholesterol, 189 mg sodium, 28 g carbohydrate, 21 g protein.

½ cup currant jelly
¼ cup sweet or semi-dry white wine (such as Riesling or Sauternes)
1 tablespoon raspberry vinegar
1 teaspoon finely shredded lime peel
1 tablespoon lime juice
¼ teaspoon grated fresh ginger
⅛ teaspoon salt
  Dash pepper
1 tablespoon margarine or butter
2 teaspoons olive oil
4 skinless, boneless duck breasts (about 12 ounces) or 4 medium skinless, boneless chicken breast halves (about 1 pound total)
Fresh red raspberries (optional)

Barbecued Turkey with Fruit Sauce

Roasting the bird with the skin on keeps the turkey moist. If you're watching fat and calories, remove the skin before serving.

Prep: 15 minutes   **Grill:** 2½ hours   **Stand:** 20 minutes   **Makes:** 10 to 14 servings

1 8- to 12-pound fresh
  or frozen turkey
1 medium onion, quartered
1 medium apple, quartered
1 14-ounce can reduced-
  sodium chicken broth
½ cup dried cranberries,
  cherries, or apricots
1 cup low-calorie orange
  marmalade spread
2 teaspoons cornstarch
1 teaspoon grated fresh
  ginger or ¼ teaspoon
  ground ginger

1. Thaw turkey, if frozen. Remove neck and giblets from turkey. Place onion and apple pieces in cavity of turkey. Skewer neck skin to back. Tie legs to tail. Twist wing tips under back. Place turkey, breast side up, on a rack in a roasting pan. Insert an oven-going meat thermometer into the center of an inside thigh muscle, making sure bulb does not touch bone.

2. In a grill with a cover arrange medium-hot coals around edge of grill. Test for medium heat above center of grill (not over coals). Place turkey in roasting pan on the grill rack in center of grill. Reserve 1 cup broth for sauce. Brush the turkey with some of the remaining broth.

3. Cover and grill 2½ to 3½ hours or until meat thermometer registers 180°, brushing occasionally with remaining chicken broth. At this time, drumsticks move easily in their sockets and turkey is no longer pink. Add additional coals as needed.

4. Meanwhile, for sauce, in a medium saucepan combine the 1 cup broth and the cranberries, cherries, or apricots. Bring to boiling; reduce heat. Cover and simmer for 10 minutes. Cool slightly. Transfer to blender container. Cover and blend until nearly smooth. Return to saucepan; stir in marmalade spread, cornstarch, and ginger. Heat and stir until bubbly.

5. Remove bird from grill. Cover with foil; let stand 20 minutes before carving. Discard onion and apple. Pass sauce with turkey.

Nutrition Facts per serving: 265 calories, 6 g total fat, 95 mg cholesterol, 229 mg sodium, 15 g carbohydrate, 37 g protein.

Turkey Breast with Raspberry Salsa

Raspberry jam and mustard add just a little touch of fruity flavor and bite to the salsa.

Prep: 10 minutes **Grill:** 1¼ hours **Stand:** 15 minutes **Makes:** 8 servings

1. Thaw turkey, if frozen. In a small bowl stir together raspberry jam, mustard, and shredded orange peel. In a small bowl stir 3 tablespoons of the jam mixture into salsa. Cover and chill jam mixture and salsa mixture in the refrigerator. If desired, skin turkey breast. Insert an oven-going meat thermometer into the center of turkey breast, making sure bulb does not touch bone.

2. In a grill with a cover arrange medium-hot coals around a drip pan. Test for medium heat above the pan. Place turkey breast, bone side down, on grill rack over pan. Cover and grill for 1¼ to 2 hours or until meat thermometer registers 170°, brushing occasionally with jam mixture during the last 30 minutes of grilling. Add additional coals as needed. Discard any remaining jam mixture.

3. Remove turkey from grill. Cover with foil; let stand 15 minutes before carving. Serve turkey with salsa mixture. If desired, garnish with orange peel strips.

Nutrition Facts per serving: 149 calories, 3 g total fat, 46 mg cholesterol, 147 mg sodium, 11 g carbohydrate, 20 g protein.

1 2- to 2½-pound fresh or
  frozen bone-in turkey breast
  half
⅓ cup seedless raspberry jam
1 tablespoon Dijon-style
  mustard
1 teaspoon finely shredded
  orange peel
½ cup bottled mild salsa
  Orange peel strips (optional)

Fueling the Fire

If the food you're grilling cooks for a long time, like Turkey Breast with Raspberry Salsa (above), you'll need to replenish the coals to keep the fire hot. To add fresh charcoal, gently tap the burning coals with tongs to remove excess ash. Then move the coals closer together with tongs and place new briquettes on top of the coals. You'll need to add 8 to 10 additional briquettes every 30 to 45 minutes. The number of briquettes will depend on the weather. If it is cold and/or windy, you'll probably need more. Never add charcoal starters to burning coals. If you're grilling with soaked wood chips, add more drained chips when you add fresh briquettes.

Curry-Glazed Turkey Thighs

Dark meat enthusiasts, here's a recipe for you—turkey thighs brushed with an orange and mustard glaze and topped with a creamy yogurt sauce.

Prep: 15 minutes **Grill:** 50 minutes **Makes:** 4 servings

2 small fresh or frozen turkey thighs (about 2 pounds total)

⅓ cup orange marmalade

1 tablespoon Dijon-style mustard

½ to 1 teaspoon curry powder

⅛ teaspoon salt

½ cup plain yogurt

   Hot cooked rice (optional)

   Raisins, peanuts, and/or chopped apple (optional)

1. Thaw turkey, if frozen; set aside. For glaze, in a small bowl stir together marmalade, mustard, curry powder, and salt. For sauce, stir 3 tablespoons of the glaze into the yogurt; refrigerate until serving time.

2. If desired, skin turkey thighs. Insert an oven-going meat thermometer into the center of 1 of the turkey thighs, making sure bulb does not touch bone. In a grill with a cover arrange medium-hot coals around a drip pan. Test for medium heat above pan. Place turkey thighs on grill rack over pan. Cover and grill for 50 to 60 minutes or until meat thermometer registers 180°, turning once halfway through grilling and brushing once or twice with glaze during the last 10 minutes of grilling. Discard any remaining glaze.

3. To serve, slice turkey thighs. Serve with sauce and, if desired, rice and raisins, peanuts, and/or apple.

Nutrition Facts per serving: **157 calories, 4 g total fat, 30 mg cholesterol, 209 mg sodium, 21 g carbohydrate, 9 g protein.**

Thawing Turkey Safely

The safest way to thaw turkey is in the refrigerator. Never thaw turkey at room temperature, in the microwave, or in warm water because these methods can allow harmful bacteria to grow quickly to dangerous levels. Thawing turkey in the refrigerator means you'll need to allow plenty of time. Today's newer refrigerators hold temperatures more precisely, so plan on 24 hours of thawing for every 5 pounds of meat. (Don't count the day you plan to grill.) To thaw, leave the turkey in its wrapping and place on a tray in the refrigerator. Thaw turkey pieces for 24 hours. (Thawed turkey will keep for 1 to 2 days in the refrigerator.) To thaw a whole 12-pound turkey, allow about 60 hours. For a 15-pound bird, allow 72 hours. So if you plan to grill on Sunday, you'll need to start thawing on Thursday. If the turkey isn't completely thawed when you plan to grill it, place the wrapped bird in a clean sink of cold water. Change the water every 30 minutes until the turkey is thawed. A whole turkey is thawed when the giblets can be removed easily and there are no ice crystals in the body and neck cavities. Before grilling, rinse the turkey and pat dry.

Apricot-Stuffed Grilled Turkey Breast

The apricot and pecan stuffing picks up wonderful flavor from the turkey as it grills.

Prep: 25 minutes **Grill:** 1¼ hours **Stand:** 15 minutes **Makes:** 8 servings

1. Thaw turkey, if frozen. In a small bowl soak 4 to 6 wooden picks in water for 10 minutes. Remove bone from turkey breast. Cut a horizontal slit into thickest part of turkey breast to form a 5×4-inch pocket. Set aside.

2. For stuffing, in a medium bowl combine bread crumbs, apricots, pecans, apple juice or water, oil, rosemary, and garlic salt. Spoon stuffing into pocket. Securely fasten the opening with water-soaked wooden picks. In a small bowl stir together mustard and the water; set aside.

3. In a grill with a cover arrange medium-hot coals around a drip pan. Test for medium heat above pan. Place turkey breast on the grill rack over pan. Cover and grill 1¼ to 2 hours or until turkey is tender and no longer pink (an instant-read thermometer inserted in stuffing should register 165°), brushing with mustard mixture during the last 15 minutes of grilling. Add additional coals as needed. Discard any remaining mustard mixture. Cover turkey with foil and let stand 15 minutes before slicing.*

Nutrition Facts per serving: 237 calories, 11 g total fat, 59 mg cholesterol, 205 mg sodium, 10 g carbohydrate, 24 g protein.

Note: Most grilling recipes for large pieces of poultry (or meat) give directions for letting the poultry stand before carving. This allows the internal temperature to rise 5° to 10° so the poultry is completely cooked without being overcooked. And it gives the poultry time to firm up slightly, allowing you to carve neat, even slices that hold together. To keep the poultry warm while it stands, cover it with foil.

1 2- to 2½-pound fresh
   or frozen bone-in turkey
   breast half
1½ cups soft bread crumbs
   (2 slices)
½ cup snipped dried apricots
¼ cup chopped pecans, toasted
2 tablespoons apple juice or
   water
1 tablespoon cooking oil
¼ teaspoon dried rosemary,
   crushed
¼ teaspoon garlic salt
1 tablespoon Dijon-style
   mustard
1 tablespoon water

Turkey with Tomatillo Guacamole

In this low-fat version of guacamole, tomatillos—sometimes called Mexican green tomatoes—replace part of the traditional avocado.

Prep: 20 minutes **Grill:** 1¼ hours **Stand:** 15 minutes **Makes:** 8 servings

1 2- to 2½-pound fresh
   or frozen bone-in turkey
   breast half
2 teaspoons ground coriander
½ teaspoon onion powder
¼ teaspoon chili powder
   Dash ground red pepper
1 tablespoon margarine
   or butter, melted
1 tablespoon lemon juice
1 recipe Tomatillo Guacamole
   Tomato wedges (optional)
   Lime peel strips (optional)

1. Thaw turkey breast half, if frozen. Skin turkey breast half. In a small saucepan cook coriander, onion powder, chili powder, and ground red pepper in hot margarine or butter for 1 minute. Remove from heat; stir in lemon juice. Spread spice mixture on all sides of turkey breast half.

2. In a grill with a cover arrange medium-hot coals around a drip pan. Test for medium heat above the pan. Insert an oven-going meat thermometer into the thickest part of turkey breast, making sure bulb does not touch bone. Place turkey breast, bone side down, on grill rack over pan. Cover and grill for 1¼ to 2 hours or until meat thermometer registers 170°. Add additional coals as needed.

3. Remove turkey from grill. Cover with foil; let stand 15 minutes before carving. Serve turkey with Tomatillo Guacamole. If desired, garnish with tomato wedges and lime peel strips.

Tomatillo Guacamole: In a small bowl combine 2 canned tomatillos, rinsed, drained, and finely chopped (¼ cup); 1 plum tomato, chopped; ½ of a small avocado, pitted, peeled, and chopped (about ½ cup); 1 tablespoon canned diced green chili peppers; 2 teaspoons lemon juice; and ⅛ teaspoon garlic salt. Makes about 1 cup.

Nutrition Facts per serving: **156 calories, 6 g total fat, 50 mg cholesterol, 157 mg sodium, 3 g carbohydrate, 22 g protein.**

Stuffed Turkey Tenderloins

Turkey tenderloins stuffed with spinach and goat cheese make a delicious headliner for a dinner party.

Prep: 15 minutes **Grill:** 16 minutes **Makes:** 4 servings

1. Make a pocket in each turkey breast tenderloin by cutting lengthwise from 1 side almost to, but not through, the opposite side; set aside. In a medium bowl combine spinach, goat cheese, and black pepper. Spoon spinach mixture into pockets. Tie 100%-cotton kitchen string around each tenderloin in 3 or 4 places to hold in stuffing. In a small bowl combine oil, paprika, salt, and ground red pepper; brush evenly over tenderloins.

2. Lightly grease the rack of an uncovered grill. Place turkey on rack. Grill directly over medium coals for 16 to 20 minutes or until turkey is tender and no longer pink in center of the thickest part, turning once halfway through grilling. Remove and discard strings; slice tenderloins crosswise.

Nutrition Facts per serving: 220 calories, 12 g total fat, 68 mg cholesterol, 458 mg sodium, 1 g carbohydrate, 26 g protein.

- 2 8-ounce turkey breast tenderloins
- 2 cups chopped fresh spinach leaves
- 3 ounces semisoft goat cheese (chèvre) or feta cheese, crumbled (about ¾ cup)
- ½ teaspoon ground black pepper
- 1 tablespoon olive oil
- 1 teaspoon paprika
- ½ teaspoon salt
- ⅛ to ¼ teaspoon ground red pepper

Grilled Turkey with Cherry Sauce

These turkey steaks get a triple-dose of cherry flavor from the sweet-tart sauce.

Prep: 25 minutes **Grill:** 12 minutes **Makes:** 4 servings

½ cup cherry jelly or jam

⅓ cup dried tart cherries, cut up

2 tablespoons cherry liqueur or orange juice

1 tablespoon lemon juice

¼ teaspoon salt

⅛ teaspoon coarsely ground black pepper

4 medium turkey breast tenderloin steaks (about 1 pound total)*

Hot cooked rice pilaf (optional)

1. For sauce, in a small saucepan combine the jelly or jam, dried cherries, liqueur or orange juice, lemon juice, salt, and pepper. Cook over low heat about 15 minutes or until jelly is melted and sauce is slightly thickened, stirring occasionally.

2. Grill turkey on the rack of an uncovered grill directly over medium coals for 12 to 15 minutes or until turkey is tender and no longer pink, turning once halfway through grilling and brushing once with sauce after 6 minutes of grilling.

3. To serve, reheat remaining sauce until bubbly; spoon over turkey. If desired, serve with rice pilaf.

Nutrition Facts per serving: 268 calories, 2 g total fat, 50 mg cholesterol, 185 mg sodium, 37 g carbohydrate, 22 g protein.

Note: If you can't find turkey breast tenderloin steaks, buy two turkey breast tenderloins and split them in half lengthwise.

Turkey-Peach Salad

To make peach "bowls" for the salad, cut two large peaches in half crosswise; remove pits. Using a spoon, scoop out some of the pulp to create shallow "bowls."

Prep: 10 minutes   **Grill:** 12 minutes   **Makes:** 4 servings

1. Rub both sides of turkey with oil. Sprinkle with salt and pepper. Grill turkey on the rack of an uncovered grill directly over medium coals for 12 to 15 minutes or until turkey is tender and no longer pink, turning once halfway through grilling. Cool turkey slightly; cut into bite-size strips.

2. Meanwhile, in a medium bowl combine the cut-up peaches and plums. Add the 2 tablespoons lemon juice; toss gently to coat. For dressing, in a small bowl combine yogurt, green onion, and poppy seeds. If necessary, stir in 1 to 2 teaspoons lemon juice to reach drizzling consistency.

3. Divide greens among 4 dinner plates. Arrange turkey and fruit on top of greens. Drizzle with dressing.

Nutrition Facts per serving: 209 calories, 4 g total fat, 51 mg cholesterol, 96 mg sodium, 20 g carbohydrate, 24 g protein.

Note: If you can't find turkey breast tenderloin steaks, buy two turkey breast tenderloins and split them in half lengthwise.

4 turkey breast tenderloin steaks (about 1 pound total)*
1 teaspoon olive oil
  Salt
  Pepper
2 peaches, pitted and cut up
2 plums, pitted and sliced
2 tablespoons lemon juice
½ cup lemon low-fat yogurt
2 tablespoons thinly sliced green onion
¼ teaspoon poppy seeds
  Lemon juice (optional)
  Torn mixed salad greens

Caesar Turkey and Penne Salad

Tired of ordinary Caesar salad? Try this new spin on the classic.

Prep: 20 minutes **Grill:** 12 minutes **Makes:** 4 servings

6 ounces dried gemelli
    or penne pasta
4 turkey breast tenderloin
    steaks (about 1 pound
    total)*
¾ cup bottled Caesar salad
    dressing
6 cups torn romaine lettuce
12 yellow and/or red cherry
    tomatoes, halved
¼ cup finely shredded
    Parmesan cheese
    Cracked black pepper
    (optional)

1. Cook pasta according to package directions; drain. Rinse with cold water; drain again.

2. Meanwhile, grill turkey on the rack of an uncovered grill directly over medium coals for 12 to 15 minutes or until turkey is tender and no longer pink, turning once halfway through grilling and brushing occasionally with ¼ cup of the salad dressing during the first 5 minutes of grilling. Discard remainder of the ¼ cup salad dressing used as a brush-on. Transfer turkey to a cutting board; cool slightly.

3. In a large salad bowl combine cooked pasta, romaine, and tomatoes. Add the remaining salad dressing; toss gently to coat. Slice turkey diagonally across the grain and arrange on greens mixture. Sprinkle with Parmesan cheese and, if desired, cracked black pepper.

Nutrition Facts per serving: **538 calories, 26 g total fat, 55 mg cholesterol, 138 mg sodium, 41 g carbohydrate, 32 g protein.**

Note: If you can't find turkey breast tenderloin steaks, buy two turkey breast tenderloins and spilt them in half lengthwise.

Cajun Turkey Steaks

These spicy turkey steaks have a kick reminiscent of Buffalo wings.

Prep: 15 minutes **Marinate:** 4 to 6 hours **Grill:** 15 minutes **Makes:** 5 to 7 servings

1. For marinade, in a medium bowl combine salad dressing, onion, lemon juice, ground red pepper, garlic, taco seasoning, Cajun seasoning, and black pepper. Place tenderloin steaks in a heavy, large self-sealing plastic bag set in a large bowl. Pour marinade over turkey. Seal bag; turn to coat turkey. Marinate in refrigerator for at least 4 hours or up to 6 hours, turning the bag occasionally.

2. Drain tenderloin steaks, discarding marinade. In a grill with a cover arrange medium-hot coals around drip pan. Test for medium heat above drip pan. Place tenderloin steaks on rack over pan. Cover and grill for 15 to 18 minutes or until turkey is tender and no longer pink. If desired, garnish with chile peppers.

Nutrition Facts per serving: **256 calories, 15 g total fat, 59 mg cholesterol, 374 mg sodium, 5 g carbohydrate, 25 g protein.**

Note: If you can't find turkey breast tenderloin steaks, buy 1½ to 2 pounds turkey breast tenderloins and split each tenderloin in half lengthwise.

- 1 cup bottled Italian salad dressing
- ½ cup finely chopped onion
- ⅓ cup lemon juice
- 1½ to 2 teaspoons ground red pepper
- 4 cloves garlic, minced
- 1 teaspoon taco seasoning
- 1 teaspoon Cajun seasoning
- ⅛ to ¼ teaspoon ground black pepper
- 1½ to 2 pounds turkey breast tenderloin steaks*
- Fresh chile peppers (optional)

Orange Barbecued Turkey

Add your favorite rice pilaf, some steamed broccoli, and a loaf of crusty bread to these turkey steaks and you have a meal to brag about.

Prep: 10 minutes **Marinate:** 30 minutes **Grill:** 12 minutes **Makes:** 4 servings

1 teaspoon finely shredded
  orange peel
½ cup orange juice
1 tablespoon cooking oil
2 teaspoons Worcestershire
  sauce
1 teaspoon dry mustard
½ teaspoon lemon-pepper
  seasoning
⅛ teaspoon garlic powder
4 turkey breast tenderloin
  steaks (about 1 pound
  total)*

1. For marinade, in a small bowl combine the orange peel, orange juice, oil, Worcestershire sauce, mustard, lemon-pepper seasoning, and garlic powder.

2. Place the turkey steaks in a nonmetallic shallow pan. Pour marinade over the turkey steaks. Turn turkey to coat. Cover and marinate in the refrigerator for 30 minutes.

3. Drain turkey, reserving marinade. Grill steaks on the rack of an uncovered grill directly over medium coals for 12 to 15 minutes or until tender and no longer pink, turning once halfway through grilling and brushing frequently with reserved marinade during the first 6 minutes of grilling. Discard any remaining marinade.

Nutrition Facts per serving: 162 calories, 6 g total fat, 50 mg cholesterol, 206 mg sodium, 4 g carbohydrate, 22 g protein.

Note: If you can't find turkey breast tenderloin steaks, buy two turkey breast tenderloins and split them in half lengthwise.

Marinade Safety

Many recipes, such as Orange Barbecued Turkey (above), call for marinades to be brushed on during grilling. This technique is a great way to add extra flavor and moistness to grilled foods, but you need to take some safety precautions. Because the marinade has been in contact with the raw food, it contains bacteria that may be harmful. For this reason, brush on the marinade only during the first part of grilling so there is at least 5 minutes of grilling after the last brushing with marinade—this gives enough time to thoroughly cook the surface of the food. Also, because of the bacteria in the marinade, discard any that remains after you finishing brushing it on.

Tandoori Turkey

The blend of cumin, coriander, turmeric, and other seasonings gives the turkey a tongue-tingling flavor similar to classic Indian tandoori chicken, which is traditionally cooked in a special oven.

Prep: 15 minutes **Marinate:** 8 to 24 hours **Grill:** 12 minutes **Makes:** 4 servings

1. For marinade, in a food processor bowl or blender container combine onion, lime juice, oil, cumin, coriander seed, salt, ginger, turmeric, and crushed red pepper. Cover and process or blend until mixture is almost smooth. Pour mixture into a shallow nonmetallic dish or pan; stir in yogurt.

2. Cut small slits in both sides of the tenderloin steaks. Place steaks in the yogurt mixture, turning to coat both sides. Cover; marinate in the refrigerator for at least 8 hours or up to 24 hours, turning steaks occasionally.

3. Remove turkey breast tenderloin steaks from marinade; discard marinade. Lightly coat the rack of an uncovered grill with nonstick cooking spray. Place turkey on rack. Grill directly over medium coals for 12 to 15 minutes or until turkey is tender and no longer pink, turning once halfway through grilling. If desired, serve over hot cooked couscous.

Nutrition Facts per serving: **143 calories, 4 g total fat, 50 mg cholesterol, 192 mg sodium, 3 g carbohydrate, 22 g protein.**

Note: If you can't find turkey breast tenderloin steaks, buy two turkey breast tenderloins and split them in half lengthwise.

½ cup chopped onion
2 tablespoons lime juice
1 tablespoon cooking oil
1 teaspoon ground cumin
1 teaspoon coriander seed
½ teaspoon salt
½ teaspoon ground ginger
½ teaspoon ground turmeric
¼ teaspoon crushed red pepper
½ cup plain fat-free yogurt
4 medium turkey breast
   tenderloin steaks
   (about 1 pound total)*
   Nonstick cooking spray
   Hot cooked couscous
   (optional)

Fish & Seafood

Whether it's fish, shrimp, lobster, or crab you enjoy, grill one of these fresh-from-the-water specialties, and you can have the fun of a seaside or lake getaway in your backyard.

Caramelized Salmon with Citrus Salsa, page 122

Caramelized Salmon With Citrus Salsa

The sugar coating caramelizes to a golden brown as the salmon grills.

Prep: 15 minutes **Chill:** 8 to 24 hours **Grill:** 14 minutes **Makes:** 6 servings

1½ pounds fresh or frozen
   salmon fillet (with skin),
   about 1 inch thick
2 tablespoons sugar
1½ teaspoons grated orange
   peel
1 teaspoon salt
¼ teaspoon freshly ground
   black pepper
1 teaspoon finely shredded
   orange peel
2 oranges, peeled, sectioned,
   and chopped
1 cup chopped fresh pineapple
   or canned crushed
   pineapple, drained
2 tablespoons snipped
   fresh cilantro
1 small shallot, finely chopped
   (1 tablespoon)
1 small fresh jalapeño pepper,
   seeded and finely chopped*
Nonstick cooking spray

1. Thaw fish, if frozen. Rinse fish; pat dry with paper towels. For rub, in a small bowl combine sugar, grated orange peel, salt, and pepper. Sprinkle rub evenly over flesh side of salmon; rub in with your fingers. Place fish, sugar side up, in a nonmetallic baking dish. Cover and chill in the refrigerator for at least 8 hours or up to 24 hours.

2. For salsa, in a small bowl combine the shredded orange peel, chopped oranges, pineapple, cilantro, shallot, and jalapeño pepper. Cover; refrigerate until serving time (up to 24 hours).

3. Remove fish from dish; discard liquid in dish. Coat the unheated grill rack of a grill with a cover with nonstick cooking spray. Arrange medium-hot coals around a drip pan. Test for medium heat above the pan. Place fish, skin side down, on grill rack over pan. Cover and grill 14 to 18 minutes or just until fish flakes easily with a fork.

4. To serve, cut fish into 6 serving-size pieces, cutting to but not through the skin. Carefully slip a metal spatula between fish and skin, lifting fish up and away from skin. Serve with salsa.

Nutrition Facts per serving: 145 calories, 4 g total fat, 20 mg cholesterol, 424 mg sodium, 10 g carbohydrate, 17 g protein.

*Note: Because chile peppers, such as jalapeños, contain volatile oils that can burn your skin and eyes, avoid direct contact with them as much as possible. When working with chile peppers, wear plastic or rubber gloves. If your bare hands do touch the chile peppers, wash your hands and nails well with soap and warm water.

Speedy Salmon Fillet

You can choose any of four different fish to grill with this lemon, garlic, basil, and soy sauce brush-on.

Prep: 15 minutes **Grill:** 8 minutes **Makes:** 6 servings

1. Thaw fish, if frozen. Rinse fish; pat dry with paper towels. In a small bowl combine lemon juice, garlic, basil, oil, soy sauce, Worcestershire sauce, and pepper; brush mixture over fish.

2. Lightly grease the rack of an uncovered grill or a wire grill basket. Place fish fillets on the grill rack or in the grill basket, turning thin ends under to make an even thickness. Grill directly over medium coals 8 to 12 minutes or just until fish flakes easily with a fork, carefully turning once halfway through grilling and brushing with remaining sauce after 3 minutes grilling. Discard any remaining sauce.

3. If desired, serve fish on ti leaves. If desired, garnish with lemon wedges.

Nutrition Facts per serving: 130 calories, 6 g total fat, 20 mg cholesterol, 248 mg sodium, 1 g carbohydrate, 16 g protein.

Note: If using ti leaves, be sure they have not been sprayed or treated in a way that would make them unsafe for contact with food. Wash them thoroughly before using. Although they are not toxic, they should not be eaten.

1½ pounds fresh or frozen boneless, skinless salmon fillet, about 1 inch thick, or tuna, halibut, or swordfish steaks, cut 1 inch thick
3 tablespoons lemon juice
2 cloves garlic, minced
2 tablespoons snipped fresh basil or 1 teaspoon dried basil, crushed
1 tablespoon cooking oil
1 tablespoon soy sauce
1 teaspoon Worcestershire sauce
¼ teaspoon pepper
Ti leaves (optional)*
Lemon wedges (optional)

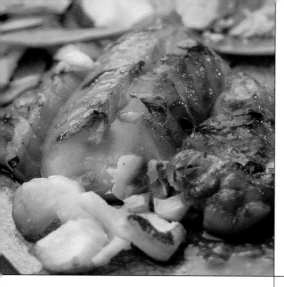

Wasabi-Glazed Whitefish With Vegetable Slaw

Wasabi—the vibrant green condiment made from Japanese horseradish—can be purchased at Asian specialty stores or large supermarkets. Be sure to get the powdered form for this recipe.

Prep: 15 minutes **Grill:** 6 minutes **Makes:** 4 servings

4 4-ounce fresh or frozen white-fleshed skinless fish fillets (such as whitefish, sea bass, or orange roughy), about ¾ inch thick

2 tablespoons light soy sauce

1 teaspoon toasted sesame oil

½ teaspoon sugar

¼ teaspoon wasabi powder or 1 tablespoon prepared horseradish

1 medium zucchini, coarsely shredded (about 1⅓ cups)

1 cup sliced radishes

1 cup fresh pea pods

3 tablespoons snipped fresh chives

3 tablespoons rice vinegar

1. Thaw fish, if frozen. Rinse fish; pat dry with paper towels. In small bowl combine soy sauce, ½ teaspoon of the sesame oil, ¼ teaspoon of the sugar, and the wasabi powder or horseradish. Brush soy mixture over fish.

2. Lightly grease the grill rack of an uncovered grill. Place fish on rack. Grill directly over medium coals for 6 to 9 minutes or just until fish flakes easily with a fork, carefully turning once halfway through grilling.

3. Meanwhile, for vegetable slaw, in a medium bowl combine zucchini, radishes, pea pods, and chives. In a small bowl combine the remaining sesame oil, the remaining sugar, and the vinegar. Drizzle over the zucchini mixture; toss to coat. Serve vegetable slaw with fish.

Nutrition Facts per serving: 141 calories, 3 g total fat, 60 mg cholesterol, 363 mg sodium, 6 g carbohydrate, 24 g protein.

Citrus-Honey Swordfish

Any firm-fleshed fish will taste great with the sweet-tart flavor of this marinade.

Prep: 15 minutes **Marinate:** 1 to 2 hours **Grill:** 8 minutes **Makes:** 4 servings

1. Thaw fish, if frozen. Rinse fish; pat dry with paper towels. Cut fish into 4 serving-size pieces. Place fish in a heavy, large self-sealing plastic bag set in a shallow dish. For marinade, in a small bowl combine orange juice, lemon juice, mustard, honey, and soy sauce. Pour over fish. Seal bag; turn to coat fish. Marinate in the refrigerator for at least 1 hour or up to 2 hours, turning bag occasionally.

2. Drain fish, reserving marinade. Lightly grease the rack of an uncovered grill. Place fish on rack. Grill directly over medium coals for 8 to 12 minutes or just until fish flakes easily with a fork, carefully turning once halfway through grilling and brushing once with reserved marinade after 3 minutes of grilling. Transfer the remaining marinade to a small saucepan; bring to boiling.

3. Meanwhile, cook pasta according to package directions; drain. Toss the pasta with heated marinade. Serve with the grilled fish.

Nutrition Facts per serving: 303 calories, 6 g total fat, 34 mg cholesterol, 550 mg sodium, 34 g carbohydrate, 27 g protein.

1 pound fresh or frozen
  swordfish steaks, cut
  1 inch thick
¼ cup orange juice
2 tablespoons lemon juice
2 tablespoons Dijon-style
  mustard
2 tablespoons honey
1 tablespoon soy sauce
4 ounces dried vermicelli

Thawing Fish and Seafood

To ensure that frozen fish and seafood are at their prime and are safe to eat, thaw them slowly in the refrigerator. Defrosting fish or seafood at room temperature or in warm water is unsafe because it can allow harmful bacteria to grow at a rapid rate. For best results, place the fish or seafood, still in its original wrapping, in a container in the refrigerator. Thaw a 1-pound package overnight. If the package is still icy, run it under cold running water for 1 to 2 minutes or until you can separate the pieces. Never refreeze thawed fish or seafood.

Grilled Chorrillos-Style Sea Bass

The jalapeño-onion relish gives the sea bass or halibut fillets a spunky Tex-Mex twist.

Prep: 10 minutes **Chill:** 15 minutes **Grill:** 6 minutes **Makes:** 4 servings

4 6-ounce fresh or frozen sea bass or halibut fillets, ¾ to 1 inch thick

2 teaspoons toasted sesame oil

4 cloves garlic, minced

1 tablespoon grated fresh ginger

¾ teaspoon salt

½ teaspoon ground cardamom

4 teaspoons lemon juice

1 medium red onion, cut into ¼-inch-thick slices

1 tablespoon olive oil

2 fresh jalapeño peppers, seeded and finely chopped*

3 small yellow or red tomatoes, halved and cut into wedges

1 tablespoon snipped fresh oregano

¾ teaspoon snipped fresh thyme

¼ teaspoon ground black pepper

Fresh herb sprigs (optional)

Lemon slices, halved (optional)

1. Thaw fish, if frozen. Rinse fish; pat dry with paper towels. Set aside. For paste, in a small bowl stir together sesame oil, half of the garlic, the ginger, ½ teaspoon of the salt, and the cardamom. Rub both sides of fish evenly with paste. Chill in the refrigerator for 15 minutes.

2. Just before grilling, drizzle lemon juice over fish. Lightly grease the rack of an uncovered grill. Place fish on rack. Grill directly over medium coals for 6 to 12 minutes or just until fish flakes easily with a fork, carefully turning fish once halfway through grilling.

3. Meanwhile, in a heavy, large skillet cook onion slices in hot oil over medium-high heat until tender, stirring frequently. Add remaining garlic and the jalapeño peppers; continue cooking until onions are golden. Add tomatoes, oregano, thyme, black pepper, and remaining salt. Stir gently until heated through.

4. To serve, place fish fillets on a serving platter; top with the tomato-onion mixture. If desired, garnish with herb sprigs and lemon slices.

Nutrition Facts per serving: 293 calories, 7 g total fat, 29 mg cholesterol, 978 mg sodium, 8 g carbohydrate, 49 g protein.

Note: Because chile peppers, such as jalapeños, contain volatile oils that can burn your skin and eyes, avoid direct contact with them as much as possible. When working with chile peppers, wear plastic or rubber gloves. If your bare hands do touch the chile peppers, wash your hands and nails well with soap and warm water.

Grilled Red Snapper with Tropical Salsa

A simple lime juice marinade delicately seasons the snapper, while a mango and black bean salsa adds a powerful flavor punch.

Prep: 10 minutes **Marinate:** 2 hours **Grill:** 45 minutes **Makes:** 6 servings

1. Thaw fish, if frozen. Rinse fish; pat dry with paper towels. Sprinkle garlic inside cavity of fish. Place fish in a large nonmetallic baking dish; pour lime juice over fish. Cover and marinate in the refrigerator for 2 hours.

2. Remove fish from baking dish; discard lime juice. Cut several slits in a piece of heavy foil large enough to hold fish. Lightly grease foil; place fish on greased side.

3. In a grill with a cover arrange medium-hot coals around a drip pan. Test for medium heat above the pan. Place foil with fish on grill rack over pan. Cover and grill for 45 to 60 minutes or just until fish flakes easily with a fork, carefully turning once halfway through grilling.

4. If desired, line a serving platter with ti leaves. Transfer fish to platter. Serve with Tropical Salsa.

Tropical Salsa: Seed and finely chop 2 fresh jalapeño peppers (see note on opposite page). In a medium bowl combine the finely chopped peppers; 1 small mango, chopped; ¼ of a fresh pineapple, peeled and chopped; 1 medium tomato, chopped; 1 small cucumber, seeded and chopped; ½ of a 15-ounce can black beans, rinsed and drained; 2 tablespoons snipped fresh cilantro; and 2 tablespoons lime juice. Cover and refrigerate for up to 24 hours.

Nutrition Facts per serving: 256 calories, 3 g total fat, 69 mg cholesterol, 212 mg sodium, 17 g carbohydrate, 42 g protein.

1 2½- to 3-pound fresh
   or frozen whole dressed
   red snapper
2 cloves garlic, minced
3 tablespoons lime juice
   Ti leaves (optional) (see note
   on page 123)
1 recipe Tropical Salsa

Orange Roughy with Nectarine Salsa

Using a wire grill basket helps you turn fish fillets or fish steaks on the grill with ease.

Prep: 20 minutes **Grill:** 8 minutes **Makes:** 4 servings

1 1-pound fresh or frozen orange roughy fillet, about 1 inch thick
1 large nectarine, cut into ½-inch pieces
1 small cucumber, seeded and cut into ½-inch pieces
1 kiwi fruit, peeled and cut into ½-inch pieces
¼ cup thinly sliced green onions
3 tablespoons orange juice
1 tablespoon white wine vinegar
1 teaspoon olive oil
¼ teaspoon freshly ground black pepper
Fresh kale leaves (optional)
Fresh herb sprigs (optional)

1. Thaw fish, if frozen. For salsa, in a medium bowl combine nectarine, cucumber, kiwi fruit, green onions, orange juice, and vinegar. Cover and refrigerate until ready to serve.

2. Rinse fish; pat dry with paper towels. Rub oil over both sides of fish; sprinkle with pepper. Well grease a wire grill basket. Place fish in grill basket. Place basket on rack of an uncovered grill directly over medium coals. Grill for 8 to 12 minutes or just until fish flakes easily with a fork, carefully turning basket once halfway through grilling.

3. To serve, cut fish into 4 pieces. If desired, place on kale leaves. Spoon salsa over fish. If desired, garnish with herb sprigs.

Nutrition Facts per serving: **158 calories, 3 g total fat, 60 mg cholesterol, 94 mg sodium, 10 g carbohydrate, 22 g protein.**

Grilled Catfish with Horseradish Sauce

This spritely horseradish sauce livens up roast beef just as deliciously as it does fish.

Prep: 10 minutes **Grill:** 5 minutes **Makes:** 4 servings

1. Thaw fish, if frozen. Measure thickness of fish. Rinse fish; pat dry with paper towels. Cut fish into 4 serving-size portions. Set aside.

2. For horseradish sauce, place flour in a small saucepan. Stir in milk until smooth. Cook and stir until thickened and bubbly. Cook 1 minute more; remove from heat. Stir in snipped chives, horseradish, lemon juice, and salt. Cover and set aside.

3. Brush fish with oil; sprinkle with seasoning blend and, if desired, pepper. Lightly grease a wire grill basket. Place fish in grill basket. Place grill basket on the rack of an uncovered grill directly over medium coals. Grill just until fish flakes easily with a fork (allow 4 to 6 minutes per ½-inch thickness of fish), carefully turning once halfway through grilling.

4. To serve, spoon horseradish sauce over fish. If desired, garnish with whole fresh chives.

Nutrition Facts per serving: 208 calories, 10 g total fat, 73 mg cholesterol, 210 mg sodium, 4 g carbohydrate, 23 g protein.

1 pound fresh or frozen
   skinless catfish or other
   firm fish fillets, ¾ to
   1 inch thick
1 tablespoon all-purpose flour
¾ cup fat-free milk
1 tablespoon snipped fresh
   chives or 1 teaspoon
   dried snipped chives
2 teaspoons prepared
   horseradish
1 teaspoon lemon juice
⅛ teaspoon salt
1 teaspoon olive oil
   or cooking oil
½ teaspoon salt-free
   seasoning blend
⅛ teaspoon pepper (optional)
   Whole fresh chives (optional)

Blackened Catfish with Roasted Potatoes

Vegetables roasted in olive oil add color and variety to this version of a Cajun classic.

Prep: 20 minutes **Grill:** 35 minutes **Makes:** 4 servings

4 4- to 5-ounce fresh or frozen
   catfish or red snapper
   fillets, ½ to 1 inch thick
1 tablespoon olive oil
¼ teaspoon salt
   Several dashes bottled
   hot pepper sauce
1½ pounds tiny new potatoes,
   thinly sliced
4 medium carrots, thinly
   sliced
1 medium green sweet pepper,
   cut into thin strips
1 medium onion, sliced
½ teaspoon Cajun seasoning
   Nonstick cooking spray
1 tablespoon snipped fresh
   chervil or parsley

1. Thaw fish, if frozen. Measure thickness of fish. Fold a
48×18-inch piece of heavy foil in half to make a 24×18-inch
rectangle. In a large bowl combine oil, salt, and hot pepper
sauce. Add the potatoes, carrots, sweet pepper, and onion; toss
to coat. Place in the center of foil. Bring up 2 opposite edges of
foil; seal with a double fold. Fold remaining ends to completely
enclose vegetables, leaving space for steam to build.

2. Grill vegetable packet on the rack of an uncovered grill
directly over medium coals for 35 to 40 minutes or until
potatoes and carrots are tender.

3. Meanwhile, rinse fish; pat dry with paper towels. Sprinkle
both sides of fish with Cajun seasoning and lightly coat with
nonstick cooking spray.

4. Well grease a wire grill basket. Place fish in grill basket. While
the vegetables grill, place grill basket on the grill rack next to
the vegetable packet and grill just until fish flakes easily with
a fork (allow 4 to 6 minutes per ½-inch thickness of fish),
carefully turning grill basket once halfway through grilling.

5. To serve, sprinkle fish and vegetables with snipped chervil
or parsley.

Nutrition Facts per serving: 352 calories, 6 g total fat, 42 mg cholesterol,
266 mg sodium, 48 g carbohydrate, 28 g protein.

Citrus-Tarragon Salmon Steaks

Don't marinate fish any longer than the time suggested or it may become tough.

Prep: 20 minutes **Marinate:** 45 minutes **Grill:** 6 minutes **Makes:** 4 servings

1. Thaw fish, if frozen. Rinse fish; pat dry with paper towels. For marinade, in a small bowl combine shredded orange peel, orange juice, lime juice, vinegar, tarragon, oil, salt, and pepper.

2. Place fish in a shallow nonmetallic baking dish. Pour marinade over fish. Cover and marinate in the refrigerator for 45 minutes, turning the fish once halfway through marinating.

3. Drain fish, reserving marinade. Coat the unheated rack of an uncovered grill with nonstick cooking spray. Place fish on rack. Grill directly over medium coals for 6 to 9 minutes or just until fish flakes easily with a fork, carefully turning once halfway through grilling and brushing once with reserved marinade after 2 minutes of grilling. Discard any remaining marinade. If desired, garnish with orange peel strips.

Nutrition Facts per serving: **179** calories, **8** g total fat, **42** mg cholesterol, **184** mg sodium, **4** g carbohydrate, **24** g protein.

4 fresh or frozen salmon steaks, cut ¾ inch thick (about 1 pound)
1 teaspoon finely shredded orange peel
¼ cup orange juice
¼ cup lime juice
1 tablespoon champagne vinegar or white wine vinegar
1 tablespoon snipped fresh tarragon or ½ teaspoon dried tarragon, crushed
1 teaspoon olive oil or salad oil
¼ teaspoon salt
⅛ teaspoon pepper
  Nonstick cooking spray
  Orange peel strips (optional)

Honey-Glazed Tuna And Greens

Quick-grilled tuna with a soy sauce and pepper glaze adds up to a fabulous entrée.

Prep: 15 minutes **Grill:** 4 minutes **Makes:** 4 servings

4 **5-ounce fresh or frozen tuna steaks, cut ½ to 1 inch thick**

¼ **cup honey**

¼ **cup reduced-sodium soy sauce**

1 **teaspoon toasted sesame oil**

½ **teaspoon crushed red pepper**

12 **cups mesclun or torn mixed bitter salad greens (about 8 ounces)**

10 **to 12 tiny pear-shaped yellow or red tomatoes, halved**

1. Thaw fish, if frozen. Measure thickness of fish. Rinse fish; pat dry with paper towels. In a small bowl combine honey, soy sauce, sesame oil, and red pepper. Set aside 2 tablespoons of the honey mixture to brush on the fish. Reserve remaining honey mixture for dressing.

2. Brush both sides of fish with the 2 tablespoons honey mixture. Lightly grease the rack of an uncovered grill. Place fish on rack. Grill directly over medium coals just until fish flakes easily with a fork (allow 4 to 6 minutes per ½-inch thickness of fish). Carefully turn 1-inch-thick steaks over once halfway through grilling.

3. In a large bowl toss together mesclun or salad greens and tomatoes; arrange on 4 dinner plates. Cut tuna across the grain into ½-inch-thick slices; arrange on greens. Drizzle with reserved honey mixture.

Nutrition Facts per serving: 279 calories, 2 g total fat, 24 mg cholesterol, 1,015 mg sodium, 22 g carbohydrate, 42 g protein.

Grilled Salmon Steaks with Mustard-Jalapeño Glaze

Orange juice concentrate adds a hint of citrus to the zingy glaze.

Prep: 10 minutes **Grill:** 6 minutes **Makes:** 4 servings

1. Thaw fish, if frozen. Rinse fish; pat dry with paper towels. For glaze, in a small bowl stir together mustard, orange juice concentrate, corn syrup, jalapeño peppers, and lemon-pepper seasoning. Set aside.

2. Lightly brush both sides of fish with oil. Grill fish on rack of an uncovered grill directly over medium coals for 6 to 9 minutes or just until fish flakes easily with a fork, carefully turning once halfway through grilling. Brush fish with glaze frequently during the last 2 to 3 minutes of grilling. Discard any remaining glaze.

Nutrition Facts per serving: **178 calories, 7 g total fat, 25 mg cholesterol, 608 mg sodium, 7 g carbohydrate, 21 g protein.**

Note: Because chile peppers, such as jalapeños, contain volatile oils that can burn your skin and eyes, avoid direct contact with them as much as possible. When working with chile peppers, wear plastic or rubber gloves. If your bare hands do touch the chile peppers, wash your hands and nails well with soap and warm water.

- 4 fresh or frozen salmon steaks, cut ¾ inch thick (about 1¼ pounds total)
- 3 tablespoons Dijon-style mustard
- 1 tablespoon frozen orange juice concentrate, thawed
- 1 tablespoon light-colored corn syrup
- 3 canned jalapeño peppers, seeded and finely chopped*
- ½ teaspoon lemon-pepper seasoning
- 1 teaspoon olive oil

Cooking Fish Just Right

Here's a way to test fish for doneness that eliminates much of the guesswork. Insert a fork into the fish and twist gently. If the fish is cooked properly, it will look opaque and begin to flake easily when you twist the fork. The flesh should come away from the bones readily, and the juices should be milky white. If the fish is undercooked, it will resist flaking, will look translucent, and the juices will be clear and watery. If the fish is overcooked, it will look dry and mealy with few juices. It also will fall apart easily when you twist the fork.

Salmon with Apricot Sauce

To give the sauce a little extra flavor, grill the fresh apricot halves, cut sides down, over medium coals a few minutes or just until they begin to brown. Cut up the apricots and add to the sauce.

Prep: 25 minutes **Grill:** 6 minutes **Makes:** 4 servings

4 fresh or frozen salmon
  or halibut steaks, cut
  ¾ inch thick (about
  1¼ pounds total)
4 fresh apricots, halved and
  pitted, or 8 dried apricot
  halves
½ cup apricot nectar
⅓ cup apricot preserves
3 tablespoons sliced green
  onions
1½ teaspoons snipped fresh
  oregano or ½ teaspoon
  dried oregano, crushed
⅛ teaspoon salt
  Few dashes bottled
  hot pepper sauce
1 tablespoon olive oil
1 to 2 teaspoons bottled
  hot pepper sauce
  Salt
  Pepper
  Nonstick cooking spray
  Fresh oregano sprigs
  (optional)

1. Thaw fish, if frozen. Rinse fish; pat dry. Cut up fresh apricot halves; set aside. (Or halve the dried apricots; cover with boiling water. Let stand for 10 minutes. Drain well.)

2. For sauce, in a small saucepan combine apricot nectar, apricot preserves, green onions, snipped oregano, and the ⅛ teaspoon salt. Bring just to boiling, stirring frequently; reduce heat. Boil gently, uncovered, about 8 minutes or until slightly thickened. Remove from heat; reserve ¼ cup of the preserves mixture to brush on fish. In a small bowl combine remaining preserves mixture, apricot quarters or halves, and the few dashes bottled hot pepper sauce. Cover sauce and keep warm.

3. In a small bowl stir together the oil and 1 to 2 teaspoons bottled hot pepper sauce. Brush both sides of fish with the oil mixture. Sprinkle fish lightly with salt and pepper.

4. Coat the unheated rack of an uncovered grill with nonstick cooking spray. Place salmon on rack. Grill directly over medium coals for 6 to 9 minutes or just until fish flakes easily with a fork, carefully turning once halfway through grilling. Brush salmon with the reserved preserves mixture during the last 2 to 3 minutes of grilling. Discard remainder of preserves mixture used as brush-on.

5. To serve, transfer salmon to a platter. Spoon sauce over salmon. If desired, garnish with oregano sprigs.

Nutrition Facts per serving: 304 calories, 8 g total fat, 73 mg cholesterol, 260 mg sodium, 27 g carbohydrate, 29 g protein.

Salmon with Fresh Pineapple Salsa

A wide spatula makes it easier to turn the salmon on the grill.

Prep: 20 minutes **Grill:** 8 minutes **Makes:** 4 servings

1. Thaw salmon, if frozen. Rinse fish; pat dry with paper towels.

2. For salsa, in a medium bowl combine the pineapple, sweet pepper, red onion, 2 tablespoons of the lime juice, the jalapeño pepper, cilantro or chives, and honey. Set aside. Brush both sides of fish with the remaining lime juice; sprinkle with cumin.

3. Lightly grease the rack of an uncovered grill. Place fish on rack. Grill directly over medium coals for 8 to 12 minutes or just until fish flakes easily with a fork, carefully turning once halfway through grilling. Serve salmon steaks with salsa.

Nutrition Facts per serving: 170 calories, 4 g total fat, 20 mg cholesterol, 70 mg sodium, 17 g carbohydrate, 17 g protein.

Note: Because chile peppers, such as jalapeños, contain volatile oils that can burn your skin and eyes, avoid direct contact with them as much as possible. When working with chile peppers, wear plastic or rubber gloves. If your bare hands do touch the chile peppers, wash your hands and nails well with soap and warm water.

4 4- to 6-ounce fresh or frozen salmon steaks, cut 1 inch thick
2 cups coarsely chopped fresh pineapple
½ cup chopped red sweet pepper
¼ cup finely chopped red onion
3 tablespoons lime juice
1 small fresh jalapeño pepper, seeded and finely chopped*
1 tablespoon snipped fresh cilantro or fresh chives
1 tablespoon honey
¼ teaspoon ground cumin

Sizzling Salmon with Minted Lentils

This all-purpose Cucumber Sauce tastes terrific with all kinds of white fish and chicken too.

Prep: 45 minutes   **Chill:** 2 hours   **Grill:** 8 minutes   **Makes:** 4 servings

4   6- to 8-ounce fresh or frozen
     salmon steaks, cut 1 inch
     thick
8   cups lightly salted water
12   ounces fresh green beans
     or long beans
1   recipe Cucumber Sauce
1   14-ounce can reduced-
     sodium chicken broth
⅔   cup dry brown lentils,
     rinsed and drained
     Salt
     Pepper
     Lemon wedges (optional)
     Fresh mint sprigs (optional)

1. Thaw fish steaks, if frozen. Rinse fish steaks; pat dry with paper towels.

2. In a large saucepan bring the lightly salted water to boiling. Add beans. Cover and cook about 4 minutes or just until crisp-tender. Drain well. In a medium bowl combine beans with ½ cup of the Cucumber Sauce. Set aside.

3. In a medium saucepan combine broth and lentils. Bring to boiling; reduce heat. Cover and simmer for 20 to 25 minutes or until lentils are tender. Drain, discarding cooking liquid. Return lentils to saucepan; stir in half (about 1 cup) of the remaining Cucumber Sauce. Set aside.

4. Sprinkle fish with salt and pepper. Lightly grease the grill rack of an uncovered grill. Place fish on rack. Grill directly over medium coals for 8 to 12 minutes or just until fish flakes easily with a fork, carefully turning once halfway through grilling.

5. Serve fish with lentil mixture and bean mixture. Pass the remaining Cucumber Sauce. If desired, garnish with lemon wedges and mint sprigs.

Cucumber Sauce: Seed and chop 2 medium cucumbers. In a medium bowl combine cucumbers, ¼ cup snipped fresh parsley, ¼ cup lemon juice, 2 tablespoons salad oil, 2 tablespoons thinly sliced green onion, 2 tablespoons snipped fresh mint, and ¼ teaspoon salt. Cover and chill in the refrigerator for at least 2 hours or up to 24 hours. Makes about 2½ cups.

Nutrition Facts per serving: 397 calories, 14 g total fat, 31 mg cholesterol, 308 mg sodium, 34 g carbohydrate, 37 g protein.

Grilled Tuna with Roasted Pepper Sauce

A roasted red pepper sauce contributes both color and a lively zing to the tuna steaks.

Prep: 25 minutes **Grill:** 8 minutes **Makes:** 4 servings

1. Thaw fish, if frozen. Rinse fish; pat dry with paper towels. Brush both sides of fish with some of the oil. Grill fish on the rack of an uncovered grill directly over medium coals for 8 to 12 minutes or just until fish flakes easily with a fork, carefully turning once and brushing with remaining oil halfway through grilling. Discard any remaining oil.

2. Meanwhile, for sauce, in blender container or food processor bowl combine red peppers, lime juice, the water, thyme or dill, salt, and black pepper. Cover; blend or process until smooth. Pour into a small saucepan. Cook and stir over low heat until heated through. Stir in margarine or butter.

3. Serve sauce with fish. If desired, garnish with lime slices.

Nutrition Facts per serving: 316 calories, 17 g total fat, 59 mg cholesterol, 262 mg sodium, 4 g carbohydrate, 36 g protein.

4 5- to 6-ounce fresh or frozen
   tuna or halibut steaks,
   cut 1 inch thick
1 tablespoon olive oil
   or cooking oil
1 7-ounce jar roasted
   red peppers, drained
3 tablespoons lime juice
2 tablespoons water
2 teaspoons snipped fresh
   thyme or dill or ½ teaspoon
   dried thyme, crushed,
   or dried dillweed
¼ teaspoon salt
⅛ teaspoon ground
   black pepper
2 tablespoons margarine
   or butter
4 lime slices (optional)

Swordfish with Cucumber Sauce

The refreshing sauce for these grilled fish steaks pairs yogurt and cucumber with mint.

Prep: 10 minutes **Grill:** 6 minutes **Makes:** 4 servings

 2 fresh or frozen swordfish or halibut steaks, cut ¾ inch thick (about 1 pound total)
⅓ cup plain low-fat yogurt
¼ cup finely chopped cucumber
 1 teaspoon snipped fresh mint or dill or ¼ teaspoon dried mint, crushed, or dried dillweed
Dash pepper
Nonstick cooking spray
Fresh mint sprigs (optional)

1. Thaw fish, if frozen. Rinse fish; pat dry with paper towels. Cut each fish steak in half. For cucumber sauce, in a small bowl stir together yogurt, cucumber, mint or dill, and pepper. Cover and refrigerate until serving time.

2. Coat the unheated rack of an uncovered grill with nonstick cooking spray. Place fish on rack. Grill directly over medium coals for 6 to 9 minutes or just until fish flakes easily with a fork, carefully turning once halfway through grilling.

3. Serve the fish with the cucumber sauce. If desired, garnish with mint sprigs.

Nutrition Facts per serving: **151 calories, 5 g total fat, 46 mg cholesterol, 115 mg sodium, 2 g carbohydrate, 23 g protein.**

Grilled Tuna with Tuscan Beans

Canned beans make this Italian favorite extra easy.

Prep: 15 minutes **Grill:** 6 minutes **Makes:** 4 servings

1. Thaw fish steaks, if frozen. For beans, in a medium skillet cook garlic in the 1 tablespoon hot oil for 15 seconds. Stir in the undrained tomatoes and the snipped or dried sage. Bring to boiling; reduce heat. Simmer, uncovered, for 5 minutes. Stir in white beans; heat through.

2. Meanwhile, rinse fish; pat dry with paper towels. Brush both sides of each fish steak with the 2 teaspoons oil and the lemon juice; sprinkle with pepper.

3. Coat the unheated rack of an uncovered grill or a grill basket with nonstick cooking spray. Place fish on rack or in grill basket. Grill directly over medium coals for 6 to 9 minutes or just until fish flakes easily with a fork, carefully turning once halfway through grilling.

4. To serve, remove the skin from fish steaks. Divide beans among 4 dinner plates; top with fish steaks. If desired, garnish with sage sprigs.

Nutrition Facts per serving: 298 calories, 7 g total fat, 49 mg cholesterol, 536 mg sodium, 25 g carbohydrate, 33 g protein.

- 4 fresh or frozen tuna, swordfish, halibut, shark, or salmon steaks, cut ¾ inch thick (about 1 pound total)
- 2 cloves garlic, minced
- 1 tablespoon olive oil
- 1 14½-ounce can Italian-style stewed tomatoes, cut up
- 2 teaspoons snipped fresh sage or ¼ teaspoon ground sage
- 1 15-ounce can small white beans, rinsed and drained
- 2 teaspoons olive oil
- 2 teaspoons lemon juice
- ⅛ teaspoon pepper
  Nonstick cooking spray
  Fresh sage sprigs (optional)

Island Grilled Tuna and Tropical Fruit

Because of their firm texture, tuna, marlin, and swordfish steaks are ideal for grilling. Here the fish steaks pick up a calypso beat with a pineapple and ginger glaze.

Prep: 20 minutes   **Grill:** 14 minutes   **Makes:** 4 servings

4 4- to 6-ounce fresh or frozen
    tuna, marlin, or swordfish
    steaks, cut 1 inch thick
4 slices bacon
1 recipe Tropical Glaze
4 ½-inch-thick slices fresh
    pineapple or 4 slices
    canned pineapple, drained
1 small papaya (ripe but firm),
    peeled, seeded, and
    quartered
    Lime wedges (optional)
    Star anise (optional)
    Thin slices lemon, orange,
    and grapefruit peel
    (optional)

1. Thaw fish, if frozen. In a small bowl soak 4 wooden picks in water for 10 minutes. Rinse fish; pat dry with paper towels. In a large skillet cook bacon for 2 to 3 minutes or until partially cooked but not crisp. Wrap a piece of bacon around the outside of each fish steak and secure with a water-soaked wooden pick.

2. In a grill with a cover arrange medium-hot coals around a drip pan. Test for medium heat above pan. Lightly grease grill rack. Place fish on grill rack over pan. Brush with some of the Tropical Glaze. Cover and grill for 14 to 18 minutes or just until fish flakes easily with a fork, carefully turning once halfway through grilling and brushing once with glaze after 8 minutes of grilling. Brush pineapple and papaya with glaze. For the last 5 minutes of grilling, arrange fruit on the grill rack around the fish directly over the coals; turn fruit once.

3. To serve, reheat remaining glaze until bubbly; drizzle over fish and fruit. If desired, garnish with lime wedges, star anise, and citrus peels.

Tropical Glaze: In a medium saucepan combine 1 cup pineapple juice, ⅓ cup sugar, 4 teaspoons grated fresh ginger, 1 tablespoon finely shredded lemon peel, ⅓ cup lemon juice, 1 tablespoon cornstarch, and 1 to 2 teaspoons habanero chili sauce or other Caribbean-style hot sauce. Cook and stir until thickened and bubbly. Cook and stir for 2 minutes more. Remove from heat. Stir in 1 teaspoon vanilla. Makes 1½ cups.

Nutrition Facts per serving: 374 calories, 11 g total fat, 53 mg cholesterol, 158 mg sodium, 38 g carbohydrate, 31 g protein.

Lime-Marinated Swordfish With Southwestern Pesto

Be sure to marinate the fish only 1 hour before grilling so the lime juice will have enough time to flavor the fish but won't soften its texture.

Prep: 30 minutes **Marinate:** 1 hour **Grill:** 6 minutes **Makes:** 6 servings

1. Thaw fish, if frozen. Rinse fish; pat dry with paper towels. Place fish in a heavy, large self-sealing plastic bag set into a shallow dish. For marinade, in a small bowl combine lime peel, lime juice, cilantro, oil, garlic, pepper, and salt. Pour marinade over fish. Seal bag; turn to coat fish. Marinate in the refrigerator for 1 hour, turning bag occasionally.

2. Drain fish, discarding marinade. Lightly grease the rack of an uncovered grill. Place fish on rack. Grill directly over medium coals. Grill 6 to 9 minutes or just until fish flakes easily with a fork, carefully turning once halfway through grilling.

3. Serve fish with Southwestern Pesto. If desired, garnish with basil.

Southwestern Pesto: Seed and quarter 1 fresh jalapeño pepper (see note on page 135). In a blender container or food processor bowl combine the jalapeño pepper quarters; 2 ounces Mexican grating cheese (at room temperature), cut up; and 2 cloves garlic, peeled. Cover; blend or process until finely grated. Add two 4-ounce cans diced green chili peppers, drained; ¼ cup pine nuts or slivered almonds; ¼ cup packed fresh parsley; and ¼ cup packed fresh cilantro leaves. With machine running, gradually add 2 tablespoons olive oil. Blend or process until nearly smooth. Chill pesto in the refrigerator for up to 3 days or freeze for up to 1 month. Makes 1⅓ cups.

Nutrition Facts per serving: 212 calories, 11 g total fat, 49 mg cholesterol, 306 mg sodium, 3 g carbohydrate, 25 g protein.

- 6 4-ounce fresh or frozen swordfish or tuna steaks, cut ¾ inch thick
- ½ teaspoon finely shredded lime peel
- ¼ cup lime juice
- 1 tablespoon snipped fresh cilantro
- 2 teaspoons cooking oil
- 2 cloves garlic, minced
- 1 teaspoon coarsely ground black pepper
- ¼ teaspoon salt
- 1 recipe Southwestern Pesto
  Fresh basil sprigs (optional)

Lemon-Herb Swordfish Steaks

Lemon and rosemary team up with garlic and tarragon in this versatile marinade that works equally well with swordfish, tuna, or shark steaks.

Prep: 10 minutes **Marinate:** 30 minutes **Grill:** 8 minutes **Makes:** 4 to 6 servings

4 to 6 fresh or frozen swordfish, tuna, or shark steaks (about 1½ pounds total), cut 1 inch thick
¼ cup snipped fresh parsley
¼ cup chicken broth
1 teaspoon finely shredded lemon peel
2 tablespoons lemon juice
1 tablespoon snipped fresh rosemary
1 tablespoon olive oil
1 shallot, finely chopped
3 cloves garlic, minced
1½ teaspoons snipped fresh tarragon
¼ teaspoon salt
Fresh tarragon sprigs (optional)

1. Thaw fish, if frozen. Rinse fish; pat dry with paper towels. Place fish steaks in a heavy, large self-sealing plastic bag set in a shallow dish. For marinade, in a small bowl combine parsley, chicken broth, lemon peel, lemon juice, rosemary, oil, shallot, garlic, snipped tarragon, and salt. Pour marinade over fish. Seal bag; turn to coat fish. Marinate in the refrigerator for 30 minutes, turning bag occasionally.

2. Drain fish, reserving marinade. Lightly grease the rack of an uncovered grill. Place fish on rack. Grill directly over medium coals for 8 to 12 minutes, carefully turning once halfway through grilling and brushing once with reserved marinade after 3 minutes of grilling. Discard any remaining marinade. If desired, garnish with tarragon sprigs.

Nutrition Facts per serving: 248 calories, 10 g total fat, 22 mg cholesterol, 337 mg sodium, 2 g carbohydrate, 34 g protein.

Two-Pepper Halibut

For a smoky flavor, toast the oregano by cooking and stirring it in a skillet over medium heat about 1 minute or until fragrant. Serve the grilled fish with your favorite rice pilaf.

Prep: 20 minutes **Marinate:** 30 minutes **Grill:** 8 minutes **Makes:** 4 to 6 servings

1. Thaw fish, if frozen. Rinse fish; pat dry with paper towels. For marinade, in a blender container combine chipotle peppers, adobo sauce, sweet pepper, lime juice, garlic, and oregano. Cover and blend until smooth. Transfer half of the marinade to a shallow nonmetallic baking dish. Set aside remaining marinade for sauce.

2. Add fish steaks to baking dish, spooning some of the marinade over fish. Cover and marinate in the refrigerator for 30 minutes.

3. Drain fish, discarding marinade. Sprinkle fish with salt. Lightly grease the rack of an uncovered grill. Place fish on rack. Grill directly over medium coals for 8 to 12 minutes or just until fish flakes easily with a fork, carefully turning once halfway through grilling.

4. For sauce, in a small saucepan heat reserved marinade until bubbly; serve with fish.

Nutrition Facts per serving: **199 calories, 4 g total fat, 55 mg cholesterol, 284 mg sodium, 3 g carbohydrate, 36 g protein.**

- **4 to 6** fresh or frozen halibut, swordfish, or shark steaks (about 1½ pounds total), cut 1 inch thick
- **2** canned chipotle peppers in adobo sauce
- **2** tablespoons adobo sauce
- **1** medium red sweet pepper, cut up
- **2** tablespoons lime juice
- **2** cloves garlic, halved
- **1** teaspoon dried Mexican oregano or oregano, toasted
- **¼** teaspoon salt

Rock Lobster Tails

The dill dipping sauce adds plenty of flavor without overpowering the succulent lobster.

Prep: 45 minutes **Grill:** 6 minutes **Makes:** 4 servings

4 medium fresh or frozen
   rock lobster tails
   (about 1½ pounds total)
1 lemon or lime
2 tablespoons olive oil
2 cloves garlic, minced
1 teaspoon chili powder
½ cup light mayonnaise
   dressing or salad dressing
1 teaspoon snipped fresh dill
   or ¼ teaspoon dried
   dillweed
   Lemon or lime wedges
   Fresh tarragon sprigs
   (optional)

1. Thaw lobster, if frozen. Rinse lobster; pat dry with paper towels. Using kitchen shears or a large sharp knife, cut through center of hard topshell and meat of lobster. Do not cut through undershell. Spread tails open, butterfly style, to expose meat on top. Set lobster aside.

2. Finely shred enough lemon or lime peel to measure ½ teaspoon shredded peel; set peel aside. Squeeze enough juice from lemon or lime to measure 4 to 5 teaspoons juice. For brush-on, in a small bowl combine half of the lemon or lime juice, the oil, garlic, and chili powder; brush on exposed lobster meat, reserving extra brush-on.

3. Grill lobster tails, meaty sides down, on the rack of an uncovered grill directly over medium coals for 6 to 10 minutes or until meat is opaque, turning once halfway through grilling and brushing with remaining brush-on after 3 minutes of grilling. Do not overcook. Discard any remaining brush-on.

4. Meanwhile, for dill sauce, in a small bowl combine light mayonnaise dressing or salad dressing, dill, reserved lemon or lime peel, and the remaining lemon or lime juice. If desired, split lobster tails in half lengthwise. Serve with dill sauce and fresh lemon or lime wedges. If desired, garnish with tarragon sprigs.

Nutrition Facts per serving: 272 calories, 18 g total fat, 78 mg cholesterol, 640 mg sodium, 5 g carbohydrate, 22 g protein.

Zucchini Crab Cakes

You'll need to start with about 1¼ pounds of crab legs to end up with 8 ounces of crabmeat. Be sure to discard any small pieces of shell or cartilage from the crabmeat.

Prep: 20 minutes **Grill:** 6 minutes **Makes:** 4 servings

1. In a large skillet cook and stir the zucchini and green onions in 2 teaspoons of the hot oil about 3 minutes or until the vegetables are just tender and the liquid is evaporated. Cool slightly.

2. In a large bowl combine the egg, bread crumbs, mustard, thyme, and, if desired, red pepper. Add the zucchini mixture and crabmeat; mix well. Using about ¼ cup of the mixture for each crab cake, shape into 8 patties, each about 2½ inches in diameter. Brush both sides of each patty lightly with the remaining oil.

3. Grease the rack of an uncovered grill or a grilling tray. Carefully place crab cakes on rack or tray. Grill directly over medium-hot coals for 6 to 8 minutes or until golden brown, carefully turning once halfway through grilling.

4. For each serving, overlap 2 patties on individual salad plates along with sliced tomatoes. If desired, garnish with cherry tomatoes and fresh chives. Serve with the Tomato-Sour Cream Dipping Sauce.

Tomato-Sour Cream Dipping Sauce: In a small bowl stir together ½ cup dairy sour cream, 3 tablespoons finely chopped yellow and red tomatoes, 1 to 2 tablespoons lemon juice or lime juice, and ⅛ teaspoon seasoned salt. Cover and chill in the refrigerator until serving time (up to 2 hours).

Nutrition Facts per serving: **277 calories, 16 g total fat, 123 mg cholesterol, 424 mg sodium, 16 g carbohydrate, 17 g protein.**

- 1 cup coarsely shredded zucchini (about 5 ounces)
- ¼ cup thinly sliced green onions
- 6 teaspoons cooking oil
- 1 beaten egg
- ½ cup seasoned fine dry bread crumbs
- 1 tablespoon Dijon-style mustard
- ½ teaspoon snipped fresh lemon thyme or snipped fresh thyme
- ⅛ to ¼ teaspoon ground red pepper (optional)
- 8 ounces cooked crabmeat, chopped (1½ cups)
- 2 red and/or yellow tomatoes, cut into ¼-inch-thick slices
  Red and/or yellow cherry tomatoes (optional)
  Fresh chives with blossoms (optional)
- 1 recipe Tomato-Sour Cream Dipping Sauce

Burgers, Sandwiches & Pizzas

If the day's activities have everyone starved, fire up the grill and satisfy those hunger pangs with these belt-busting burgers, two-fisted sandwiches, or spunky pizzas.

Pork Burgers with Tangy-Sweet Barbecue Sauce, page 158

Terrific Teriyaki Burgers

Soy sauce and ginger—two essentials for teriyaki sauce—give an Asian twist to all-American burgers.

Prep: 15 minutes **Grill:** 14 minutes **Makes:** 6 servings

1½ cups soft bread crumbs
¼ cup chopped onion
¼ cup water
2 tablespoons sugar
1 tablespoon soy sauce
1 clove garlic, minced
Dash ground ginger
1½ pounds lean ground beef
6 hamburger buns, split and toasted
Sliced cucumbers (optional)
Lettuce leaves (optional)

1. In a large bowl stir together soft bread crumbs, onion, water, sugar, soy sauce, garlic, and ginger. Add the ground beef; mix well. Shape into six ¾-inch-thick patties.

2. Grill patties on rack of an uncovered grill directly over medium coals for 14 to 18 minutes or until done (160°),* turning once halfway through grilling.

3. Serve burgers in buns topped, if desired, with sliced cucumbers and lettuce.

Nutrition Facts per serving: 353 calories, 13 g total fat, 71 mg cholesterol, 475 mg sodium, 32 g carbohydrate, 25 g protein.

Note: The internal color of a ground meat patty is not a reliable doneness indicator. A beef patty cooked to 160°, regardless of color, is safe. Use an instant-read thermometer to check the internal temperature. To measure the doneness of a patty, insert an instant-read thermometer through the side of the patty to a depth of 2 to 3 inches.

Burger Safety

Serving burgers that are not thoroughly cooked can be unsafe because ground meats may contain bacteria that can make you sick. Burgers need to cook long enough that these bacteria are destroyed. To make sure a burger is done, don't rely on color. Instead, check the internal temperature with an instant-read thermometer. An internal temperature of at least 160° is safe for beef, pork, and lamb burgers, no matter what the meat color. For ground turkey or chicken patties, the temperature should be 165°. For the most accurate reading, insert the thermometer 2 to 3 inches into the side of the burger.

Spanish Meat Loaves

Melted jalapeño pepper jelly gives these olive-stuffed loaves a glossy glaze and sweet-hot flavor.

Prep: 15 minutes   **Grill:** 18 minutes   **Makes:** 4 servings

1. In a medium bowl combine the egg, rolled oats, the ½ cup olives, the parsley, tomato paste, and pepper. Add the ground beef; mix well. Shape meat mixture into four 4×2½×1-inch meat loaves.

2. Grill meat loaves on the rack of an uncovered grill directly over medium coals for 16 to 20 minutes or until done (160°),* turning once halfway through grilling. Brush with melted jelly; grill for 2 minutes more.

3. Meanwhile, for relish, in a small bowl combine the chopped tomato, salsa, chopped cucumber, and, if desired, the 2 tablespoons olives.

4. Divide the lettuce and, if desired, bread slices among 4 dinner plates. Top with the meat loaves and relish.

Nutrition Facts per serving: 362 calories, 16 g total fat, 125 mg cholesterol, 479 mg sodium, 31 g carbohydrate, 26 g protein.

Note: The internal color of a meat loaf is not a reliable doneness indicator. A beef loaf cooked to 160°, regardless of color, is safe. Use an instant-read thermometer to check the internal temperature. To measure the doneness of the loaf, insert an instant-read thermometer through one end into the center of the loaf to a depth of 2 to 3 inches.

  1 beaten egg
¾ cup quick-cooking rolled oats
½ cup pimiento-stuffed green
      olives, sliced
¼ cup snipped fresh flat-leaf
      parsley or curly parsley
¼ cup tomato paste
¼ teaspoon pepper
  1 pound lean ground beef
¼ cup jalapeño pepper jelly
      or apple jelly, melted
  1 medium tomato, chopped
⅓ cup bottled chunky salsa
¼ cup chopped, seeded
      cucumber
  2 tablespoons sliced pimiento-
      stuffed green olives
      (optional)
      Lettuce leaves
  8 thin slices bread, toasted
      (optional)

Gorgonzola and Garlic-Stuffed Burgers

With creamy centers of blue cheese and fresh basil, these burgers are company-special fare.

Prep: 20 minutes   **Grill:** 14 minutes   **Makes:** 4 servings

½ cup crumbled Gorgonzola cheese or other blue cheese (2 ounces)

¼ cup snipped fresh basil

1 clove garlic, minced

1¼ pounds lean ground beef

  Salt

  Pepper

4 kaiser rolls, split and toasted

1½ cups arugula or fresh spinach leaves

1 large tomato, sliced

1. For burgers, in a small bowl combine Gorgonzola cheese, basil, and garlic; press into 4 slightly flattened mounds. Shape ground beef into eight ¼-inch-thick patties. Place a cheese mound in center of each of 4 of the patties. Top with remaining patties; press edges to seal. Reshape patties as necessary. Sprinkle with salt and pepper.

2. Grill burgers on the rack of an uncovered grill directly over medium coals for 14 to 18 minutes or until done (160°),* turning once halfway through grilling. Serve burgers on kaiser rolls with arugula and tomato.

Nutrition Facts per serving: 467 calories, 21 g total fat, 102 mg cholesterol, 675 mg sodium, 33 g carbohydrate, 35 g protein.

Note: The internal color of a ground meat patty is not a reliable doneness indicator. A beef patty cooked to 160°, regardless of color, is safe. Use an instant-read thermometer to check the internal temperature. To measure the doneness of a patty, insert an instant-read thermometer through the side of the patty to a depth of 2 to 3 inches.

Grilled Burgers with Caramelized Onions

For outstanding flavor choose Vidalia, Walla Walla, Maui, or another type of sweet onion.

Prep: 15 minutes **Grill:** 10 minutes **Makes:** 4 servings

1. In a medium bowl combine beef, honey mustard, and the ½ teaspoon salt; mix lightly until combined. Shape meat mixture into four ½-inch-thick patties. Sprinkle both sides of each patty with pepper; press in lightly.

2. Grill patties on the rack of an uncovered grill directly over medium coals for 10 to 13 minutes or until done (160°),* turning once halfway through grilling.

3. Meanwhile, for caramelized onions, in a covered large skillet cook onions in hot margarine or butter over medium-low heat until tender. (To make sure the steam stays trapped in the skillet and helps cook the onions, uncover the skillet only occasionally to stir the onions.) Uncover skillet; stir in brown sugar and the ¼ teaspoon salt. Cook, stirring constantly, over medium-high heat for 5 to 6 minutes or until onions are golden. Remove from heat. Add balsamic vinegar; stir to scrape up browned bits from bottom of skillet.

4. Serve burgers on toasted hamburger buns topped with the caramelized onions.

Nutrition Facts per serving: **476 calories, 23 g total fat, 61 mg cholesterol, 834 mg sodium, 40 g carbohydrate, 26 g protein.**

Note: The internal color of a ground meat patty is not a reliable doneness indicator. A beef patty cooked to 160°, regardless of color, is safe. Use an instant-read thermometer to check the internal temperature. To measure the doneness of a patty, insert an instant-read thermometer through the side of the patty to a depth of 2 to 3 inches.

1 pound lean ground beef

2 tablespoons honey mustard

½ teaspoon salt

1 teaspoon coarsely ground black pepper

2 large sweet onions, halved lengthwise and thinly sliced

2 tablespoons margarine or butter

4 teaspoons brown sugar

¼ teaspoon salt

2 tablespoons balsamic vinegar

4 onion hamburger buns, split and toasted

Basil Cheeseburgers

Fresh basil leaves and a roasted red pepper relish are refreshing changes from the standard burger toppings of lettuce and catsup.

Prep: 15 minutes **Grill:** 14 minutes **Makes:** 4 servings

¼ **cup finely chopped red onion**

2 **tablespoons fine dry bread crumbs**

2 **tablespoons catsup**

1 **tablespoon prepared horseradish**

1 **tablespoon prepared mustard**

¼ **teaspoon salt**

¼ **teaspoon ground black pepper**

1 **pound lean ground beef**

4 **slices Monterey Jack cheese**

4 **whole wheat hamburger buns, split and toasted**

Fresh basil leaves

¼ **cup Red Sweet Pepper Relish**

1. In a medium bowl combine red onion and bread crumbs. Stir in the catsup, prepared horseradish, mustard, salt, and black pepper. Add ground beef; mix well. Shape meat mixture into four ¾-inch-thick patties.

2. Grill patties on the rack of an uncovered grill directly over medium coals for 14 to 18 minutes or until done (160°),* turning once halfway through grilling and topping each burger with a slice of cheese for the last 2 minutes of grilling.

3. Serve burgers on buns with fresh basil leaves and the Red Sweet Pepper Relish.

Red Sweet Pepper Relish: In a food processor bowl combine ½ cup purchased roasted red sweet pepper strips; 1 tablespoon finely chopped pitted ripe olives; 2 teaspoons olive oil; 2 teaspoons snipped fresh thyme or ½ teaspoon dried thyme, crushed; and ¼ teaspoon ground black pepper. Cover and process with several on-off turns until coarsely chopped. Cover; store in the refrigerator for up to 1 week. Makes about ⅔ cup.

Nutrition Facts per serving: **446 calories, 23 g total fat, 96 mg cholesterol, 792 mg sodium, 28 g carbohydrate, 32 g protein.**

Note: The internal color of a ground meat patty is not a reliable doneness indicator. A beef patty cooked to 160°, regardless of color, is safe. Use an instant-read thermometer to check the internal temperature. To measure the doneness of a patty, insert an instant-read thermometer through the side of the patty to a depth of 2 to 3 inches.

Creole Carnival Burgers

Add extra kick to these stuffed burgers by substituting mozzarella cheese with jalapeño peppers for the Monterey Jack cheese.

Prep: 25 minutes **Grill:** 14 minutes **Makes:** 6 servings

1. In a large bowl combine beef, Cajun seasoning, and salt. Shape meat mixture into twelve ¼-inch-thick patties.

2. In a medium bowl combine onion, sweet pepper, and cheese. Spoon ¼ cup of cheese mixture into center of each of 6 of the patties. Top with remaining patties; press edges to seal. Reshape patties as necessary.

3. Grill burgers on the rack of an uncovered grill directly over medium coals for 14 to 18 minutes or until done (160°),* turning once halfway through grilling. Serve on buns. If desired, serve with your choice of accompaniments.

Nutrition Facts per serving: 460 calories, 24 g total fat, 103 mg cholesterol, 626 mg sodium, 24 g carbohydrate, 37 g protein.

Note: The internal color of a ground meat patty is not a reliable doneness indicator. A beef patty cooked to 160°, regardless of color, is safe. Use an instant-read thermometer to check the internal temperature. To measure the doneness of a patty, insert an instant-read thermometer through the side of the patty to a depth of 2 to 3 inches.

2 pounds ground beef

2 teaspoons Cajun seasoning

½ teaspoon salt

1 medium onion, chopped

1 small green sweet pepper, chopped

½ cup shredded Monterey Jack cheese (2 ounces)

6 hamburger buns, split
Desired accompaniments (such as lettuce, sliced tomatoes, sliced cucumber, pickles, carrot sticks, and celery sticks) (optional)

Double Salsa Burgers

The fresh tomato and sweet and hot pepper salsa adds zesty flavor.

Prep: 25 minutes   **Grill:** 10 minutes   **Makes:** 6 servings

1 large tomato, seeded
   and finely chopped
½ cup finely chopped green
   sweet pepper
¼ cup finely chopped red onion
2 fresh jalapeño peppers,
   seeded and finely chopped*
1 clove garlic, minced
1 tablespoon snipped fresh
   cilantro
¼ teaspoon salt
1½ pounds lean ground beef
2 cups shredded lettuce
⅓ cup finely shredded cheddar
   cheese
¼ cup dairy sour cream
   and/or guacamole

1. For salsa, in a small bowl combine tomato, sweet pepper, onion, jalapeño peppers, garlic, cilantro, and salt. Set aside 2 tablespoons of the salsa. Cover and chill remaining salsa in refrigerator until serving time.

2. In another bowl combine ground beef and the 2 tablespoons salsa; mix well. Shape mixture into six ½-inch-thick oval patties.

3. Grill patties on an uncovered grill directly over medium coals for 10 to 13 minutes or until done (160°),** turning once halfway through grilling. Arrange shredded lettuce on individual plates. Top with burgers, remaining salsa, and cheddar cheese. Serve with sour cream and/or guacamole.

Nutrition Facts per serving: **298 calories, 19 g total fat, 87 mg cholesterol, 350 mg sodium, 6 g carbohydrate, 24 g protein.**

Note: Because chile peppers, such as jalapeños, contain volatile oils that can burn your skin and eyes, avoid direct contact with them as much as possible. When working with chile peppers, wear plastic or rubber gloves. If your bare hands do touch the chile peppers, wash your hands and nails well with soap and warm water.

****Note:*** The internal color of a ground meat patty is not a reliable doneness indicator. A beef patty cooked to 160°, regardless of color, is safe. Use an instant-read thermometer to check the internal temperature. To measure the doneness of a patty, insert an instant-read thermometer through the side of the patty to a depth of 2 to 3 inches.

Outdoor Burgers

Whenever you're grilling burgers, use an instant-read thermometer to assure that the meat is thoroughly cooked.

Prep: 20 minutes   **Grill:** 14 minutes   **Makes:** 8 servings

1. In a medium bowl combine onion, bread crumbs, sweet pepper, catsup, horseradish, mustard, salt, and black pepper. Add ground beef; mix well. Shape meat mixture into eight ¾-inch-thick patties.

2. Grill patties on the rack of an uncovered grill directly over medium coals for 14 to 18 minutes or until done (160°),* turning once halfway through grilling and topping each burger with a slice of mozzarella for the last 2 minutes of grilling. Remove from grill; sprinkle with basil.

3. Serve on toasted Italian bread slices. If desired, serve with onion slices and lettuce leaves.

Nutrition Facts per serving: 396 calories, 18 g total fat, 83 mg cholesterol, 695 mg sodium, 28 g carbohydrate, 30 g protein.

Note: The internal color of a ground meat patty is not a reliable doneness indicator. A beef patty cooked to 160°, regardless of color, is safe. Use an instant-read thermometer to check the internal temperature. To measure the doneness of a patty, insert an instant-read thermometer through the side of the patty to a depth of 2 to 3 inches.

½ cup finely chopped onion

¼ cup fine dry bread crumbs

¼ cup finely chopped green
   sweet pepper

¼ cup catsup

2 tablespoons prepared
   horseradish

2 tablespoons prepared
   mustard

½ teaspoon salt

½ teaspoon ground
   black pepper

2 pounds extra-lean
   ground beef

8 slices smoked or regular
   mozzarella cheese

   Fresh basil leaves, sliced

8 ¾-inch-thick slices Italian
   bread, toasted

   Red onion slices (optional)

   Lettuce leaves (optional)

Red River Burgers

These juicy burgers are seasoned just right with two kinds of chile peppers.

Prep: 20 minutes **Grill:** 14 minutes **Makes:** 4 servings

½ cup chopped green onions or finely chopped white onion

2 tablespoons fine dry bread crumbs

2 fresh red serrano peppers, seeded and finely chopped*

3 canned chipotle peppers in adobo sauce, chopped

½ teaspoon salt

1 pound lean ground beef

8 1-inch-thick slices bread, toasted, or 4 whole wheat hamburger buns, split and toasted

Roasted red pepper catsup, roasted garlic catsup, or other purchased flavored catsup (optional)

4 green or red tomato slices (optional)

Sliced red onion (optional)

Fresh red serrano peppers (optional)

1. In a large bowl combine green onions or white onion, bread crumbs, the finely chopped serrano peppers, the chipotle peppers, and salt. Add ground beef; mix well. Shape beef mixture into four ¾-inch-thick patties.

2. Grill patties on the rack of an uncovered grill directly over medium coals for 14 to 18 minutes or until done (160°),** turning once halfway through grilling.

3. Serve burgers on toasted bread or buns. If desired, top with flavored catsup, tomato slices, red onion slices, and additional serrano peppers.

Nutrition Facts per serving: 352 calories, 13 g total fat, 71 mg cholesterol, 756 mg sodium, 32 g carbohydrate, 25 g protein.

*Note: Because chile peppers, such as serrano peppers, contain volatile oils that can burn your skin and eyes, avoid direct contact with them as much as possible. When working with chile peppers, wear plastic or rubber gloves. If your bare hands do touch the chile peppers, wash your hands and nails well with soap and warm water.

**Note: The internal color of a ground meat patty is not a reliable doneness indicator. A beef patty cooked to 160°, regardless of color, is safe. Use an instant-read thermometer to check the internal temperature. To measure the doneness of a patty, insert an instant-read thermometer through the side of the patty to a depth of 2 to 3 inches.

Dried Tomato Burgers

To add moistness as well as flavor to the burgers, be sure to use oil-packed dried tomatoes.

Prep: 15 minutes **Grill:** 10 minutes **Makes:** 4 servings

1. In a medium bowl combine the ground beef, tomatoes, lemon peel, salt, and black pepper; mix well. Shape into four ½-inch-thick patties. Grill patties on the rack of an uncovered grill directly over medium coals for 10 to 13 minutes or until done (160°),** turning once halfway through grilling.

2. Meanwhile, in a small bowl combine mayonnaise dressing or salad dressing, basil, and jalapeño pepper.

3. Serve burgers on buns topped with mayonnaise dressing mixture and arugula or spinach.

Nutrition Facts per serving: 450 calories, 20 g total fat, 71 mg cholesterol, 784 mg sodium, 40 g carbohydrate, 26 g protein.

*****Note:** Because chile peppers, such as jalapeños, contain volatile oils that can burn your skin and eyes, avoid direct contact with them as much as possible. When working with chile peppers, wear plastic or rubber gloves. If your bare hands do touch the chile peppers, wash your hands and nails well with soap and warm water.

******Note:** The internal color of a ground meat patty is not a reliable doneness indicator. A beef patty cooked to 160°, regardless of color, is safe. Use an instant-read thermometer to check the internal temperature. To measure the doneness of a patty, insert an instant-read thermometer through the side of the patty to a depth of 2 to 3 inches.

- **1 pound lean ground beef**
- **1 tablespoon finely chopped, drained, oil-packed dried tomatoes**
- **1 teaspoon finely shredded lemon peel or lime peel**
- **½ teaspoon salt**
- **¼ teaspoon ground black pepper**
- **¼ cup light mayonnaise dressing or salad dressing**
- **2 tablespoons snipped fresh basil**
- **1 fresh jalapeño pepper, seeded and finely chopped***
- **4 onion hamburger buns, split and toasted**
- **1 cup lightly packed arugula or fresh spinach leaves**

Pork Burgers with Tangy-Sweet Barbecue Sauce

You'll find sausage seasoning—a mixture of salt, sage, and other herbs—in the spice section of most large supermarkets.

Prep: 10 minutes **Grill:** 14 minutes **Makes:** 4 servings

1 **pound lean ground pork**

1 **teaspoon sausage seasoning**

1 **recipe Tangy-Sweet Barbecue Sauce**

8 **1-inch-thick slices bread, toasted, or 4 hamburger buns or kaiser rolls, split and toasted**

Leaf lettuce

Tomato slices

Onion slices

1. In a large bowl combine ground pork and sausage seasoning. Shape mixture into four ¾-inch-thick patties.

2. Grill patties on the rack of an uncovered grill directly over medium coals for 14 to 18 minutes or until done (160°),* turning once halfway through grilling and brushing once with Tangy-Sweet Barbecue Sauce after 7 minutes of grilling.

3. Serve burgers on toasted bread or buns with lettuce, tomato slices, and onion slices. Reheat remaining Tangy-Sweet Barbecue Sauce until bubbly; serve with burgers.

Tangy-Sweet Barbecue Sauce: In a medium saucepan combine 1 cup catsup, ½ cup packed brown sugar, ⅓ cup granulated sugar, 3 tablespoons cooking oil, 2 tablespoons vinegar, 1 tablespoon honey, and 2 teaspoons Worcestershire sauce. Stir over medium heat until the sugars dissolve and sauce is bubbly. Cover and store in the refrigerator for up to 1 week. Makes 1¾ cups.

Nutrition Facts per serving: **613 calories, 20 g total fat, 53 mg cholesterol, 1,144 mg sodium, 91 g carbohydrate, 20 g protein.**

Note: The internal color of a ground meat patty is not a reliable doneness indicator. A pork patty cooked to 160°, regardless of color, is safe. Use an instant-read thermometer to check the internal temperature. To measure the doneness of a patty, insert an instant-read thermometer through the side of the patty to a depth of 2 to 3 inches.

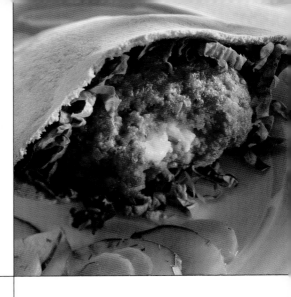

Feta-Stuffed Pita Burgers

A savory combination of ground lamb and ground beef distinguishes these feta-filled burgers.

Prep: 15 minutes **Grill:** 14 minutes **Makes:** 4 servings

1. In a medium bowl combine the milk, cornmeal, onion, garlic, salt, oregano, cumin, ground red pepper, and lemon-pepper seasoning. Add ground lamb and ground beef; mix well. Shape into eight ¼-inch-thick oval patties. Place 1 tablespoon of the feta in center of each of 4 of the patties. Top with remaining patties; press edges to seal. Reshape patties as necessary.

2. Grill patties on the rack of an uncovered grill directly over medium coals for 14 to 18 minutes or until done (160°).* turning once halfway through grilling. Serve in pitas with shredded spinach.

Nutrition Facts per serving: 345 calories, 17 g total fat, 80 mg cholesterol, 493 mg sodium, 22 g carbohydrate, 25 g protein.

Note: The internal color of a ground meat patty is not a reliable doneness indicator. A beef and lamb patty cooked to 160°, regardless of color, is safe. Use an instant-read thermometer to check the internal temperature. To measure the doneness of a patty, insert an instant-read thermometer through the side of the patty to a depth of 2 to 3 inches.

2 tablespoons milk
2 tablespoons cornmeal
1 tablespoon finely chopped onion
1 clove garlic, minced
¼ teaspoon salt
¼ teaspoon dried oregano, crushed
¼ teaspoon ground cumin
⅛ teaspoon ground red pepper
⅛ teaspoon lemon-pepper seasoning
8 ounces lean ground lamb
8 ounces lean ground beef
¼ cup finely crumbled feta cheese (1 ounce)
2 large pita bread rounds, halved crosswise and split horizontally
1½ cups shredded fresh spinach

Turkey Burgers

Another time, try the mustard and fruit preserves glaze on grilled or broiled chicken breasts.

Prep: 25 minutes **Grill:** 14 minutes **Makes:** 4 servings

1 tablespoon prepared
   mustard
1 tablespoon cherry, apricot,
   peach, or pineapple
   preserves
1 beaten egg
¼ cup quick-cooking
   rolled oats
¼ cup finely chopped celery
2 tablespoons chopped dried
   tart cherries or snipped
   dried apricots (optional)
¼ teaspoon salt
⅛ teaspoon pepper
1 pound uncooked ground
   turkey or chicken
4 kaiser rolls or hamburger
   buns, split and toasted
   Shredded lettuce (optional)
   Chopped tomato (optional)

1. For glaze, in a small bowl combine mustard and preserves. Set aside.

2. In a medium bowl combine egg, oats, celery, cherries or apricots (if desired), salt, and pepper. Add turkey or chicken; mix well. Shape into four ¾-inch-thick patties.

3. Grill patties on the rack of an uncovered grill directly over medium coals for 14 to 18 minutes or until done (165°),* turning once halfway through grilling and brushing both sides of patties with glaze during the last 1 minute of grilling. Serve on rolls or buns with remaining glaze and, if desired, lettuce and tomato.

Nutrition Facts per serving: 376 calories, 13 g total fat, 95 mg cholesterol, 560 mg sodium, 40 g carbohydrate, 23 g protein.

Note: The internal color of a ground poultry patty is not a reliable doneness indicator. A poultry patty cooked to 165°, regardless of color, is safe. Use an instant-read thermometer to check the internal temperature. To measure the doneness of a patty, insert an instant-read thermometer through the side of the patty to a depth of 2 to 3 inches.

Basil Turkey Burgers

Use the extra dried tomato mayonnaise to dress up roast beef or chicken sandwiches.

Prep: 20 minutes **Grill:** 14 minutes **Makes:** 4 servings

1. In a medium bowl combine the milk, onion, bread crumbs, basil, salt, and pepper. Add ground turkey; mix well. Shape mixture into four ¾-inch-thick patties.

2. Grill patties on the rack of an uncovered grill directly over medium coals for 14 to 18 minutes or until done (165°),* turning once halfway through grilling.

3. Serve burgers on toasted buns with lettuce and the Dried Tomato Mayonnaise.

Dried Tomato Mayonnaise: In small bowl pour enough boiling water over 2 tablespoons snipped dried tomatoes (not oil-packed) to cover. Let stand about 10 minutes or until tomatoes are pliable. Drain well. Stir tomatoes into ⅓ cup fat-free mayonnaise dressing or light mayonnaise dressing. Cover and store in the refrigerator for up to 1 week. Makes about ½ cup.

Nutrition Facts per serving: **251 calories, 9 g total fat, 32 mg cholesterol, 488 mg sodium, 27 g carbohydrate, 16 g protein.**

Note: The internal color of a ground poultry patty is not a reliable doneness indicator. A poultry patty cooked to 165°, regardless of color, is safe. Use an instant-read thermometer to check the internal temperature. To measure the doneness of a patty, insert an instant-read thermometer through the side of the patty to a depth of 2 to 3 inches.

¼ cup fat-free milk

2 tablespoons finely chopped onion

1 tablespoon fine dry bread crumbs

1 tablespoon snipped fresh basil or 1 teaspoon dried basil, crushed

⅛ teaspoon salt

⅛ teaspoon pepper

12 ounces uncooked ground turkey

4 hamburger buns, split and toasted

4 lettuce leaves

¼ cup Dried Tomato Mayonnaise

Grilled Greek-Style Turkey Burgers

Kalamatas are rich, fruity Greek olives typically packed in vinegar or oil. If you can't find kalamatas, any ripe olives will work for the refreshing burger topper.

Prep: 20 minutes **Grill:** 14 minutes **Makes:** 4 servings

⅓ cup fine dry wheat
    bread crumbs

1 slightly beaten egg white

1 tablespoon milk

1 0.7-ounce envelope Italian
    salad dressing mix
    (5 teaspoons)

1 pound uncooked ground
    turkey or chicken

4 pita bread rounds, toasted,
    or 4 whole wheat
    hamburger buns, split
    and toasted

1 recipe Tomato-Olive Topper

¼ cup crumbled feta cheese

1. In a medium bowl combine wheat bread crumbs, egg white, milk, and half of the dry salad dressing mix. Add ground turkey; mix well. (Set aside the remaining dry salad dressing mix for the Tomato-Olive Topper.) Shape turkey mixture into four ¾-inch-thick patties.

2. Grill patties on the rack of an uncovered grill directly over medium coals for 14 to 18 minutes or until done (165°),* turning once halfway through grilling.

3. Serve the burgers on pita bread rounds. Top with Tomato-Olive Topper and sprinkle with feta cheese.

Tomato-Olive Topper: In a small bowl stir together 2 tablespoons white wine vinegar, 2 teaspoons olive oil, and the remaining dry salad dressing mix. Stir in 1 cup finely chopped tomato, ¼ cup finely chopped cucumber, and ¼ cup finely chopped, pitted kalamata or ripe olives. Makes about 1⅓ cups.

Nutrition Facts per serving: 403 calories, 18 g total fat, 96 mg cholesterol, 1,177 mg sodium, 32 g carbohydrate, 28 g protein.

Note: The internal color of a ground poultry patty is not a reliable doneness indicator. A poultry patty cooked to 165°, regardless of color, is safe. Use an instant-read thermometer to check the internal temperature. To measure the doneness of a patty, insert an instant-read thermometer through the side of the patty to a depth of 2 to 3 inches.

Grilled Lambburger Roll-Ups

In recent years, the Middle Eastern spread known as hummus has become popular served with pita bread or chips. Check in the supermarket's dairy section or deli for prepared hummus.

Prep: 15 minutes **Grill:** 14 minutes **Makes:** 4 servings

1. In a large bowl combine egg, bread crumbs, oregano, the water, garlic, salt, and pepper. Add lamb; mix well. Shape into eight 4-inch-long logs.

2. Grill lamb logs on the rack of an uncovered grill directly over medium coals for 14 to 18 minutes or until done (160°),* turning once halfway through grilling.

3. Meanwhile, spread the cracker bread or tortillas with hummus. Sprinkle with spinach or lettuce, feta cheese, and olives. If using cracker bread, place 4 lamb pieces, end to end, near an edge of each bread round. Roll up, beginning with edge closest to lamb. Slice each roll-up diagonally into fourths. (If using tortillas, place 2 lamb pieces, end to end, on each tortilla. Roll up. Slice each roll-up diagonally in half.)

Nutrition Facts per serving: 625 calories, 26 g total fat, 135 mg cholesterol, 1,225 mg sodium, 64 g carbohydrate, 34 g protein.

Note: The internal color of a ground meat burger is not a reliable doneness indicator. A lambburger cooked to 160°, regardless of color, is safe. Use an instant-read thermometer to check the internal temperature. To measure the doneness of a lamb log, insert an instant-read thermometer through one end of the log to a depth of 2 to 3 inches.

- 1 beaten egg
- 3 tablespoons fine dry bread crumbs
- 2 tablespoons snipped fresh oregano
- 1 tablespoon water
- 2 cloves garlic, minced
- ¾ teaspoon salt
- ½ teaspoon freshly ground black pepper
- 1 pound lean ground lamb
- 2 14- to 15-inch soft cracker bread rounds or four 7- to 8-inch flour tortillas
- ⅓ cup prepared hummus [chickpea (garbanzo bean) spread]
- 4 cups torn fresh spinach or red-tipped leaf lettuce
- ¼ cup crumbled feta cheese (1 ounce)
- 3 tablespoons sliced pitted kalamata or ripe olives

Steak Rémoulade Sandwiches

A five-ingredient version of the classic mayonnaise-based French sauce known as rémoulade and a prepared garlic spread complement the grilled steak and sweet peppers.

Prep: 15 minutes **Grill:** 11 minutes **Makes:** 2 servings

2 tablespoons light
   mayonnaise dressing
   or salad dressing
1 teaspoon finely minced
   cornichons or sweet
   pickles
½ teaspoon drained capers,
   chopped
¼ teaspoon lemon juice
   Freshly ground black pepper
1 8-ounce boneless beef top
   loin steak, cut 1 inch thick
1 teaspoon prepared garlic
   spread or 1 teaspoon
   bottled minced garlic
1 large yellow sweet pepper,
   cut lengthwise into 8 strips
2 French-style or kaiser rolls,
   split and toasted
½ cup arugula or fresh
   spinach leaves

1. For rémoulade, in a small bowl combine the mayonnaise dressing or salad dressing, cornichons or sweet pickles, capers, lemon juice, and a dash black pepper. Cover and refrigerate until ready to serve.

2. Pat steak dry with paper towels. Using your fingers, rub the garlic spread or minced garlic over steak. Sprinkle with additional freshly ground black pepper. Grill steak and sweet pepper strips on the rack of an uncovered grill directly over medium coals until steak is desired doneness and pepper strips are crisp-tender, turning once halfway through grilling. [For steak, allow 11 to 15 minutes for medium-rare (145°) and 14 to 18 minutes for medium doneness (160°).] Cut the steak into ¼-inch-thick slices.

3. To assemble, spread the rémoulade on cut sides of toasted rolls. Fill rolls with the arugula or spinach, steak slices, and sweet pepper strips.

Nutrition Facts per serving: 430 calories, 18 g total fat, 70 mg cholesterol, 512 mg sodium, 36 g carbohydrate, 30 g protein.

Beef Fajitas

Onions and sweet peppers grill in a foil packet placed alongside the steak.

Prep: 30 minutes   **Marinate:** 6 to 12 hours   **Grill:** 17 minutes   **Makes:** 6 servings

1. For marinade, in a small bowl stir together the ¼ cup lime juice, the soy sauce, 1 tablespoon oil, and the garlic. Score both sides of steak in a diamond pattern by making shallow diagonal cuts at 1-inch intervals. Place steak in a heavy, large self-sealing plastic bag set in a shallow dish. Pour marinade over steak. Seal bag; turn to coat steak. Marinate in the refrigerator for at least 6 hours or up to 12 hours, turning steak occasionally.

2. Meanwhile, combine the avocado, salsa, cilantro, the 1 tablespoon juice, and the hot pepper sauce. Cover; chill in the refrigerator until serving time. Wrap tortillas in foil; set aside.

3. Tear off a 36×18-inch piece of heavy foil. Fold in half to make an 18-inch square. Place onions and sweet peppers in center of the foil. Drizzle with 1 tablespoon oil. Bring up 2 opposite edges of foil and seal. Fold up remaining edges to completely enclose the vegetables, leaving space for steam to build.

4. Drain steak, reserving marinade. Grill steak and vegetable packet on the rack of an uncovered grill directly over medium coals for 10 minutes. Brush steak with reserved marinade; turn steak. Discard any remaining marinade. Add wrapped tortillas to grill. Grill for 7 to 11 minutes more or until steak is medium doneness (160°) and vegetables are crisp-tender.

5. To serve, cut steak into thin bite-size strips. Arrange beef, onions, and sweet peppers on tortillas. Top with avocado mixture and tomato. Fold tortillas around filling.

Nutrition Facts per serving: **506 calories, 26 g total fat, 59 mg cholesterol, 659 mg sodium, 39 g carbohydrate, 29 g protein.**

- ¼ cup lime juice
- 2 tablespoons soy sauce
- 1 tablespoon cooking oil
- 1 clove garlic, minced
- 1½ pounds beef flank steak
- 1 avocado, pitted, peeled, and coarsely chopped
- ¼ cup bottled salsa
- 1 tablespoon snipped fresh cilantro
- 1 tablespoon lime juice
- ¼ teaspoon bottled hot pepper sauce
- 12 8-inch flour tortillas
- 2 medium onions, sliced
- 2 medium green sweet peppers, cut into bite-size strips
- 1 tablespoon cooking oil
- 1 medium tomato, coarsely chopped

Italian Steak Sandwiches

The robustly flavored olive oil sauce adds an authentic Italian touch to this hearty sandwich.

Prep: 20 minutes **Grill:** 16 minutes **Makes:** 4 servings

1 1-pound boneless beef top
   sirloin steak, cut 1 inch
   thick
1 cup loosely packed fresh
   flat-leaf parsley
3 tablespoons olive oil
4 teaspoons lemon juice
1 tablespoon capers, drained
2 cloves garlic, minced
   Dash salt
   Dash bottled hot pepper
   sauce
4 1-inch-thick slices
   sourdough bread
1 medium onion, thinly sliced
   and separated into rings
1 cup mesclun

1. Trim fat from steak. For sauce, in a blender container or food processor bowl combine parsley, olive oil, lemon juice, capers, garlic, salt, and hot pepper sauce. Cover and blend or process until nearly smooth, stopping and scraping side as necessary. Set aside.

2. Grill steak on the rack of an uncovered grill directly over medium coals to desired doneness, turning once halfway through grilling. [Allow 14 to 18 minutes for medium-rare (145°) or 18 to 22 minutes for medium doneness (160°).] Remove steak from grill. Add bread slices, cut sides down, to grill. Grill for 2 to 4 minutes or until bread is lightly browned, turning once halfway through grilling.

3. Thinly slice steak. To serve, arrange onion rings and mesclun on bread slices; top with steak slices. Drizzle with sauce.

Nutrition Facts per serving: **314 calories, 15 g total fat, 69 mg cholesterol, 318 mg sodium, 17 g carbohydrate, 27 g protein.**

Savory Mushroom Burgers

The produce sections of many supermarkets carry a variety of "wild" mushrooms, including chanterelle, porcini, and shiitake.

Prep: 35 minutes **Grill:** 14 minutes **Makes:** 4 servings

1. Remove stems and finely chop half of the mushrooms; slice remaining mushrooms and set aside. In a small saucepan cook finely chopped mushrooms and garlic in ½ cup of the chicken broth for 4 to 5 minutes or until tender. Stir in bulgur. Return to boiling; reduce heat. Cover and simmer about 10 minutes or until liquid is absorbed and bulgur is tender.

2. Remove from heat; cool slightly. In a large bowl combine turkey, green onion, Worcestershire sauce, and pepper. Add bulgur mixture; mix until combined. Shape turkey mixture into four ¾-inch-thick patties.

3. Lightly coat the unheated rack of an uncovered grill with nonstick cooking spray. Place patties on rack. Grill directly over medium coals for 14 to 18 minutes or until done (165°),* turning once halfway through grilling.

4. Meanwhile, in covered saucepan cook sliced mushrooms in remaining broth for 4 to 5 minutes or until tender.

5. If desired, spread mustard on bottom halves of buns or rolls. Serve burgers and sliced mushrooms on buns or rolls.

Nutrition Facts per serving: 292 calories, 10 g total fat, 67 mg cholesterol, 520 mg sodium, 30 g carbohydrate, 21 g protein.

Note: The internal color of a ground poultry patty is not a reliable doneness indicator. A poultry patty cooked to 165°, regardless of color, is safe. Use an instant-read thermometer to check the internal temperature. To measure the doneness of a patty, insert an instant-read thermometer through the side of the patty to a depth of 2 to 3 inches.

7 ounces wild mushrooms (such as chanterelle, porcini, or shiitake) or button mushrooms
2 cloves garlic, minced
¾ cup chicken broth
3 tablespoons bulgur
12 ounces uncooked ground turkey breast
2 tablespoons thinly sliced green onion
2 teaspoons Worcestershire sauce
¼ teaspoon pepper
Nonstick cooking spray
Dijon-style mustard (optional)
4 hamburger buns or kaiser rolls, split and toasted

Taco Steak Sandwich

Give the steak a sophisticated margarita flavor by substituting 2 tablespoons lime juice plus ¼ cup tequila for the ¼ cup lime juice in the marinade.

Prep: 20 minutes **Marinate:** 6 to 24 hours **Grill:** 17 minutes **Makes:** 5 or 6 servings

1¼ to 1½ pounds beef flank steak
¼ cup lime juice
1 tablespoon cooking oil
2 cloves garlic, minced
½ teaspoon ground cumin
Salt
5 or 6 French-style rolls, warmed
Lettuce leaves
½ cup bottled salsa
2 medium tomatoes, chopped
Desired toppings (such as shredded lettuce, thin strips jicama, dairy sour cream, and/or snipped fresh cilantro) (optional)

1. Score both sides of the steak in a diamond pattern by making shallow diagonal cuts at 1-inch intervals. Place steak in a heavy, large self-sealing plastic bag set in a shallow dish. For marinade, in a small bowl combine lime juice, oil, garlic, and cumin. Pour marinade over steak. Seal bag; turn to coat steak. Marinate in the refrigerator for at least 6 hours or up to 24 hours, turning bag occasionally. Drain steak, discarding marinade. Season steak lightly with salt.

2. Grill steak on the rack of an uncovered grill directly over medium coals for 17 to 21 minutes for medium doneness (160°), turning once halfway through grilling. Carve steak, across the grain, into thin slices. Serve sliced steak in rolls with lettuce leaves, salsa, tomatoes, and desired toppings (if using).

Nutrition Facts per serving: 329 calories, 14 g total fat, 58 mg cholesterol, 476 mg sodium, 23 g carbohydrate, 26 g protein.

Texas Teriyaki Fajita Steaks With Honey Pickle Salsa

Grilled steak and a chile pepper-pickle salsa star in these two-fisted sandwiches.

Prep: 25 minutes **Grill:** 17 minutes **Makes:** 6 servings

1. For glaze, in a small saucepan heat vinegar, brown sugar, lime peel, lime juice, soy sauce, mustard, and ginger over medium heat until boiling. Boil gently about 10 minutes or until reduced by half (should measure about ⅓ cup).

2. Grill steak on the rack of an uncovered grill directly over medium coals for 17 to 21 minutes or until medium doneness (160°), turning once halfway through grilling and generously brushing with glaze for the first 10 minutes of grilling. Discard any remaining glaze. Remove from grill; let steak stand for 5 minutes before thinly slicing across the grain.

3. Serve sliced steak in rolls with lettuce, tomato slices, and Honey Pickle Salsa or bottled salsa. If desired, pass sour cream.

Honey Pickle Salsa: In a small bowl combine one 4-ounce can chopped green chile peppers, drained; ½ cup chopped dill pickle; 3 tablespoons finely chopped red onion; 2 tablespoons snipped fresh cilantro; 4 teaspoons lime juice; and 2 teaspoons honey. Cover and chill in refrigerator for up to 8 hours. Makes about 1 cup.

Nutrition Facts per serving: **296 calories, 9 g total fat, 38 mg cholesterol, 672 mg sodium, 28 g carbohydrate, 25 g protein.**

¼ cup rice vinegar
2 tablespoons brown sugar
½ teaspoon finely shredded lime peel
2 tablespoons lime juice
1 tablespoon soy sauce
1 tablespoon Dijon-style mustard
1 teaspoon grated fresh ginger
1¼ pounds beef flank steak or skirt steak
6 French-style rolls, split and toasted
Lettuce leaves
Tomato slices
1 recipe Honey Pickle Salsa or 1 cup bottled salsa
Dairy sour cream (optional)

Beef and Avocado Tacos

In Mexican cuisine, carne asada (grilled meat) is a popular choice for tacos and burritos.

Prep: 20 minutes **Grill:** 10 minutes **Makes:** 4 servings

---

2 tablespoons lemon juice

1 avocado, pitted, peeled, and cut into ½-inch cubes

1 pound boneless beef sirloin or eye round steak, cut 1 inch thick

1 medium onion, cut into wedges

2 fresh Anaheim or poblano peppers, cut into 1-inch squares*

1 tablespoon olive oil

½ cup bottled picante sauce

2 cups shredded lettuce

4 7- to 8-inch flour tortillas Bottled picante sauce (optional)

1. Drizzle lemon juice over avocado; toss gently to coat. Set aside.

2. Cut steak into 2×1-inch strips. On four 12-inch skewers, thread steak strips, accordion-style. On four 12-inch skewers, alternately thread onion wedges and pepper squares. Brush vegetables with oil.

3. Grill the kabobs on the rack of an uncovered grill directly over medium coals for 10 to 12 minutes or until steak is done, turning kabobs once halfway through grilling and brushing occasionally with the ½ cup picante sauce during the first 5 minutes grilling. Discard the remainder of the ½ cup picante sauce used as a brush-on.

4. To serve, divide the steak, onion, peppers, avocado, and lettuce among the tortillas. Fold tortillas over filling. If desired, serve with additional picante sauce.

Nutrition Facts per serving: 425 calories, 24 g total fat, 76 mg cholesterol, 403 mg sodium, 24 g carbohydrate, 30 g protein.

Note: Because chile peppers, such as Anaheim or poblano peppers, contain volatile oils that can burn your skin and eyes, avoid direct contact with them as much as possible. When working with chile peppers, wear plastic or rubber gloves. If your bare hands do touch the chile peppers, wash your hands and nails well with soap and warm water.

Italian Pizza Sandwiches

It's easy to adapt this recipe to suit lovers of spicy food as well as those who prefer milder fare. Just grill both hot and mild Italian sausage links.

Prep: 15 minutes **Grill:** 20 minutes **Makes:** 4 servings

1. Tear off a 36×18-inch piece of heavy foil. Fold in half to make an 18-inch square. Place sweet pepper and onion in the center of the foil. Dot with margarine or butter. Bring up 2 opposite edges of foil and seal. Fold up remaining edges to completely enclose vegetables, leaving space for steam to build. Prick the Italian sausage links in several places with a fork or the tip of a sharp knife.

2. In a grill with a cover arrange medium-hot coals around a drip pan. Test for medium heat above the pan. Place sausage links and the foil packet on grill rack over pan. Cover and grill for 20 to 30 minutes or until sausages are cooked through (an instant-read thermometer inserted from an end into the center of sausage should register 160°) and vegetables are tender.

3. Meanwhile, in a small saucepan heat pizza sauce.

4. To serve, halve sausage links lengthwise, cutting to but not through the other side. Place sausage links in the toasted rolls. Top with pepper mixture and pizza sauce. Sprinkle with Parmesan cheese.

Nutrition Facts per serving: **376 calories, 22 g total fat, 51 mg cholesterol, 1,067 mg sodium, 26 g carbohydrate, 18 g protein.**

- 1 medium green sweet pepper, cut into thin strips
- 1 medium onion, thinly sliced
- 1 tablespoon margarine or butter
- 4 uncooked sweet (mild) or hot Italian sausage links (12 ounces to 1 pound total)
- ½ cup pizza sauce
- 4 French-style rolls, split and toasted
- 2 tablespoons grated Parmesan cheese

Grilled Chicken Mole Sandwich

A little chocolate is traditional to round out the flavor in mole, a delicious Mexican sauce.

Prep: 30 minutes   **Grill:** 12 minutes   **Chill:** 30 minutes to 24 hours   **Makes:** 4 servings

3 dried New Mexico peppers
    or dried pasilla peppers
¼ cup chopped onion
3 cloves garlic, chopped
1 tablespoon cooking oil
½ cup water
1½ ounces Mexican-style sweet
    chocolate or semisweet
    chocolate, chopped
    (about 3 tablespoons)
4 medium skinless, boneless
    chicken breast halves
    (about 1 pound total)
    Salt (optional)
1 small avocado, pitted,
    peeled, and mashed
2 tablespoons light
    mayonnaise dressing
    or salad dressing
⅛ teaspoon salt
¼ teaspoon ground red pepper
    (optional)
2 bolitos, bollilos, or other
    Mexican rolls or hard rolls
    (approximately 6 inches
    in diameter), split
    Baby romaine or other
    green lettuce leaves
    Tomato slices
½ of a medium papaya, peeled,
    seeded, and sliced

1. For mole, remove stem and seeds from dried peppers; coarsely chop peppers and set aside. In large skillet cook onion and garlic in hot oil over medium-high heat 4 to 5 minutes or until onion is browned. Add dried peppers and the water; reduce heat. Stir in chocolate. Cook and stir over medium heat 3 to 5 minutes or until thickened and bubbly. Cool slightly. Transfer mixture to a food processor bowl or blender container; cover and process or blend until a smooth paste forms. Set aside to cool. Transfer 1 to 2 tablespoons of the mole to a small bowl.

2. If desired, sprinkle chicken with salt. Using a sharp knife, butterfly-cut each breast by cutting a slit horizontally two-thirds of the way through; spread open. Spread inside of each breast with mole from food processor bowl or blender container. Fold closed. Rub the outside of each breast with the reserved mole. Grill breasts on the rack of an uncovered grill directly over medium coals for 12 to 15 minutes or until tender and no longer pink, turning once halfway through grilling. Cover and chill in the refrigerator for at least 30 minutes or up to 24 hours.

3. In a small bowl stir together avocado, light mayonnaise dressing or salad dressing, the ⅛ teaspoon salt, and, if desired, the ground red pepper. Cut chicken into ¼- to ½-inch-thick slices. Spread avocado mixture on split rolls. Layer each roll half with chicken, romaine, and tomato. Top with papaya.

Nutrition Facts per serving: 524 calories, 24 g total fat, 59 mg cholesterol, 448 mg sodium, 52 g carbohydrate, 28 g protein.

Barbecued Turkey Tenderloins

Grilled tomatillos (also called Mexican green tomatoes) add a gourmet touch to these sandwiches. If you can't find fresh tomatillos, spoon salsa verde (green salsa) onto the turkey.

Prep: 10 minutes **Grill:** 20 minutes **Makes:** 4 servings

1. For sauce, in a small bowl combine barbecue sauce, jalapeño pepper, and tahini. Transfer half of the sauce to another bowl for basting sauce. Reserve remaining sauce until ready to serve. On two 8- to 10-inch skewers thread tomatillos, if using. Set aside.

2. Brush both sides of each turkey tenderloin with basting sauce. Lightly grease the rack of an uncovered grill. Place turkey on rack. Grill directly over medium coals about 20 minutes or until tender and no longer pink (170°), turning and brushing once with basting sauce halfway through grilling time. Discard any remaining basting sauce. For the last 8 minutes of grilling, grill tomatillos (if using) on the grill rack next to the turkey until tender, turning once halfway through grilling. Thinly slice turkey and chop tomatillos.

3. To serve, fill rolls with a few spinach leaves, grilled turkey, and tomatillos or salsa verde. Spoon reserved sauce over.

Nutrition Facts per serving: 378 calories, 8 g total fat, 50 mg cholesterol, 776 mg sodium, 45 g carbohydrate, 30 g protein.

Note: Because chile peppers, such as jalapeños, contain volatile oils that can burn your skin and eyes, avoid direct contact with them as much as possible. When working with chile peppers, wear plastic or rubber gloves. If your bare hands do touch the chile peppers, wash your hands and nails well with soap and warm water.

****Note:*** Tahini is a thick paste that is made by crushing sesame seeds. It is often used in Middle Eastern dishes and can be found in the ethnic foods section of most supermarkets.

½ cup bottled onion-hickory barbecue sauce
1 small fresh jalapeño pepper, seeded and finely chopped*
1 tablespoon tahini**
4 tomatillos, husked and halved lengthwise, or ½ cup salsa verde
2 turkey breast tenderloins (about 1 pound total)
4 French-style rolls, split and toasted
Fresh spinach leaves

Grilled Tuna Fajitas

Heat the tortillas and grill the sweet peppers alongside the tuna.

Prep: 30 minutes **Marinate:** 30 minutes to 1 hour **Grill:** 8 minutes **Makes:** 4 servings

2 5- to 6-ounce fresh or frozen tuna steaks, cut 1 inch thick
¼ cup lemon juice
2 tablespoons snipped fresh cilantro or parsley
2 teaspoons olive oil
2 cloves garlic, minced
¼ teaspoon coarsely ground black pepper
⅛ teaspoon ground red pepper
8 8-inch fat-free flour tortillas
   Nonstick cooking spray
2 medium red sweet peppers, quartered and stems and membranes removed
1 recipe Tomatillo Salsa
   Sliced fresh serrano or jalapeño peppers (optional) (see note on page 173)

1. Thaw fish, if frozen. Rinse fish; pat dry. Place fish in a heavy, large self-sealing plastic bag set in a shallow dish. For marinade, mix juice, cilantro, oil, garlic, and ground peppers. Pour over fish. Seal bag; turn to coat fish. Marinate in refrigerator for at least 30 minutes or up to 1 hour; turn bag occasionally.

2. Wrap tortillas in foil. Drain fish, reserving marinade. Lightly coat unheated rack of uncovered grill with nonstick cooking spray. Place fish and sweet pepper quarters on rack. Grill directly over medium coals 8 to 12 minutes or just until fish flakes easily with a fork, turning once halfway through grilling and brushing once with reserved marinade after 3 minutes of grilling. Discard any remaining marinade. Grill sweet peppers for 8 to 10 minutes or until tender, turning occasionally. Place wrapped tortillas on rack for the last 5 minutes of grilling.

3. Flake fish into large chunks. Cut sweet peppers into ½-inch-wide strips. Quickly fill tortillas with fish and sweet peppers. Serve with Tomatillo Salsa. If desired, garnish with pepper slices.

Tomatillo Salsa: Seed and finely chop 2 fresh serrano peppers (see note on page 156). Husk and finely chop 3 fresh tomatillos. In a medium bowl combine chopped peppers; tomatillos; 3 green onions, thinly sliced; 2 tablespoons finely chopped onion; 1 tablespoon lemon juice; 1 tablespoon snipped fresh cilantro or parsley; ¼ teaspoon salt; and 1 clove garlic, minced. Makes about 2 cups.

Nutrition Facts per serving: 384 calories, 6 g total fat, 30 mg cholesterol, 846 mg sodium, 56 g carbohydrate, 23 g protein.

Salmon Wraps With Jicama Slaw

These grill-and-wrap bundles make a refreshing meal on a hot summer evening. Serve them with a fresh fruit salad and a glass of white wine.

Prep: 25 minutes **Chill:** 30 minutes **Grill:** 11 minutes **Makes:** 4 servings

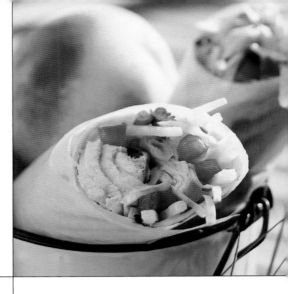

1. Thaw fish, if frozen. Rinse fish; pat dry with paper towels. For slaw, in a large bowl combine the jicama, cabbage, tomato, green onion, cilantro, and serrano peppers. In a small bowl combine the apple juice or apple cider, ½ teaspoon of the lime peel, the lime juice, 1 tablespoon oil, and the ⅛ teaspoon salt. Add to the jicama mixture and toss to combine. Cover and chill in the refrigerator for 30 minutes, stirring once or twice.

2. For rub, in a small bowl combine the remaining lime peel, the ¼ teaspoon salt, the black pepper, and oregano. Sprinkle rub evenly over fish; rub in with your fingers.

3. Lightly grease the grill rack of an uncovered grill. Place fish on rack. Grill directly over medium coals for 8 to 12 minutes or just until fish flakes easily with a fork, carefully turning once halfway through grilling.

4. To serve, break salmon into pieces. Place one-quarter of the salmon just below the center of each tortilla. Using a slotted spoon, top each salmon portion with one-quarter of the slaw. Fold bottom edge of each tortilla up over filling. Fold opposite sides in; roll up from the bottom. If necessary, secure with wooden toothpicks. Brush filled tortillas lightly with 1 tablespoon oil; place on grill rack directly over medium coals. Grill for 3 to 4 minutes or until heated through, turning once halfway through grilling. Cut each in half to serve.

Nutrition Facts per serving: 419 calories, 21 g total fat, 70 mg cholesterol, 457 mg sodium, 31 g carbohydrate, 28 g protein.

1 1-pound fresh or frozen
   skinless salmon fillet,
   about 1 inch thick
1 cup jicama cut into thin,
   bite-size pieces
1 cup shredded cabbage
1 small tomato, seeded
   and chopped (⅓ cup)
2 tablespoons thinly sliced
   green onion
1 tablespoon snipped
   fresh cilantro
1 or 2 fresh serrano peppers,
   seeded and finely chopped
   (see note on page 156)
¼ cup apple juice or apple cider
1½ teaspoons finely shredded
   lime peel
2 tablespoons lime juice
1 tablespoon salad oil
⅛ teaspoon salt
¼ teaspoon salt
¼ teaspoon ground
   black pepper
¼ teaspoon dried oregano,
   crushed
4 10-inch flour tortillas
1 tablespoon salad oil

Grilled Tuna Panini

Look in the pickle section of your supermarket for giardiniera, a mixture of marinated vegetables.

Prep: 15 minutes **Grill:** 8 minutes **Makes:** 4 servings

4 4- to 6-ounce tuna steaks, cut 1 inch thick
2 tablespoons garlic-flavored oil or roasted garlic-flavored oil
Salt
Pepper
1 12-inch Italian flatbread (focaccia), quartered and split horizontally
1½ cups torn mesclun or mixed baby salad greens
1 recipe Giardiniera Rémoulade
1 medium tomato, sliced

1. Brush tuna steaks with the oil. Sprinkle with salt and pepper. Lightly grease the rack of an uncovered grill or a grilling basket. Place fish on rack or in basket. Grill directly over medium coals for 8 to 12 minutes or just until fish flakes easily with a fork, turning once halfway through grilling. Grill bread, cut sides down, on grill rack for last 1 to 2 minutes of grilling or until golden brown.

2. Line each of 4 bread pieces with one-quarter of the greens. Top greens with tuna steaks. Top each steak with a generous 2 tablespoons of the Giardiniera Rémoulade and tomato. Top with remaining bread pieces, grilled sides down. Pass remaining Giardiniera Rémoulade.

Giardiniera Rémoulade: In a small bowl stir together ⅓ cup giardiniera, drained; 3 tablespoons chopped pitted green olives; 3 cloves garlic, minced; ⅓ cup fat-free mayonnaise or salad dressing; ½ teaspoon finely shredded lemon peel; and ¼ teaspoon pepper.

Nutrition Facts per serving: 510 calories, 13 g total fat, 19 mg cholesterol, 813 mg sodium, 56 g carbohydrate, 42 g protein.

Sizzling Vegetable Sandwiches

Please vegetarians and nonvegetarians alike with these grilled vegetable sandwiches.

Prep: 20 minutes **Grill:** 17 minutes **Makes:** 3 servings

1. Brush eggplant, zucchini, yellow squash, sweet pepper, and onion with some of the olive oil. Place onion slices on a long metal skewer. Grill onions on rack of uncovered grill directly over medium coals for 5 minutes. Arrange remaining vegetables on grill rack; grill for 12 to 15 minutes more or until vegetables are tender, turning once halfway through grilling. (If some vegetables cook more quickly than others, remove them and keep warm.)

2. Meanwhile, brush the cut sides of the rolls with remaining olive oil; grill rolls, cut sides down, on grill rack for last 1 to 2 minutes or until golden brown.

3. Layer roasted vegetables on the bottom halves of the rolls. Spread the top halves of the rolls with the Cumin Mayo; place on sandwiches.

Cumin Mayo: In a small bowl stir together 1 cup light mayonnaise dressing or salad dressing; 2 tablespoons lime juice; 1 clove garlic, minced; and 1 teaspoon cumin seeds, crushed. Cover and store in the refrigerator for up to 1 week. Makes about 1 cup.

Nutrition Facts per serving: **504 calories, 33 g total fat, 7 mg cholesterol, 437 mg sodium, 46 g carbohydrate, 8 g protein.**

- 1 small eggplant, cut lengthwise into ½-inch-thick slices
- 1 medium zucchini, cut lengthwise into ¼-inch-thick slices
- 1 medium yellow summer squash, cut lengthwise into ¼-inch-thick slices
- 1 medium red sweet pepper, seeded and cut into ½-inch-wide strips
- 1 small onion, cut into ½-inch-thick slices
- ⅓ cup olive oil
- 3 wheat French-style rolls or kaiser rolls, split
- ¼ cup Cumin Mayo

Smoked Cheese and Vegetable Tostadas

A medley of grilled vegetables and cheese tops grilled tortillas for this open-face sandwich.

Prep: 30 minutes **Grill:** 15 minutes **Makes:** 4 servings

1 medium sweet potato, peeled and cut lengthwise into ½-inch-thick slices

2 medium zucchini and/or yellow summer squash, cut lengthwise into ¾-inch-thick slices

1 small red onion, cut crosswise into ½-inch-thick slices

1 medium red or yellow sweet pepper, quartered

1 or 2 medium fresh Anaheim or New Mexico chili peppers, halved lengthwise and seeded (see note on page 170)

1 recipe Cilantro Vinaigrette

1 cup frozen whole kernel corn, thawed

8 6-inch corn tortillas

6 ounces smoked Gouda or other smoked cheese, shredded (1½ cups)

Tomato, diced (optional)

2 cups torn mixed salad greens

Avocado, pitted, peeled, and sliced (optional)

Cherry and/or baby pear-shaped tomatoes (optional)

1. Cook sweet potato in boiling water for 5 minutes; drain. Lightly grease a vegetable grilling tray or the rack of a grill with a cover. Place sweet potato, zucchini, red onion, sweet pepper, and chili peppers on grilling tray or grill rack. Brush with some of the Cilantro Vinaigrette. Grill on uncovered grill directly over medium coals for 12 to 15 minutes or until vegetables are lightly golden and just tender, turning occasionally. (If some vegetables cook more quickly than others, remove and keep warm.) Transfer vegetables to cutting board and cut into chunks; place in a bowl. Toss with the corn and remaining Cilantro Vinaigrette.

2. Grill the tortillas on rack directly over medium coals for 30 seconds to 1 minute or just until warm; turn. Divide vegetable mixture and cheese evenly among the tortillas. Cover and grill about 2 minutes more or until cheese softens and tortillas become crisp. Place on serving plates. If desired, top with diced tomato. Top with salad greens. If desired, garnish with avocado and cherry and/or pear-shaped tomatoes.

Cilantro Vinaigrette: In a small bowl combine 1 teaspoon finely shredded lime peel; 3 tablespoons lime juice; 3 tablespoons olive oil; 3 tablespoons snipped fresh cilantro; 1 fresh jalapeño pepper, seeded and finely chopped (see note on page 173); 2 cloves garlic, minced; ¼ teaspoon salt; and ¼ teaspoon ground black pepper.

Nutrition Facts per serving: **447 calories, 24 g total fat, 49 mg cholesterol, 579 mg sodium, 46 g carbohydrate, 16 g protein.**

Grilled Sicilian-Style Pizza

For extra color, substitute 1 small yellow tomato and 1 small red tomato for the large tomato.

Prep: 20 minutes **Grill:** 8 minutes **Makes:** 4 servings

1. Top bread shell with tomatoes, mozzarella cheese, and olives. Drizzle oil over all. Fold a 24×18-inch piece of heavy foil in half lengthwise. Place pizza on foil, turning edges of foil up to edge of pizza.

2. In a grill with a cover arrange medium-hot coals around edge of grill. Test for medium heat above center of grill (not over coals). Place pizza on the grill rack over center of grill. Cover and grill about 8 minutes or until pizza is heated through, topping with escarole for the last 2 minutes of grilling. To serve, sprinkle shredded cheese and pepper over pizza.

Nutrition Facts per serving: **459 calories, 19 g total fat, 26 mg cholesterol, 893 mg sodium, 54 g carbohydrate, 24 g protein.**

1 16-ounce Italian bread shell (Boboli)
2 plum tomatoes, thinly sliced
1 large yellow or red tomato, thinly sliced
4 ounces fresh mozzarella or buffalo mozzarella cheese, thinly sliced
⅓ cup halved pitted kalamata olives or ripe olives
1 tablespoon olive oil
1 cup coarsely chopped escarole or curly endive
¼ cup shredded Pecorino Romano or Parmesan cheese (1 ounce)
Freshly ground black pepper

Pizza-on-the-Beach

Bring the fun of a beach party to your backyard by grilling this shrimp and scallop pizza.

Prep: 25 minutes **Grill:** 9 minutes **Stand:** 5 minutes **Makes:** 4 servings

4 ounces fresh or frozen
    medium shrimp in shells
4 ounces fresh or frozen
    sea scallops
1 large fennel bulb
    (1 to 1½ pounds), thinly
    sliced
2 teaspoons olive oil
½ cup water
    Nonstick cooking spray
1 10-ounce package
    refrigerated pizza dough
½ of a 10-ounce container
    refrigerated light Alfredo
    sauce (about ½ cup)
½ teaspoon fennel seed,
    crushed (optional)
1 cup shredded provolone,
    scamorze, mozzarella,
    and/or other cheese
    (4 ounces)
    Snipped fennel leaves
    (optional)

1. Thaw shrimp and scallops, if frozen. Peel and devein shrimp. Halve scallops. Rinse shrimp and scallops; pat dry. Set aside.

2. In a large nonstick skillet cook and stir shrimp and scallops in hot oil over medium-high heat for 2 to 3 minutes or until opaque. Remove shrimp mixture from skillet. Set aside. Add sliced fennel and the water to skillet. Bring to boiling; reduce heat. Cover and simmer for 2 to 3 minutes or just until tender; drain and set aside.

3. Coat a 16-inch grill pizza pan or 12- to 13-inch metal pizza pan with nonstick cooking spray; set aside. Unroll pizza dough; divide into 4 pieces. On lightly floured surface, roll out each dough piece to ¼-inch thickness. Transfer to pan. (If necessary, cook only 2 pizzas at a time.)

4. In a grill with a cover place pan on grill rack directly over medium coals. Cover; grill 6 to 8 minutes or until bottoms of crusts turn slightly golden, giving pan half turn after 4 minutes. Remove pan from grill; cool slightly. Carefully turn crusts over.

5. Spread Alfredo sauce on crusts to within ½ inch of edges. Top with shrimp, scallops, and sliced fennel. If desired, sprinkle with fennel seed. Top with cheese. Return pizzas to grill. Cover; grill 3 to 4 minutes more or until cheese is melted and crust bottoms are golden. Remove from grill. If desired, sprinkle with fennel leaves. Let stand 5 minutes before serving.

Nutrition Facts per serving: 436 calories, 18 g total fat, 76 mg cholesterol, 1,048 mg sodium, 46 g carbohydrate, 24 g protein.

Canadian Bacon Pizza

Grilling pizza gives you an at-home version of the restaurant favorite, with a crunchy crust reminiscent of pizza baked in a wood-fired oven.

Prep: 20 minutes   **Grill:** 8 minutes   **Makes:** 4 servings

1. Drain artichoke hearts, reserving marinade. Halve artichoke hearts lengthwise; set aside.

2. Brush the bread shells with some of the reserved marinade. Sprinkle fontina or mozzarella cheese over shells. Divide artichoke hearts, Canadian-style bacon, tomatoes, feta cheese, green onion, and oregano or basil among bread shells.

3. Transfer the bread shells to a large piece of double-thickness foil. In a grill with a cover arrange medium-hot coals around edge of grill. Test for medium heat above center of grill (not over coals). Place foil with bread shells on grill rack over center of grill. Cover and grill about 8 minutes or until cheese is melted and pizza is heated through.

Nutrition Facts per serving: **465 calories, 19 g total fat, 44 mg cholesterol, 1,264 mg sodium, 56 g carbohydrate, 23 g protein.**

1 6-ounce jar marinated artichoke hearts
4 6-inch Italian bread shells (Boboli)
½ cup shredded fontina or mozzarella cheese (2 ounces)
4 slices Canadian-style bacon, cut into strips (2 ounces)
2 plum tomatoes, sliced
¼ cup crumbled feta cheese (1 ounce)
1 green onion, thinly sliced
2 teaspoons snipped fresh oregano or basil

Kabobs

Caught in that steak or burger grilling rut?
Break out with one of these skewered sensations.
From Asian satays to Tex-Mex fajitas
to tropical shrimp, there's a kabob here
to tantalize your tastebuds.

Curried Pork Satay with Mint Chutney, page 192

Chutney Beef Kabobs

Rice studded with chopped papaya and mango chutney makes a delicious serve-along.

Prep: 25 minutes **Marinate:** 2 to 8 hours **Grill:** 8 minutes **Makes:** 4 servings

12 ounces boneless beef sirloin steak, cut into 1-inch cubes

1 8-ounce can pineapple chunks (juice-pack)

⅓ cup mango chutney

1 teaspoon curry powder

½ teaspoon ground ginger

½ teaspoon ground cumin

¼ teaspoon ground black pepper

1 clove garlic, quartered

1 medium green sweet pepper, cut into 1-inch squares

2 cups hot cooked rice

½ cup chopped, peeled papaya

2 tablespoons mango chutney, snipped

1. Place beef cubes in a heavy, large self-sealing plastic bag set in a shallow bowl.

2. For marinade, drain pineapple chunks, reserving juice. Cover; refrigerate pineapple. In a food processor bowl or blender container combine the reserved pineapple juice, the ⅓ cup chutney, the curry powder, ginger, cumin, black pepper, and garlic. Cover and process or blend until smooth. Pour marinade over beef in bag. Seal bag; turn to coat beef. Marinate in the refrigerator for at least 2 hours or up to 8 hours, turning bag occasionally.

3. Drain beef, reserving marinade. On metal skewers, alternately thread beef, pineapple chunks, and sweet pepper pieces, leaving about ¼ inch of space between pieces.

4. Grill kabobs on rack of an uncovered grill directly over medium coals to desired doneness, turning once halfway through grilling and brushing frequently with reserved marinade during the first 3 minutes of grilling. [Allow 8 to 12 minutes for medium-rare (145°) or 12 to 15 minutes for medium doneness (160°).] Discard any remaining marinade.

5. Meanwhile, in a medium saucepan stir together the rice, papaya, and the 2 tablespoons snipped chutney. Heat through. Serve with kabobs.

Nutrition Facts per serving: 366 calories, 8 g total fat, 57 mg cholesterol, 51 mg sodium, 50 g carbohydrate, 22 g protein.

Fajita Kabobs

Grilling the beef steak and vegetables—and even heating the tortillas on the grill— turns fajitas into a cookout special.

Prep: 40 minutes   **Marinate:** 2 to 24 hours   **Grill:** 5 minutes   **Makes:** 6 servings

1. Cut steak into ¼-inch-thick strips. Place steak strips, sweet peppers, and onion wedges in a heavy, large self-sealing plastic bag set in a shallow bowl. For marinade, in a small bowl combine salad dressing, cumin, and crushed red pepper. Pour over steak and vegetables. Seal bag; turn to coat steak and vegetables. Marinate in the refrigerator for at least 2 hours or up to 24 hours, turning bag occasionally.

2. Wrap tortillas in foil; set aside. Drain steak and vegetables, discarding marinade. On long metal skewers, alternately thread steak strips (accordion style), sweet peppers, and onion, leaving about ¼ inch of space between pieces. Grill kabobs on rack of an uncovered grill directly over medium coals for 5 to 6 minutes or until steak is done and vegetables are tender, turning once halfway through grilling. Place tortillas to side of grill while grilling kabobs; turn tortillas occasionally.

3. In a small bowl stir together sour cream and cilantro. Serve kabobs with warmed tortillas, Pico de Gallo Salsa, and sour cream mixture.

Pico de Gallo Salsa: In a medium bowl combine 2 medium tomatoes, peeled and finely chopped; 2 tablespoons finely chopped onion; 2 tablespoons snipped fresh cilantro or parsley; 1 fresh serrano pepper, finely chopped (see note on page 156); and dash sugar. Makes about 1 cup.

Nutrition Facts per serving: 450 calories, 20 g total fat, 66 mg cholesterol, 367 mg sodium, 38 g carbohydrate, 28 g protein.

1¼ pounds beef top sirloin steak, cut 1 inch thick
3 red and/or green sweet peppers, cut into 1-inch squares
1 red onion, cut into wedges
½ cup vinegar and oil salad dressing
½ teaspoon ground cumin
¼ teaspoon crushed red pepper
12 7- to 8-inch flour tortillas
½ cup light dairy sour cream
2 tablespoons snipped fresh cilantro
1 recipe Pico de Gallo Salsa

Beef Brochettes Tamarind

Look for tamarind concentrate at your local Asian food market.

Prep: 30 minutes   **Marinate:** 2 to 24 hours   **Grill:** 12 minutes   **Makes:** 6 servings

1½ pounds boneless beef
   sirloin steak, cut into
   1½-inch cubes
¼ cup honey
¼ cup water
1 to 2 tablespoons grated
   fresh ginger
1 tablespoon tamarind
   concentrate (no water
   added)
¼ teaspoon salt
2 cups assorted fresh
   vegetables (such as whole
   mushrooms, ½-inch-thick
   slices zucchini or yellow
   summer squash, and/or
   1-inch pieces sweet
   pepper)

1. Place beef in a heavy, large self-sealing plastic bag set in a shallow bowl. For marinade, in a small bowl combine honey, the water, ginger, tamarind concentrate, and salt. Pour over beef. Seal bag; turn to coat beef. Marinate in the refrigerator for at least 2 hours or up to 24 hours, turning bag occasionally.

2. Drain beef, reserving marinade. On long metal skewers, alternately thread beef and vegetable pieces, leaving about ¼ inch of space between pieces.

3. Grill kabobs on rack of an uncovered grill directly over medium coals for 12 to 16 minutes or until beef is done, turning once halfway through grilling and brushing with reserved marinade during first 6 minutes of grilling. Discard any remaining marinade.

Nutrition Facts per serving: 257 calories, 10 g total fat, 76 mg cholesterol, 424 mg sodium, 14 g carbohydrate, 26 g protein.

Beef Satay with Spicy Peanut Sauce

Thinly slicing steak is easier if you partially freeze it before cutting.

Prep: 20 minutes   **Marinate:** 30 minutes   **Soak:** 30 minutes   **Grill:** 3 minutes
Makes: 5 servings

1. Cut steak across the grain into thin strips. For marinade, in a medium bowl combine the ⅓ cup teriyaki sauce and ¼ teaspoon of the hot pepper sauce. Add steak; toss to coat. Marinate in the refrigerator for 30 minutes. Soak wooden skewers in enough water to cover for 30 minutes; drain skewers.

2. Drain steak strips, reserving marinade. For satay, on soaked skewers alternately thread steak strips (accordion style), green onion pieces, and sweet pepper squares, leaving about ¼ inch of space between pieces. Brush with the reserved marinade. Discard any remaining marinade.

3. Grill satay on the rack of an uncovered grill directly over medium coals for 3 to 4 minutes or until done, turning once halfway through grilling.

4. For peanut sauce, in a small saucepan combine the remaining hot pepper sauce, the peanut butter, the water, and the 2 tablespoons teriyaki sauce. Cook and stir over medium heat just until smooth and heated through.

5. Serve satay with warm peanut sauce. If desired, garnish with pomegranate seeds and peanuts.

Nutrition Facts per serving: 217 calories, 10 g total fat, 43 mg cholesterol, 567 mg sodium, 10 g carbohydrate, 21 g protein.

1 1- to 1¼-pound beef
   flank steak
⅓ cup light teriyaki sauce
½ teaspoon bottled hot
   pepper sauce
10 8-inch wooden skewers
4 green onions, cut into
   1-inch-long pieces
1 green or red sweet pepper,
   cut into ¾-inch squares
3 tablespoons reduced-fat
   or regular peanut butter
3 tablespoons water
2 tablespoons light teriyaki
   sauce
   Pomegranate seeds
   (optional)
   Chopped peanuts (optional)

Jalapeño Beef Kabobs

These kabobs get their zesty flavor from the sweet-hot jalapeño pepper jelly glaze.

Prep: 25 minutes **Grill:** 8 minutes **Makes:** 4 servings

1 10-ounce jar jalapeño
   pepper jelly
2 tablespoons lime juice
½ teaspoon bottled minced
   garlic
4 small purple or white
   boiling onions
4 baby pattypan squash,
   halved crosswise
1 pound boneless beef sirloin
   steak, cut into 1-inch
   cubes
4 fresh tomatillos, husked
   and quartered
½ of a medium red or green
   sweet pepper, cut into
   1-inch squares
   Hot cooked rice (optional)

1. For glaze, in a small saucepan combine the jalapeño pepper jelly, lime juice, and garlic. Cook and stir over medium heat until jelly is melted. Remove from heat.

2. In a covered small saucepan cook onions in a small amount of boiling water for 3 minutes. Add squash; cook for 1 minute more. Drain. On long metal skewers, alternately thread onions, squash, steak, tomatillos, and sweet pepper, leaving about ¼ inch of space between pieces.

3. Grill kabobs on rack of an uncovered grill directly over medium coals for 8 to 12 minutes or until meat is done, turning once halfway through grilling and brushing occasionally with glaze during the last 5 minutes of grilling.

4. If desired, serve with hot cooked rice. Reheat any remaining glaze until bubbly; serve warmed glaze with kabobs.

Nutrition Facts per serving: 444 calories, 11 g total fat, 76 mg cholesterol, 71 mg sodium, 61 g carbohydrate, 27 g protein.

Kabob Capers

It's easy and fun to improvise kabobs using the ingredients you like. Start by cutting up meat, poultry, fish, or seafood into 1-inch pieces. Next slice similar-sized pieces of your favorite vegetables. (You may want to slightly precook carrots, onions, potatoes, parsnips, and asparagus in boiling water.) Thread the pieces on skewers, leaving about ¼ inch of space between the pieces so the heat can cook them evenly on all sides. Use the timings below as direct grilling guidelines, turning the kabobs occasionally.

- Beef and lamb: 8 to 12 minutes
- Pork and veal: 10 to 14 minutes
- Chicken and turkey: 12 to 14 minutes
- Fish: 8 to 12 minutes
- Scallops: 5 to 8 minutes
- Shrimp: 5 to 9 minutes

Meat and Vegetable Kabobs

Start with your favorite barbecue sauce and add a medley of seasonings for a flavorful sauce that complements beef, chicken, and vegetables.

Prep: 25 minutes **Marinate:** 6 to 24 hours **Grill:** 8 minutes **Makes:** 4 or 5 servings

1. Cut steak into 1-inch cubes or cut chicken into 1-inch pieces. Place steak and/or chicken in a heavy, large self-sealing plastic bag set in a deep bowl.

2. For marinade, in a small saucepan combine barbecue sauce, the water, garlic, dried onion, sugar, steak sauce, vinegar, Worcestershire sauce, oil, and salt. Bring just to boiling. Cool. Pour barbecue sauce mixture over steak and/or chicken. Seal bag; turn to coat steak and/or chicken. Marinate in the refrigerator for at least 6 hours or up to 24 hours, turning bag occasionally.

3. In a covered medium saucepan cook onions in a small amount of boiling water for 3 minutes. Add mushrooms; cook 1 minute more. Drain.

4. Drain steak and/or chicken, reserving marinade. On metal skewers, alternately thread vegetables and steak and/or chicken, leaving about ¼ inch of space between pieces. Grill kabobs on rack of uncovered grill directly over medium coals for 8 to 14 minutes or until done, turning once halfway through grilling and brushing once with reserved marinade after 3 minutes of grilling.

5. In a small saucepan heat remaining marinade to boiling; serve warmed marinade with kabobs. If desired, garnish with fresh herb sprigs.

Nutrition Facts per serving: 372 calories, 18 g total fat, 91 mg cholesterol, 652 mg sodium, 19 g carbohydrate, 34 g protein.

1½ pounds beef sirloin steak, cut 1 inch thick, and/or skinless, boneless chicken breasts and/or thighs

½ cup bottled barbecue sauce

¼ cup water

2 to 4 cloves garlic, minced

2 tablespoons dried minced onion

2 tablespoons sugar

2 tablespoons bottled steak sauce

2 tablespoons vinegar

2 tablespoons Worcestershire sauce

2 tablespoons cooking oil

½ teaspoon salt

2 medium onions, each cut into 8 wedges

10 to 12 fresh mushrooms, stems removed

1 medium zucchini, halved and cut into ½-inch-thick slices

1 large red or green sweet pepper, cut into 1-inch pieces

Fresh herb sprigs (optional)

Spicy Pork Satay with Peanut Sauce

To make a green onion brush, trim off the onion's root and most of the green portion. Thinly slash both ends of the onion to create a fringe. Let stand in ice water about 5 minutes or until ends curl.

Prep: 20 minutes   **Marinate:** 1 to 2 hours   **Grill:** 10 minutes   **Makes:** 4 servings

12 ounces pork tenderloin
⅓ cup light soy sauce
2 tablespoons lemon juice
1½ teaspoons chili powder
8 green onions, cut into
  1-inch pieces
1 recipe Peanut Sauce
  Hot cooked brown or
  white rice (optional)
  Green onion brushes
  (optional)

1. Cut pork diagonally into strips about 3 inches long and ¼ inch thick. In a shallow glass dish stir together soy sauce, lemon juice, and chili powder. Add pork strips; gently toss to coat. Cover and marinate in the refrigerator for at least 1 hour or up to 2 hours, stirring occasionally.

2. Drain pork strips, reserving marinade. On metal skewers, alternately thread pork strips and green onion pieces, leaving about ¼ inch of space between pieces.

3. Grill kabobs on rack of an uncovered grill over medium coals for 8 to 14 minutes or until pork juices run clear, turning once halfway through grilling and brushing with reserved marinade during first 3 minutes of grilling. Discard any remaining marinade.

4. Serve kabobs with Peanut Sauce for dipping. If desired, serve with hot cooked brown or white rice and garnish with green onion brushes.

Peanut Sauce: In a small bowl stir together 2 tablespoons creamy peanut butter, 2 tablespoons hot water, 4 teaspoons light soy sauce, ½ teaspoon grated fresh ginger, ½ teaspoon sugar, ¼ to ½ teaspoon bottled hot pepper sauce, and 1 small clove garlic, minced. Stir before serving.

Nutrition Facts per serving: 165 calories, 7 g total fat, 60 mg cholesterol, 925 mg sodium, 5 g carbohydrate, 22 g protein.

Sweet and Sour Pork Kabobs

Sweet pineapple juice and tangy wine vinegar complement each other in the sauce brushed on these colorful kabobs.

Prep: 35 minutes **Grill:** 10 minutes **Makes:** 4 servings

1. In a covered medium saucepan cook carrots in a small amount of boiling water for 8 minutes; drain well. Drain pineapple, reserving juice. Quarter pineapple slices; set aside.

2. For sauce, in a small saucepan combine reserved pineapple juice, wine vinegar, soy sauce, oil, cornstarch, sugar, and garlic. Cook and stir until thickened and bubbly. Cook and stir for 2 minutes more.

3. On metal skewers, alternately thread carrots, pineapple, sweet peppers, and pork, leaving about ¼ inch of space between pieces. Brush with sauce.

4. Grill kabobs on rack of an uncovered grill directly over medium coals for 10 to 14 minutes or until pork juices run clear, turning once halfway through grilling and brushing frequently with sauce during first 5 minutes of grilling. Reheat any remaining sauce until bubbly; serve with kabobs. If desired, serve over hot cooked couscous.

Nutrition Facts per serving: **203 calories, 9 g total fat, 38 mg cholesterol, 318 mg sodium, 19 g carbohydrate, 14 g protein.**

- 2 medium carrots, bias-sliced into 1-inch pieces
- 1 8-ounce can pineapple slices (juice-pack)
- ⅓ cup wine vinegar
- 2 tablespoons reduced-sodium soy sauce
- 1 tablespoon cooking oil
- 2 teaspoons cornstarch
- 1 teaspoon sugar
- 1 clove garlic, minced
- 2 small green and/or red sweet peppers, cut into 1-inch squares
- 12 ounces lean boneless pork, cut into 1-inch pieces
- Hot cooked couscous (optional)

Curried Pork Satay with Mint Chutney

Complete the meal with steamed green beans, tomatoes, and your favorite dessert.

Prep: 25 minutes **Marinate:** 4 to 24 hours **Grill:** 10 minutes **Makes:** 4 servings

¼ cup reduced-sodium
    soy sauce
¼ cup dry red or white wine
1 tablespoon cooking oil
2 teaspoons brown sugar
2 teaspoons curry powder
¼ to ½ teaspoon crushed
    red pepper
12 ounces lean boneless pork,
    cut into 1-inch cubes
    Hot cooked couscous
1 recipe Mint Chutney

1. For marinade, in a small bowl stir together soy sauce, wine, oil, brown sugar, curry powder, and crushed red pepper. Set aside. Place pork cubes in a heavy, large self-sealing plastic bag set in a shallow bowl. Pour marinade over pork. Seal bag; turn to coat pork. Marinate in the refrigerator for at least 4 hours or up to 24 hours, turning bag occasionally.

2. Drain pork, discarding marinade. Thread pork onto skewers, leaving about ¼ inch of space between pieces. Grill kabobs on the rack of an uncovered grill directly over medium coals for 10 to 14 minutes or until juices run clear, turning once halfway through grilling. Serve kabobs with hot cooked couscous and Mint Chutney.

Mint Chutney: Seed and coarsely chop 1 medium red apple. Peel, seed, and coarsely chop 1 medium orange. In a small bowl toss together apple, orange, 2 tablespoons snipped fresh mint leaves, 1 tablespoon brown sugar, and 1 tablespoon rice wine vinegar. Serve immediately or cover and chill in the refrigerator for up to 4 hours. Makes about 1½ cups chutney.

Nutrition Facts per serving: **296 calories, 9 g total fat, 38 mg cholesterol, 575 mg sodium, 33 g carbohydrate, 17 g protein.**

Jamaican Pork Kabobs

Mango chutney and Pickapeppa sauce—a Jamaican seasoning sauce—lend an air of the island to the pork and vegetables.

Prep: 25 minutes **Grill:** 10 minutes **Makes:** 4 servings

1. Cut corn crosswise into 1-inch pieces. In a covered medium saucepan cook corn pieces in a small amount of boiling water for 3 minutes; drain and rinse with cold water. On long metal skewers, alternately thread tenderloin slices, onion wedges, squash or tomatillos, and corn pieces, leaving about ¼ inch of space between pieces. In small bowl combine chutney, Pickapeppa sauce, oil, and water; set aside.

2. Grill kabobs on rack of an uncovered grill directly over medium coals for 10 to 14 minutes or until pork juices run clear and vegetables are tender, turning once halfway through grilling and brushing with the chutney mixture during the last 3 minutes of grilling. Discard any remaining chutney mixture.

Nutrition Facts per serving: 252 calories, 7 g total fat, 60 mg cholesterol, 127 mg sodium, 27 g carbohydrate, 21 g protein.

- 2 fresh ears of corn, husked and cleaned
- 1 12- to 14-ounce pork tenderloin, cut into 1-inch-thick slices
- 1 small red onion, cut into ½-inch-thick wedges
- 16 baby pattypan squash (about 1 inch in diameter) or 4 fresh tomatillos, husked and quartered
- ¼ cup mango chutney, finely chopped
- 3 tablespoons Pickapeppa sauce
- 1 tablespoon cooking oil
- 1 tablespoon water

Double Sausage Kabobs

Rolling the vegetables in an herb mixture is an easy way to add scrumptious flavor.

Prep: 30 minutes **Grill:** 15 minutes **Makes:** 6 servings

12 ounces tiny new potatoes,
    halved, or small potatoes,
    quartered
⅓ cup finely snipped fresh
    parsley
2 tablespoons finely snipped
    fresh oregano or
    2 teaspoons dried oregano
2 cloves garlic, minced
2 medium yellow sweet
    peppers, cut into 2×1-inch
    strips
2 tablespoons olive oil
8 ounces cooked Polish
    sausage links, cut into
    1½-inch-thick bias slices
4 ounces cooked Italian
    sausage links, cut into
    1½-inch-thick bias slices
Honey mustard (optional)
Fresh oregano sprigs
    (optional)

1. In a covered medium saucepan cook potatoes in a moderate amount of boiling salted water for 10 to 12 minutes or just until tender. Drain; set aside to cool slightly. In a shallow dish stir together the snipped parsley, snipped or dried oregano, and garlic; set aside.

2. Place potatoes and sweet peppers in a large bowl; drizzle with oil and toss to coat. Roll vegetables in the herb mixture, patting vegetables until lightly covered with herbs.

3. On long metal skewers, alternately thread sausage slices, sweet peppers, and potatoes, leaving about ¼ inch of space between pieces.

4. In a grill with a cover arrange medium-hot coals around a drip pan. Test for medium heat above the pan. Place kabobs on grill rack over pan. Cover and grill about 15 minutes or until sausage is heated through and sweet peppers just are tender, turning once halfway through grilling. If desired, serve with honey mustard. If desired, garnish with oregano sprigs.

Nutrition Facts per serving: 293 calories, 22 g total fat, 40 mg cholesterol, 527 mg sodium, 16 g carbohydrate, 9 g protein.

Grecian Kabobs

Suit your fancy; use lamb or pork—or even a combination of the two meats.

Prep: 25 minutes **Marinate:** 4 to 24 hours **Grill:** 12 minutes **Makes:** 4 servings

1. For marinade, in a small bowl combine oil, lemon juice, chives, oregano, water, and garlic. Place meat in a heavy, large self-sealing plastic bag set in a shallow bowl. Pour marinade over meat. Seal bag; turn to coat meat. Marinate in the refrigerator for at least 4 hours or up to 24 hours, turning bag occasionally.

2. Meanwhile, in a covered small saucepan cook onion wedges in a small amount of boiling water for 3 minutes. Drain and cool slightly.

3. Drain meat, reserving marinade. On metal skewers, alternately thread lamb or pork, onion, sweet pepper squares, and mushrooms, leaving about ¼ inch of space between pieces.

4. Grill kabobs on rack of an uncovered grill directly over medium coals until done, turning once halfway through grilling and brushing with reserved marinade once after 3 minutes of grilling. (Allow 8 to 12 minutes for lamb or 10 to 14 minutes for pork.) Discard any remaining marinade.

5. If desired, toss hot cooked couscous with chopped sweet pepper; serve with kabobs. If desired, garnish with herb sprigs.

Nutrition Facts per serving: 177 calories, 9 g total fat, 57 mg cholesterol, 46 mg sodium, 5 g carbohydrate, 19 g protein.

2 tablespoons olive oil
  or cooking oil
2 tablespoons lemon juice
1 tablespoon snipped fresh
  chives or 1 teaspoon
  dried chives
1 tablespoon snipped fresh
  oregano or 1 teaspoon
  dried oregano, crushed
1 tablespoon water
1 clove garlic, minced
1 pound lean boneless lamb
  or pork, cut into
  1-inch cubes
1 medium red onion, cut into
  wedges
1 medium green sweet pepper,
  cut into 1-inch squares
2 cups fresh mushrooms
  Hot cooked couscous
  (optional)
  Chopped red and/or green
  sweet pepper (optional)
  Fresh herb sprigs (optional)

Grilled Lamb Kabobs with Mustard Glaze

If tiny new potatoes aren't available, quarter eight small potatoes, making sure each piece has some peel. When putting the potatoes on the skewers, pierce through the peel of each piece.

Prep: 20 minutes **Marinate:** 2 to 6 hours **Soak:** 30 minutes **Grill:** 8 minutes
Makes: 4 servings

¼ cup Dijon-style mustard

3 tablespoons lemon juice

1 green onion, finely chopped

2 teaspoons snipped fresh
   thyme or ½ teaspoon
   dried thyme, crushed

12 ounces lean boneless lamb,
   cut into 1-inch cubes

16 tiny new potatoes, halved
   (about 1¼ pounds)

1 small red onion, cut into
   wedges

16 8-inch wooden skewers

1 large yellow, red, or green
   sweet pepper, cut into
   1½-inch squares

Hot cooked orzo
   (rosamarina) (optional)

1. For marinade, in a small bowl stir together mustard, lemon juice, green onion, and thyme. Place meat in a heavy, large self-sealing plastic bag set in a shallow bowl. Pour half of the marinade over meat. Seal bag; turn to coat meat. Marinate in the refrigerator for at least 2 hours or up to 6 hours, turning bag occasionally. Cover and refrigerate the remaining marinade for glaze.

2. Before grilling, place a steamer basket in a large saucepan. Add water to just below the bottom of the steamer basket. Bring to boiling. Add potatoes. Cover and steam for 10 to 12 minutes or just until potatoes are tender. Remove steamer basket from saucepan; cool potatoes for 5 minutes. Break each onion wedge into 2 or 3 layers.

3. Soak wooden skewers in enough water to cover for 30 minutes; drain. Drain meat, discarding marinade. On soaked skewers, alternately thread meat, potatoes, onion, and sweet pepper, leaving about ¼ inch of space between pieces.

4. Grill kabobs on rack of an uncovered grill directly over medium coals for 8 to 12 minutes or until done, turning once halfway through grilling and brushing frequently with glaze during the first 3 minutes of grilling. Discard any remaining glaze. If desired, serve kabobs with hot cooked orzo.

Nutrition Facts per serving: 408 calories, 22 g total fat, 78 mg cholesterol, 139 mg sodium, 28 g carbohydrate, 24 g protein.

Chicken-Tropical Fruit Kabobs

Curry powder and grated fresh ginger make these fruity chicken skewers extra flavorful.

Prep: 30 minutes **Marinate:** 30 minutes to 2 hours **Grill:** 12 minutes **Makes:** 4 servings

1. Place chicken in a nonmetallic medium bowl. For marinade, in a small bowl combine yogurt, curry powder, brown sugar, ginger, and salt. Squeeze the juice from half of 1 lime into yogurt mixture; stir to combine. Pour marinade over chicken; stir to coat. Cover; marinate in the refrigerator for at least 30 minutes or up to 2 hours. Cut the remaining limes into wedges; set aside.

2. Drain chicken pieces, discarding marinade. Thread chicken pieces onto long metal skewers, leaving about ¼ inch of space between pieces.

3. Grill kabobs on rack of an uncovered grill directly over medium coals for 12 to 14 minutes or until chicken is tender and no longer pink, turning once halfway through grilling.

4. To serve, place fruit cubes on the ends of kabobs. Serve with lime wedges.

Nutrition Facts per serving: **227 calories, 4 g total fat, 61 mg cholesterol, 138 mg sodium, 25 g carbohydrate, 24 g protein.**

- 1 pound skinless, boneless chicken breasts, cut into 1-inch pieces
- ⅓ cup plain yogurt
- 2 teaspoons curry powder
- 2 teaspoons brown sugar
- 1 teaspoon grated fresh ginger
- ⅛ teaspoon salt
- 2 limes
- 4 cups peeled and cubed mango, papaya, and/or fresh pineapple

Polynesian Chicken Kabobs

To shorten preparation, pick up a peeled and cored fresh pineapple at the supermarket.

Prep: 35 minutes   **Marinate:** 2 to 24 hours   **Grill:** 12 minutes   **Makes:** 6 servings

¼ cup soy sauce

2 tablespoons lemon juice

2 cloves garlic, minced

1 teaspoon grated fresh ginger or ⅛ teaspoon ground ginger

⅛ teaspoon dry mustard

1 pound skinless, boneless chicken breasts or thighs, cut into 1-inch pieces

1 cup fresh pineapple chunks or one 8-ounce can pineapple chunks, drained

1 medium green sweet pepper, cut into 1-inch pieces

1 medium red sweet pepper, cut into 1-inch pieces

Hot cooked rice (optional)

Green onion brushes (optional)

1. For marinade, in a small bowl combine soy sauce, lemon juice, garlic, ginger, and mustard. Place chicken in a heavy, large self-sealing plastic bag set in a shallow bowl. Pour marinade over chicken. Seal bag; turn to coat chicken. Marinate in the refrigerator for at least 2 hours or up to 24 hours, turning bag occasionally.

2. Drain chicken, reserving marinade. On long metal skewers, alternately thread chicken, pineapple, green pepper, and red pepper, leaving about ¼ inch of space between pieces.

3. Grill kabobs on rack of an uncovered grill directly over medium coals for 12 to 14 minutes or until chicken is tender and no longer pink, turning once halfway through grilling and brushing occasionally with reserved marinade during first 5 minutes of grilling. Discard any remaining marinade. If desired, serve over hot cooked rice. If desired, garnish with green onion brushes.

Nutrition Facts per serving: **110 calories, 2 g total fat, 40 mg cholesterol, 723 mg sodium, 7 g carbohydrate, 15 g protein.**

Sesame Chicken Kabob Salad

For summer-fresh dining at its best, nestle the plum sauce-glazed kabobs on a bed of red cabbage and bok choy.

Prep: 30 minutes **Soak:** 30 minutes **Grill:** 12 minutes **Makes:** 4 servings

1. Soak wooden skewers in enough water to cover for 30 minutes; drain. Cut each chicken breast half into 4 lengthwise strips. On soaked skewers, alternately thread chicken strips (accordion style), pineapple chunks, and sweet pepper pieces, leaving about ¼ inch of space between pieces.

2. For dressing, in a screw-top jar combine vinegar, water, salad oil, soy sauce, sesame oil, and dry mustard. Cover and shake well. Set aside 2 tablespoons of the dressing. Cover remaining dressing; chill in the refrigerator until needed.

3. In a small bowl stir together the reserved 2 tablespoons dressing and the plum sauce or chili sauce. Brush over kabobs. Discard any remaining plum sauce mixture.

4. Grill kabobs on rack of an uncovered grill directly over medium coals for 12 to 14 minutes or until chicken is tender and no longer pink, turning once halfway through grilling.

5. In a medium bowl combine the red cabbage, bok choy or lettuce, snow peas, mushrooms, and, if desired, radishes; divide red cabbage mixture among 4 dinner plates. Top with kabobs. Shake chilled dressing; drizzle over salads.

Nutrition Facts per serving: 229 calories, 8 g total fat, 59 mg cholesterol, 332 mg sodium, 15 g carbohydrate, 24 g protein.

- 8 6-inch wooden skewers
- 4 medium skinless, boneless chicken breast halves (1 pound total)
- 16 fresh pineapple chunks
- 1 yellow sweet pepper, cut into 1-inch pieces
- 3 tablespoons rice vinegar or white wine vinegar
- 2 tablespoons water
- 1 tablespoon salad oil
- 1 tablespoon soy sauce
- 1 teaspoon toasted sesame oil
- ½ teaspoon dry mustard
- 1 tablespoon bottled plum sauce or bottled chili sauce
- 2 cups chopped red cabbage
- 2 cups chopped bok choy or iceberg lettuce
- 16 to 24 snow peas, strings and tips removed and cut lengthwise into thin strips
- ½ cup sliced fresh mushrooms
- ½ cup sliced radishes (optional)

Pineapple-Rum Turkey Kabobs

Lemongrass, available at many supermarkets and in Asian markets, adds a delightful lemony flavor. If you can't find it, substitute finely shredded lemon peel.

Prep: 25 minutes **Marinate:** 4 to 24 hours **Soak:** 30 minutes **Grill:** 12 minutes
Makes: 4 servings

12 ounces turkey breast tenderloin, cut into 1-inch pieces

⅓ cup unsweetened pineapple juice

3 tablespoons rum or unsweetened pineapple juice

1 tablespoon brown sugar

1 tablespoon finely chopped lemongrass or 2 teaspoons finely shredded lemon peel

1 tablespoon olive oil

12 6-inch wooden skewers

1 medium red onion, cut into thin wedges

2 nectarines or 3 plums, pitted and cut into thick slices

1½ cups fresh or canned pineapple chunks

Hot cooked rice (optional)

1. Place turkey in a heavy, large self-sealing plastic bag set in a shallow bowl. For marinade, in a small bowl combine the ⅓ cup pineapple juice, the rum or additional pineapple juice, brown sugar, lemongrass or lemon peel, and oil. Pour over turkey. Seal bag; turning to coat turkey. Marinate in the refrigerator for at least 4 hours or up to 24 hours, turning bag occasionally.

2. Soak wooden skewers in enough water to cover for 30 minutes; drain. Drain turkey, reserving marinade. In a small saucepan bring reserved marinade to boiling; remove from heat. On 8 of the soaked skewers, alternately thread turkey and onion, leaving about ¼ inch of space between pieces.

3. Grill kabobs on rack of an uncovered grill directly over medium coals for 12 to 14 minutes or until turkey is tender and no longer pink, turning once halfway through grilling and brushing occasionally with heated marinade during last 5 minutes of grilling.

4. Meanwhile, on remaining soaked skewers, alternately thread nectarines or plums and pineapple. For the last 5 minutes of grilling, place fruit kabobs on grill rack alongside turkey kabobs; turn and brush once with heated marinade. If desired, serve turkey and fruit kabobs with hot cooked rice.

Nutrition Facts per serving: **229 calories, 6 g total fat, 37 mg cholesterol, 36 mg sodium, 23 g carbohydrate, 17 g protein.**

Tropical Turkey Kabobs

The tropical flair comes from pineapple juice and papaya.

Prep: 35 minutes **Marinate:** 2 to 4 hours **Grill:** 12 minutes **Makes:** 6 servings

1. Place turkey in a heavy, large self-sealing plastic bag set into a shallow bowl. For marinade, in a small bowl combine pineapple juice, lime juice, oil, soy sauce, and ginger. Pour over turkey. Seal bag; turn to coat turkey. Marinate in the refrigerator for at least 2 hours or up to 4 hours, turning bag occasionally.

2. In a covered small saucepan cook pearl onions in a small amount of boiling water for 2 minutes. Add green and red sweet peppers; cook for 1 minute more. Drain vegetables.

3. Drain turkey, reserving marinade. On long metal skewers, alternately thread turkey, onions, green pepper, red pepper, and papaya, leaving about ¼ inch of space between pieces.

4. Grill kabobs on rack of an uncovered grill directly over medium coals for 12 to 14 minutes or until turkey is tender and no longer pink, turning once halfway through grilling and brushing with reserved marinade once after 6 minutes of grilling. Discard any remaining marinade.

Nutrition Facts per serving: 252 calories, 5 g total fat, 50 mg cholesterol, 210 mg sodium, 28 g carbohydrate, 23 g protein.

1½ pounds turkey breast tenderloin, cut into 1-inch pieces
½ cup unsweetened pineapple juice
1 tablespoon lime juice
1 tablespoon cooking oil
1 tablespoon soy sauce
1 teaspoon grated fresh ginger
12 pearl onions, peeled
1 large green sweet pepper, cut into 1½-inch pieces
1 large red sweet pepper, cut into 1½-inch pieces
2 papayas, peeled, seeded, and cut into 1½-inch pieces

Yakitori Chicken Skewers

Golden to dark golden in color, toasted sesame oil is available at Asian food stores. Be sure to get toasted sesame oil rather than regular sesame oil—a paler, in both color and flavor, cousin.

Prep: 30 minutes   **Marinate:** 30 minutes to 4 hours   **Soak:** 30 minutes   **Grill:** 12 minutes
Makes: 5 servings

1 pound skinless, boneless
   chicken breasts
¼ cup reduced-sodium
   soy sauce
¼ cup dry sherry
2 teaspoons toasted
   sesame oil
2 cloves garlic, minced
1 teaspoon sugar
¼ to ½ teaspoon crushed
   red pepper (optional)
5 10- to 12-inch wooden
   skewers
4 green onions, cut into
   1-inch pieces

1. Cut chicken pieces lengthwise into ½-inch-thick strips. Place chicken in a heavy, large self-sealing plastic bag set in a shallow bowl. For marinade, in a small bowl combine soy sauce, sherry, sesame oil, garlic, sugar, and, if desired, crushed red pepper. Pour marinade over chicken. Seal bag; turn to coat chicken. Marinate in the refrigerator for at least 30 minutes or up to 4 hours.

2. Meanwhile, soak wooden skewers in enough water to cover for 30 minutes; drain. Drain chicken, discarding marinade. On soaked skewers, alternately thread green onion pieces and chicken strips (accordion style), leaving about ¼ inch of space between pieces.

3. Grill kabobs on rack of an uncovered grill directly over medium coals for 12 to 14 minutes or until chicken is no longer pink, turning once halfway through grilling.

Nutrition Facts per serving: **120 calories, 3 g total fat, 48 mg cholesterol, 255 mg sodium, 2 g carbohydrate, 18 g protein.**

Orange-Sesame Turkey Kabobs

Vary these kabobs to suit the season by using whatever fresh vegetables you find at the market.

Prep: 20 minutes **Marinate:** 1 to 2 hours **Grill:** 12 minutes **Makes:** 4 servings

1. For marinade, in a shallow dish combine orange juice concentrate, sesame seeds, thyme, sesame oil, and salt. Add turkey, stirring to coat. Cover; marinate in the refrigerator for at least 1 hour or up to 2 hours.

2. Drain turkey, reserving marinade. On long metal skewers, alternately thread turkey and vegetables, leaving about ¼ inch of space between pieces. Brush with reserved marinade. Discard any remaining marinade. (If using tomatoes, add to end of skewers for the last 1 minute of grilling.)

3. Coat the unheated grill rack of an uncovered grill with nonstick cooking spray. Place kabobs on rack. Grill directly over medium coals for 12 to 14 minutes or until turkey is tender and no longer pink, turning occasionally to cook evenly. If desired, serve over linguine and garnish with orange wedges.

Nutrition Facts per serving: 146 calories, 4 g total fat, 37 mg cholesterol, 171 mg sodium, 10 g carbohydrate, 18 g protein.

¼ cup frozen orange juice concentrate, thawed
2 teaspoons sesame seeds
1½ teaspoons snipped fresh thyme or ½ teaspoon dried thyme, crushed
1 teaspoon toasted sesame oil
¼ teaspoon salt
12 ounces turkey breast tenderloin, cut into 1-inch pieces
2 cups desired fresh vegetables (such as 1-inch pieces red and/or green sweet pepper, whole mushrooms, 1-inch-thick half-slices zucchini or yellow summer squash, and whole cherry tomatoes)
Nonstick cooking spray
Hot cooked linguine (optional)
Orange wedges (optional)

Ginger Tuna Kabobs

A touch of honey added to the reserved marinade makes a delicious brush-on for these grilled tuna, pineapple, and vegetable kabobs.

Prep: 30 minutes **Marinate:** 30 minutes **Soak:** 30 minutes **Grill:** 8 minutes
Makes: 4 servings

12 ounces skinless tuna
    steaks, cut 1 inch thick
3 tablespoons reduced-sodium
    soy sauce
3 tablespoons water
1 tablespoon snipped green
    onion tops or snipped
    fresh chives
2 teaspoons grated fresh
    ginger
12 6-inch wooden skewers
½ of a medium fresh
    pineapple, cored and cut
    into 1-inch cubes
1 medium red or green sweet
    pepper, cut into 1½-inch
    squares
6 green onions, cut into
    2-inch pieces
¼ cup honey

1. Rinse tuna; pat dry with paper towels. Cut into 1-inch cubes. Place in a heavy, large self-sealing plastic bag set in a shallow bowl. Add soy sauce, water, snipped green onion tops or chives, and ginger. Seal bag; turn gently to coat tuna. Marinate in the refrigerator for 30 minutes. Drain tuna, reserving marinade.

2. Meanwhile, soak wooden skewers in enough water to cover for 30 minutes; drain. On soaked skewers, alternately thread tuna, pineapple, sweet pepper, and green onion pieces, leaving about ¼ inch of space between pieces. Grill kabobs on the rack of an uncovered grill directly over medium coals for 8 to 12 minutes or just until tuna flakes easily with a fork, turning kabobs once halfway through grilling.

3. Meanwhile, bring reserved marinade to boiling; strain. Discard any solids. Stir honey into hot marinade. Brush tuna, fruit, and vegetables generously with honey mixture just before serving.

Nutrition Facts per serving: 251 calories, 5 g total fat, 32 mg cholesterol, 446 mg sodium, 32 g carbohydrate, 22 g protein.

Seafood Skewers

Fresh fennel—a vegetable with feathery leaves, celerylike stalks, and a bulbous base—is sometimes called sweet anise.

Prep: 35 minutes **Marinate:** 2 hours **Grill:** 8 minutes **Makes:** 6 servings

1. Thaw fish and shrimp, if frozen. Rinse fish; pat dry with paper towels. Cut fish into 1-inch cubes. Peel and devein shrimp, leaving tails intact. Rinse shrimp; pat dry with paper towels. Set aside.

2. Cut off and discard upper stalks of fennel, reserving some of the feathery leaves. Snip 2 tablespoons of the feathery leaves to use in the marinade. Remove any wilted outer layers from fennel bulbs; cut off a thin slice from base of each bulb. Wash and then cut each bulb lengthwise into 6 wedges. In a covered medium saucepan cook fennel wedges in a small amount of boiling water about 5 minutes or until almost tender. Drain.

3. Place fennel wedges, fish cubes, and shrimp in a heavy, large self-sealing plastic bag set in a deep bowl. For marinade, in a small bowl stir together olive oil, lemon juice, garlic, oregano, salt, and the snipped fennel leaves. Pour over seafood and fennel wedges. Seal bag; turn to coat seafood and fennel. Marinate in the refrigerator for 2 hours, turning bag occasionally.

4. Drain seafood and fennel, discarding marinade. On long metal skewers, alternately thread fish, shrimp, and fennel, leaving about ¼ inch of space between pieces.

5. Lightly grease the rack of an uncovered grill. Place kabobs on rack. Grill directly over medium coals for 8 to 12 minutes or just until fish flakes easily when tested with a fork and shrimp turn opaque.

Nutrition Facts per serving: **185 calories, 12 g total fat, 57 mg cholesterol, 199 mg sodium, 4 g carbohydrate, 16 g protein.**

1 pound fresh or frozen
   skinless fish fillets (such as
   salmon, halibut, sea bass,
   and/or red snapper),
   1 inch thick
8 ounces fresh or frozen
   medium shrimp in shells
2 medium fennel bulbs
¼ cup olive oil
3 tablespoons lemon juice
4 cloves garlic, minced
3 tablespoons snipped
   fresh oregano
¼ teaspoon salt

Spicy Shrimp on Skewers

To fill out the dinner plates, add some buttered peas and grilled fresh pineapple wedges.

Prep: 20 minutes **Marinate:** 1 to 2 hours **Grill:** 6 minutes **Makes:** 5 servings

1½ pounds fresh or frozen
    large shrimp in shells
½ cup frozen pineapple juice
    concentrate, thawed
1 to 2 tablespoons finely
    chopped jalapeño peppers*
1 clove garlic, minced
1 teaspoon grated fresh
    ginger or ⅛ teaspoon
    ground ginger
¼ teaspoon crushed
    red pepper
    Hot cooked rice pilaf
    (optional)

1. Thaw shrimp, if frozen. Rinse shrimp; pat dry with paper towels. Peel and devein shrimp, leaving tails intact. Place shrimp in a heavy, large self-sealing plastic bag set in a shallow bowl.

2. For marinade, in a small bowl combine pineapple juice concentrate, jalapeño peppers, garlic, ginger, and crushed red pepper. Pour marinade over shrimp. Seal bag; turn to coat shrimp. Marinate in the refrigerator for at least 1 hour or up to 2 hours, turning bag once.

3. Drain shrimp, reserving marinade. Thread shrimp on metal skewers, leaving about ¼ inch of space between pieces. Grill on rack of an uncovered grill directly over medium coals for 6 to 8 minutes or until shrimp turn opaque, turning once halfway through grilling and brushing once with reserved marinade during the first 3 minutes of grilling. Discard any remaining marinade. If desired, serve the kabobs over hot cooked rice pilaf.

Nutrition Facts per serving: 133 calories, 1 g total fat, 157 mg cholesterol, 181 mg sodium, 13 g carbohydrate, 17 g protein.

*__Note:__ Because chile peppers, such as jalapeños, contain volatile oils that can burn your skin and eyes, avoid direct contact with them as much as possible. When working with chile peppers, wear plastic or rubber gloves. If your bare hands do touch the chile peppers, wash your hands and nails well with soap and warm water.

Fiery Southwestern Seafood Skewers

Look for canned chipotle peppers in adobo sauce in the Mexican food section of the supermarket or at a Hispanic market.

Prep: 25 minutes **Grill:** 5 minutes **Makes:** 4 servings

1. Thaw shrimp and scallops, if frozen. Peel and devein shrimp, leaving tails intact. Rinse shrimp and scallops; pat dry with paper towels. On long metal skewers, alternately thread shrimp, scallops, sweet pepper, onion, and zucchini or yellow squash, leaving about ¼ inch of space between pieces.

2. In a small bowl combine chipotle peppers, lime juice, oil, brown sugar, garlic, cumin, and salt. Brush chipotle mixture over all sides of seafood and vegetables. Discard any remaining chipotle mixture.

3. Grill kabobs on rack of an uncovered grill directly over medium coals for 5 to 8 minutes or until shrimp and scallops turn opaque and vegetables are crisp-tender, turning once halfway through grilling. Sprinkle kabobs with cilantro and serve with lime wedges.

Nutrition Facts per serving: 152 calories, 5 g total fat, 104 mg cholesterol, 533 mg sodium, 10 g carbohydrate, 18 g protein.

8 ounces fresh or frozen
   medium or large shrimp
   in shells
8 ounces fresh or frozen sea
   scallops
1 red sweet pepper, cut into
   1-inch squares
1 medium onion, cut into
   8 wedges
2 medium zucchini or yellow
   summer squash, cut into
   ¾-inch-thick slices
2 tablespoons canned chipotle
   peppers in adobo sauce,
   mashed
1 tablespoon lime juice
1 tablespoon cooking oil
2 teaspoons brown sugar
2 cloves garlic, minced
½ teaspoon ground cumin
½ teaspoon salt
2 tablespoons snipped fresh
   cilantro
   Lime wedges

Curried Sea and Shore Kabobs

Shrimp represents the sea and pork the shore on these lime-curry glazed skewers.

Prep: 30 minutes **Grill:** 10 minutes **Makes:** 4 servings

8 ounces fresh or frozen
  jumbo shrimp in shells
2 tablespoons cooking oil
2 tablespoons finely chopped
  onion
¼ teaspoon shredded lime peel
4 teaspoons lime juice
¾ teaspoon curry powder
1 clove garlic, minced
8 ounces boneless pork loin,
  cut into 1-inch cubes
¼ of a fresh pineapple, cut into
  1-inch cubes (about 1 cup)
3 plums, pitted and quartered
  Salt (optional)
  Pepper (optional)
½ of a papaya, halved, seeded,
  peeled, and cut into
  1- to 1½-inch cubes

1. Thaw shrimp, if frozen. Peel and devein shrimp, leaving tails intact. Rinse shrimp; pat dry with paper towels. Set aside.

2. For the glaze, in a small bowl stir together oil, onion, lime peel, lime juice, curry powder, and garlic. On metal skewers, alternately thread pork, pineapple, and plum pieces, leaving about ¼ inch of space between pieces. If desired, season with salt and pepper.

3. Grill pork kabobs on rack of uncovered grill directly over medium coals for 10 to 14 minutes or until pork juices run clear, turning once halfway through grilling. Reserve half of the glaze; use remaining glaze to occasionally brush kabobs during last 3 minutes of grilling. Discard any remaining glaze used as brush-on for pork.

4. Meanwhile, on additional metal skewers, alternately thread the shrimp and the papaya pieces, leaving about ¼ inch of space between pieces. Grill the shrimp kabobs directly over medium coals for 7 to 9 minutes or until shrimp turn opaque, turning once halfway through grilling and brushing with the reserved glaze occasionally during last 3 minutes of grilling. Discard any remaining glaze used as brush-on for shrimp.

Nutrition Facts per serving: 201 calories, 11 g total fat, 91 mg cholesterol, 96 mg sodium, 11 g carbohydrate, 15 g protein.

Jambalaya on a Stick

The combination of shrimp, smoked sausage, chicken, and vegetables is reminiscent of the Creole classic jambalaya.

Prep: 35 minutes **Marinate:** 1 to 2 hours **Soak:** 30 minutes **Grill:** 12 minutes
Makes: 6 servings

1. Thaw shrimp, if frozen. Peel and devein shrimp. Rinse shrimp; pat dry with paper towels. Place shrimp, sausage, chicken, sweet pepper, and onion in a heavy, large self-sealing plastic bag set in a large bowl.

2. In a small bowl combine vinegar, tomato sauce, oil, thyme, bottled hot pepper sauce, and garlic. Pour half of the tomato sauce mixture over meat and vegetables. Seal bag; turn to coat pieces. Marinate in the refrigerator for at least 1 hour or up to 2 hours, turning bag occasionally. Cover and chill remaining tomato sauce mixture.

3. Meanwhile, soak wooden skewers in enough water to cover for 30 minutes; drain. Drain meat and vegetables, discarding marinade. On soaked skewers, alternately thread meat and vegetables (to secure pieces use 2 skewers per kabob), leaving about ¼ inch of space between pieces.

4. Grill kabobs on rack of an uncovered grill directly over medium coals for 12 to 14 minutes or until shrimp turn opaque and chicken is no longer pink, turning occasionally.

5. Meanwhile, in a small saucepan heat chilled tomato sauce mixture until bubbly. Combine cooked rice and parsley. Serve rice mixture and cherry tomatoes with kabobs. Pass warmed tomato sauce mixture.

Nutrition Facts per serving: 451 calories, 23 g total fat, 112 mg cholesterol, 632 mg sodium, 30 g carbohydrate, 27 g protein.

18 fresh or frozen large shrimp
   in shells (about 12 ounces)
12 ounces cooked smoked
   sausage links, cut into
   12 pieces
 8 ounces skinless, boneless
   chicken breasts, cut into
   1-inch pieces
 1 medium green sweet pepper,
   cut into 1-inch pieces
 1 medium onion, cut into
   1-inch wedges
⅓ cup white wine vinegar
⅓ cup tomato sauce
 2 tablespoons olive oil
 2 teaspoons dried thyme,
   crushed
 2 teaspoons bottled hot
   pepper sauce
¾ teaspoon dried minced garlic
24 8-inch wooden skewers
 3 cups hot cooked rice
 2 tablespoons snipped
   fresh parsley
 6 cherry tomatoes

Rosemary-Orange Shrimp Kabobs

With shrimp, turkey bacon, and a special orange-flavored couscous and sweet pepper combo, this dish is definitely company fare.

Prep: 30 minutes **Soak:** 30 minutes **Grill:** 8 minutes **Makes:** 4 servings

8 12-inch wooden skewers
16 fresh or frozen large
shrimp in shells
(about 1 pound total)
8 slices turkey bacon, halved
crosswise
2 red and/or yellow sweet
peppers, cut into 1-inch
pieces
2 teaspoons finely shredded
orange or blood orange
peel
2 tablespoons orange
or blood orange juice
2 teaspoons snipped fresh
rosemary
2 cups hot cooked couscous
¼ cup finely chopped green,
red, and/or yellow sweet
pepper

1. Soak wooden skewers in enough water to cover for 30 minutes; drain. Meanwhile, thaw shrimp, if frozen. Peel and devein shrimp, leaving tails intact. Rinse shrimp; pat dry with paper towels. Wrap each shrimp in a half slice of bacon. On soaked skewers, alternately thread bacon-wrapped shrimp and sweet pepper pieces, leaving about ¼ inch of space between pieces. In a small bowl combine 1 teaspoon of the orange peel, the orange juice, and rosemary. Brush over kabobs.

2. Lightly grease the rack of an uncovered grill. Place kabobs on rack. Grill directly over medium coals for 8 to 10 minutes or until bacon is crisp and shrimp turn opaque, turning once halfway through grilling.

3. Meanwhile, in a medium saucepan stir together the remaining orange peel, the cooked couscous, and chopped sweet pepper; heat through. Serve with kabobs.

Nutrition Facts per serving: **292 calories, 7 g total fat, 192 mg cholesterol, 553 mg sodium, 25 g carbohydrate, 31 g protein.**

BBQ Shrimp on Pineapple Planks

Jumbo shrimp are more impressive, but medium shrimp also work well for these skewers. Use 24 medium shrimp and grill them for 5 to 8 minutes or until they turn opaque.

Prep: 40 minutes **Marinate:** 30 minutes **Soak:** 30 minutes **Grill:** 10 minutes
Makes: 8 servings

1. Thaw shrimp, if frozen. Peel and devein shrimp, leaving tails intact. Rinse shrimp; pat dry. In a medium bowl combine the ¼ cup barbecue sauce, the chipotle peppers, 2 tablespoons of the melted margarine, and the garlic. Stir in shrimp. Cover and marinate in the refrigerator for 30 minutes, stirring occasionally.

2. Meanwhile, soak wooden skewers in enough water to cover for 30 minutes; drain. Cut pineapple lengthwise into ½-inch-thick slices. Chop 1 of the slices to measure ½ cup; set aside for relish. Halve each pineapple slice crosswise. Using remaining melted margarine, brush both sides of each pineapple plank; set aside.

3. For relish, in a bowl combine the chopped pineapple, the chopped cucumber, jicama, lime or lemon juice, and salt. Cover and set aside until serving time.

4. Remove shrimp from marinade; discard marinade. Thread 1 jumbo shrimp onto each soaked skewer. Grill shrimp kabobs and pineapple planks on the rack of an uncovered grill directly over medium coals until shrimp turn opaque and pineapple is heated through, turning once halfway through grilling. (Allow 10 to 12 minutes for jumbo shrimp and 6 to 8 minutes for pineapple planks.) If desired, brush kabobs with additional barbecue sauce during the last 1 minute of grilling.

5. To serve, stir cilantro into the relish. Serve relish with shrimp kabobs and pineapple planks.

Nutrition Facts per serving: 135 calories, 6 g total fat, 98 mg cholesterol, 288 mg sodium, 8 g carbohydrate, 12 g protein.

8 fresh or frozen jumbo shrimp
  in shells (about 1 pound)
¼ cup bottled barbecue sauce
1 to 2 tablespoons chopped
  canned chipotle peppers
  in adobo sauce
3 tablespoons margarine
  or butter, melted
2 cloves garlic, minced
8 6- to 8-inch wooden skewers
1 medium fresh pineapple,
  crown removed and peeled
½ cup chopped, seeded
  cucumber
½ cup chopped, peeled jicama
1 tablespoon lime juice
  or lemon juice
¼ teaspoon salt
  Bottled barbecue sauce
¼ cup snipped fresh cilantro

California Kabobs

Cheese tortellini is a surprisingly tasty addition to kabobs.

Prep: 30 minutes **Soak:** 30 minutes **Grill:** 5 minutes **Makes:** 4 servings

12 ounces fresh or frozen
   medium shrimp in shells
12 refrigerated spinach-and-
   cheese tortellini
8 6- to 8-inch wooden skewers
4 ounces white or red pearl
   onions (about 16)
1 14-ounce can artichoke
   hearts, drained and
   quartered lengthwise
1 recipe Lemon-Tarragon
   Vinaigrette
   Radicchio or red Swiss
   chard leaves (optional)
   Finely shredded Parmesan
   or Romano cheese
   (optional)

1. Thaw shrimp, if frozen. Peel and devein shrimp, leaving tails intact. Rinse shrimp; pat dry with paper towels. Set aside. Cook tortellini according to package directions; drain and set aside to cool. Meanwhile, soak wooden skewers in enough water to cover for 30 minutes; drain. Pour boiling water over the unpeeled onions and let stand for 3 minutes; drain. Trim off root ends and gently press to slip off skins.

2. On soaked skewers, alternately thread onions, artichoke hearts, shrimp, and tortellini, leaving about ¼ inch of space between pieces.

3. Grill kabobs on the rack of an uncovered grill directly over medium coals for 5 to 8 minutes or until shrimp turn opaque, turning once halfway through grilling.

4. To serve, drizzle with Lemon-Tarragon Vinaigrette. If desired, serve over radicchio or red Swiss chard leaves and pass Parmesan or Romano cheese.

Lemon-Tarragon Vinaigrette: In a small bowl combine 2 tablespoons olive oil; 2 teaspoons finely shredded lemon peel; 2 tablespoons lemon juice or dry vermouth; 1 tablespoon snipped fresh tarragon or 1½ teaspoons dried tarragon, crushed; 2 cloves garlic, minced; ¼ teaspoon crushed red pepper; ¼ teaspoon salt; and ⅛ teaspoon ground black pepper. Makes about ⅓ cup.

Nutrition Facts per serving: **332 calories, 10 g total fat, 110 mg cholesterol, 452 mg sodium, 24 g carbohydrate, 16 g protein.**

Shrimp Salsa Verde

Here's a foolproof way to keep shrimp from flipping when you grill them: use two skewers to hold the shrimp in place.

Prep: 35 minutes **Soak:** 30 minutes **Grill:** 6 minutes **Makes:** 4 servings

1. Thaw shrimp, if frozen. Peel and devein shrimp, leaving tails intact. Rinse shrimp; pat dry with paper towels. Soak wooden skewers in enough water to cover for 30 minutes; drain.

2. Meanwhile, for salsa, in a blender container or food processor bowl combine mint leaves, parsley, oil, anchovies, shallots or garlic, the water, pepper, and salt. Cover and blend or process until smooth. Use immediately or cover and chill in the refrigerator up to 24 hours; remove from refrigerator 30 minutes before grilling.

3. Thread 3 shrimp through head ends onto 1 soaked skewer; thread a second skewer through tails, leaving about ¼ inch of space between pieces. Repeat with remaining shrimp and skewers. Brush both sides of shrimp with salsa.

4. Grill skewers on the rack of an uncovered grill directly over medium coals for 6 to 9 minutes or until shrimp turn opaque and are lightly charred. If desired, serve shrimp with Cucumber Relish.

Nutrition Facts per serving: 332 calories, 21 g total fat, 218 mg cholesterol, 366 mg sodium, 4 g carbohydrate, 31 g protein.

Cucumber Relish: Peel and seed 2 medium cucumbers; halve lengthwise and cut into ¼-inch-thick crosswise slices. In a medium bowl combine sliced cucumbers, ¼ cup rice wine vinegar, 2 tablespoons thinly sliced fresh basil, 2 teaspoons sugar, 1 teaspoon kosher salt, 1 teaspoon grated lime peel, 1 teaspoon grated fresh ginger, and ¼ to ½ teaspoon crushed red pepper. Let stand for 15 minutes before serving. Makes 2½ cups.

24 fresh or frozen large shrimp
   in shells (about 1½ pounds
   total)
16 8-inch wooden skewers
 2 cups packed fresh mint
   leaves
 1 cup packed fresh flat-leaf
   parsley leaves
 ⅓ cup olive oil
 3 anchovy fillets, drained
 2 shallots or cloves garlic,
   peeled and quartered
 2 tablespoons water
 ¼ teaspoon freshly ground
   black pepper
   Pinch salt
 1 recipe Cucumber Relish
   (optional)

Pepper Shrimp in Peanut Sauce

Enjoy grilled shrimp at their best in this colorful pasta dish.

Prep: 30 minutes **Grill:** 5 minutes **Makes:** 4 servings

1 pound fresh or frozen
   medium shrimp in shells
8 ounces dried bow-tie pasta
   or linguine
½ cup water
¼ cup orange marmalade
2 tablespoons peanut butter
2 tablespoons soy sauce
2 teaspoons cornstarch
¼ teaspoon crushed
   red pepper
2 medium red, yellow, and/or
   green sweet peppers,
   cut into 1-inch pieces
Chopped peanuts (optional)

1. Thaw shrimp, if frozen. Peel and devein shrimp, leaving tails intact. Rinse shrimp; pat dry with paper towels. Set aside. Cook pasta according to package directions; drain. Return pasta to pan; keep warm.

2. Meanwhile, for sauce, in a small saucepan stir together the water, orange marmalade, peanut butter, soy sauce, cornstarch, and crushed red pepper. Bring to boiling; reduce heat. Cook and stir for 2 minutes. Remove from heat; keep warm.

3. On metal skewers, alternately thread shrimp and sweet peppers, leaving about ¼ inch of space between pieces. Grill kabobs on the rack of an uncovered grill directly over medium coals for 5 to 8 minutes or until shrimp turn opaque, turning to cook evenly.

4. To serve, add shrimp and peppers to the cooked pasta. Add the sauce; toss gently to coat. If desired, sprinkle individual servings with peanuts.

Nutrition Facts per serving: 382 calories, 7 g total fat, 180 mg cholesterol, 718 mg sodium, 57 g carbohydrate, 24 g protein.

Shrimp and Tropical Fruit

Turn fruit salad into a whole meal by adding savory grilled shrimp.

Prep: 25 minutes **Grill:** 7 minutes **Makes:** 6 servings

1. Thaw shrimp, if frozen. Peel and devein shrimp, leaving tails intact. Rinse shrimp; pat dry with paper towels. On six 10- to 12-inch metal skewers, thread shrimp, leaving about ¼ inch of space between pieces.

2. For sauce, in a medium bowl stir together barbecue sauce, pineapple juice, oil, and ginger. Brush shrimp with sauce.

3. Lightly grease the rack of an uncovered grill. Place skewers on rack. Grill directly over medium coals for 7 to 9 minutes or until shrimp turn opaque, turning once halfway through grilling and brushing occasionally with sauce during first 3 minutes of grilling. For the last 5 minutes of grilling, place pineapple on grill rack next to shrimp; turn once.

4. Serve shrimp and pineapple with papaya and kiwi fruit. In a small saucepan heat remaining sauce until bubbly; cool slightly. Pass with shrimp and fruit for dipping.

Nutrition Facts per serving: **199 calories, 6 g total fat, 116 mg cholesterol, 474 mg sodium, 21 g carbohydrate, 14 g protein.**

1¼ pounds fresh or frozen
    jumbo shrimp in shells
 1 cup bottled barbecue sauce
 ⅔ cup unsweetened
    pineapple juice
 2 tablespoons cooking oil
 4 teaspoons grated fresh
    ginger or 1½ teaspoons
    ground ginger
 ¼ of a fresh pineapple, sliced
    crosswise and quartered
 1 medium papaya, peeled,
    seeded, and cut up
 3 medium kiwi fruit, peeled
    and cut up

Peeling and Deveining Shrimp

Before you can enjoy tender, succulent shrimp in recipes, such as Shrimp and Tropical Fruit (above), you need to peel them and remove the black veins that run down the backs of the shellfish. The easiest way to get the job done is to remove the shell from each shrimp with your fingers, starting at the head end and working down the back. If you like, gently pull on the tail section to remove it. Use a sharp knife to make a shallow slit along the back of the shrimp, cutting from head to tail. Rinse the shrimp under cold running water to remove the vein. If necessary, use the tip of the knife to loosen the vein and rinse again.

On The Side

Fill out your menu with one of these remarkable
vegetable side dishes or fruit desserts.
They're easy to tuck alongside your main dish on the grill.

Grilled Sweet Potatoes and Apples, page 224

Grilled Mediterranean Vegetables over Couscous

When choosing nasturtiums or other edible flowers, make sure you get pesticide-free blossoms from your garden or the supermarket's produce section.

Prep: 25 minutes **Grill:** 10 minutes **Makes:** 6 to 8 servings

6 plum tomatoes, cut in half

1 red onion, cut into ¼-inch-thick slices

1 green sweet pepper, quartered

1 yellow sweet pepper, quartered

1 medium eggplant (about 1 pound), cut into 1-inch-thick slices

1 tablespoon olive oil

1½ cups water

2 tablespoons snipped fresh basil and/or oregano

2 teaspoons olive oil

½ teaspoon salt

1 cup quick-cooking couscous

½ cup nasturtiums, cut into thin strips

1. Lightly brush tomatoes, onion, sweet peppers, and eggplant with the 1 tablespoon olive oil. Lightly grease the rack of an uncovered grill. Place tomatoes in 2 foil pie plates. Place pie plates, peppers, onion, and eggplant on rack. Grill directly over medium coals until tomatoes are heated through and vegetables are tender, turning occasionally. (Allow 10 to 15 minutes for tomatoes and onion, 8 to 10 minutes for sweet peppers, and about 8 minutes for eggplant.) Remove vegetables from grill as they are done.

2. Meanwhile, bring the water to boiling in a medium saucepan. Add basil and/or oregano, the 2 teaspoons olive oil, and the salt. Stir in couscous. Cover; remove from heat. Let stand about 5 minutes or until liquid is absorbed.

3. Fluff couscous with a fork. Place on a serving platter. Sprinkle with nasturtiums. Top with grilled vegetables.

Nutrition Facts per serving: 192 calories, 4 g total fat, 0 mg cholesterol, 192 mg sodium, 34 g carbohydrate, 5 g protein.

Side-Dish Success

As long as you've got the grill going, it is only natural to use the fire to cook a side dish or dessert too. But before you start grilling, take a little time to choose your recipes carefully. For best results, select items that grill at the same temperature, use the same method (direct or indirect), and fit on the grill together. (If you are grilling a main dish indirectly, you can take advantage of the heat by placing a side dish that requires direct grilling directly over the coals or heat source.) Also choose a side dish or dessert that complements your entrée. For example, if the meat you're grilling is strongly flavored with garlic or jalapeño pepper, opt for a mild serve-along. And avoid dishes with flavors that are too similar. For example, you probably don't want to serve fish with a creamy dill sauce with dilled asparagus or peach-sauced pork chops with peach crisp for dessert.

Grilled Corn with Ancho-Avocado Butter

Want only a touch of heat in the velvety butter? Use only half of a small ancho pepper. If you like spicy food, use a whole pepper.

Prep: 30 minutes **Chill:** 1 hour **Grill:** 10 minutes **Makes:** 6 servings

1. In a small saucepan combine ancho pepper, lime juice, and the water. Cover and cook over low heat about 10 minutes or until pepper turns soft. Drain and cool. Remove stem and seeds of pepper.* Finely chop pepper; combine with softened butter or margarine.

2. In a small bowl slightly mash the avocado with the salt. Stir into butter mixture. If desired, spoon into small mold or cup lined with plastic wrap. Cover and chill for at least 1 hour or until firm.

3. Remove husks and silks from ears of corn. (If desired, leave a few leaves of the husks intact for presentation.) In a covered large saucepan cook corn in a small amount of boiling water for 5 to 7 minutes or until almost tender. Drain. Grill on rack of an uncovered grill directly over medium coals for 10 minutes, turning several times. Remove butter from mold; remove plastic wrap. Serve corn with butter mixture.

Nutrition Facts per serving: 246 calories, 10 g total fat, 8 mg cholesterol, 125 mg sodium, 40 g carbohydrate, 5 g protein.

Note: Because chile peppers, such as anchos, contain volatile oils that can burn your skin and eyes, avoid direct contact with them as much as possible. When working with chile peppers, wear plastic or rubber gloves. If your bare hands do touch the chile peppers, wash your hands and nails well with soap and warm water.

- ½ to 1 small dried ancho pepper
- 2 tablespoons lime juice
- 2 tablespoons water
- 3 tablespoons butter or margarine, softened
- ½ of a small avocado, pitted, peeled, and chopped
- ⅛ teaspoon salt
- 6 fresh ears of white and/or yellow sweet corn

Roasted Horseradish Corn

During the summer, keep some of the horseradish butter in the refrigerator to dress up corn on the cob or other cooked vegetables anytime. The butter will keep for up to 3 days.

Prep: 15 minutes **Grill:** 20 minutes **Makes:** 4 servings

---

6 tablespoons butter or
    margarine, softened
4 to 5 teaspoons prepared
    horseradish
1 tablespoon prepared
    mustard
2 cloves garlic, minced
¼ teaspoon pepper
4 large fresh ears of corn

1. For horseradish butter, in a small bowl stir together butter or margarine, horseradish, mustard, garlic, and pepper.

2. Remove husks and silks from ears of corn. If desired, reserve some husks to line serving platter. Rinse ears; pat dry. Tear off four 28×18-inch pieces of heavy foil. Fold each piece of foil in half to make a 14×18-inch rectangle. Place an ear of corn on each piece of foil.

3. Spread each ear of corn with one-fourth of the horseradish butter. Bring up 2 opposite edges of foil and seal edges with a double fold. Fold remaining ends to completely enclose ears of corn, leaving space for steam to build.

4. Grill foil-wrapped corn on rack of an uncovered grill directly over medium coals about 20 minutes or until corn is tender, turning occasionally. If desired, serve on platter lined with reserved husks.

Nutrition Facts per serving: 262 calories, 18 g total fat, 46 mg cholesterol, 294 mg sodium, 25 g carbohydrate, 4 g protein.

Hot-Off-the-Grill Potatoes

Seasoned with Parmesan cheese, crisp-cooked bacon, and fresh herbs, these potatoes in a packet make a wonderful side dish for grilled meat, poultry, or fish.

Prep: 20 minutes   **Grill:** 30 minutes   **Makes:** 4 servings

1. Fold a 48×18-inch piece of heavy foil in half to make a 24×18-inch rectangle. Grease the foil with 1 tablespoon of the butter.

2. Scrub and thinly slice unpeeled potatoes. Place sliced potatoes in center of foil. Sprinkle with green onions, Parmesan cheese, salt, paprika, and pepper. Dot with the remaining butter.

3. Bring up 2 opposite edges of foil and seal with a double fold. Fold remaining ends to completely enclose potatoes, leaving space for steam to build.

4. Grill potato packet on rack of an uncovered grill directly over medium coals for 30 to 40 minutes or until potatoes are tender, turning packet every 10 minutes during grilling. Before serving, sprinkle potatoes with crumbled bacon, parsley, dill, and chives.

Nutrition Facts per serving: **234 calories, 10 g total fat, 22 mg cholesterol, 337 mg sodium, 30 g carbohydrate, 7 g protein.**

- 3 tablespoons butter
- 5 medium potatoes
- ¼ cup chopped green onions
- 2 tablespoons grated Parmesan cheese
- ¼ teaspoon salt
- ¼ teaspoon paprika
- ¼ teaspoon freshly ground black pepper
- 3 slices bacon, crisp-cooked, drained, and crumbled
- 2 tablespoons snipped fresh parsley
- 2 tablespoons snipped fresh dill
- 2 tablespoons snipped fresh chives

Grillside Potato Chips

In this new take on all-American potato chips, grilling gives the potatoes irresistible smoky flavor.

Prep: 10 minutes **Grill:** 15 minutes **Stand:** 8 minutes **Makes:** 4 servings

1 pound potatoes (russet
    or long white), scrubbed
    and bias-cut into
    $\frac{1}{16}$-inch-thick slices
3 tablespoons cooking oil
$\frac{1}{2}$ teaspoon dried thyme,
    crushed
$\frac{1}{2}$ teaspoon coarse salt
    or seasoned salt

1. Place potato slices in a Dutch oven. Add enough water to cover. Bring just to boiling. Cook for 2 to 3 minutes or until crisp-tender. Drain; place in single layer on paper towels. Carefully brush both sides of potato slices with oil. Sprinkle with thyme and coarse salt or seasoned salt.

2. Line a large baking sheet with paper towels; set aside. Grill potato slices on the rack of an uncovered grill directly over medium-hot coals for 15 to 20 minutes or until browned and crisp, turning occasionally. Remove potato slices from grill; let stand for 10 minutes on prepared baking sheet. (Chips crisp as they stand.)

Nutrition Facts per serving: 209 calories, 10 g total fat, 0 mg cholesterol, 276 mg sodium, 27 g carbohydrate, 3 g protein.

Grilled Potatoes with Aioli

Aioli, a French garlic-flavored mayonnaise, makes a flavorful dipping sauce for grilled potatoes.

Prep: 30 minutes **Grill:** 16 minutes **Makes:** 12 appetizer servings or 6 side-dish servings

1. For aioli, heat a skillet over medium heat; add unpeeled garlic and toast for 15 to 18 minutes or until garlic skin is charred in spots and garlic feels soft when pressed with a spoon, turning frequently. Cool.

2. Gently squeeze garlic cloves from skins; transfer to a food processor bowl. Add bread, mayonnaise or salad dressing, lemon juice, shallot, the ¼ teaspoon salt, the ground red pepper, and saffron. Cover and process until smooth, gradually adding the water through feed tube. Transfer to a small serving bowl. Set aside.

3. In a large covered saucepan cook potatoes in enough boiling salted water to cover for 5 to 6 minutes or until potatoes are just tender. Drain in a colander; cool.

4. In a large bowl gently toss potatoes, oil, the ½ teaspoon salt, and the black pepper. Thread potatoes onto long metal skewers.

5. Lightly grease the rack of an uncovered grill. Place skewers on rack. Grill directly over medium coals for 16 to 18 minutes or until browned on all sides, turning occasionally. Slide potatoes off skewers onto a serving platter. If desired, sprinkle with parsley. Serve with aioli.

Nutrition Facts per appetizer serving: 150 calories, 9 g total fat, 5 mg cholesterol, 226 mg sodium, 16 g carbohydrate, 2 g protein.

- 2 **medium cloves garlic**
- 2 **slices firm-textured white bread, torn into bite-size pieces**
- ½ **cup mayonnaise or salad dressing**
- 1 **tablespoon lemon juice**
- ½ **teaspoon minced shallot**
- ¼ **teaspoon salt**
- ⅛ **teaspoon ground red pepper**
  Pinch saffron threads
- 3 **tablespoons water**
- 1 **pound small Yukon gold potatoes, halved**
- 1 **pound small red potatoes, halved, or 8 ounces each red potatoes and purple potatoes, halved**
- 1 **tablespoon olive oil**
- ½ **teaspoon salt**
- ½ **teaspoon freshly ground black pepper**
  Snipped fresh parsley (optional)

Grilled Sweet Potatoes And Apples

Serve these maple-glazed sweet potatoes and apples with grilled pork chops or ham.

Prep: 20 minutes **Grill:** 20 minutes **Makes:** 4 servings

2 medium sweet potatoes, peeled and cut into 1-inch cubes
2 medium cooking apples, cored and cut into eighths
¼ cup maple-flavored syrup
1 teaspoon finely shredded lemon peel
¼ teaspoon ground cinnamon
⅛ teaspoon salt
⅛ teaspoon pepper

1. In a covered medium saucepan cook sweet potatoes in a small amount of boiling water for 10 minutes. Drain.

2. Tear off a 36×18-inch piece of heavy foil. Fold foil in half to make an 18-inch square. Place the sweet potatoes and apple pieces in center of foil.

3. In a small bowl stir together the syrup, lemon peel, cinnamon, salt, and pepper. Drizzle over apples and potatoes. Bring up 2 opposite edges of foil and seal edges with a double fold. Fold remaining ends to completely enclose sweet potatoes and apples, leaving space for steam to build.

4. Grill foil packet on rack of an uncovered grill directly over medium coals for 20 to 25 minutes or until apples are tender.

Nutrition Facts per serving: **163 calories, 0 g total fat, 0 mg cholesterol, 93 mg sodium, 40 g carbohydrate, 1 g protein.**

Grilled Sweet Potatoes

Ginger accents the fruit juice-and-honey glaze.

Prep: 25 minutes   **Grill:** 8 minutes   **Makes:** 4 servings

1. In a medium saucepan cook potatoes in enough boiling water to cover about 15 minutes or until nearly tender; drain. Rinse with cold water; drain again. Pat dry with paper towels. Lightly coat with nonstick cooking spray.

2. Meanwhile, for glaze, in a small bowl stir together pineapple-orange juice concentrate, parsley, margarine or butter, honey, and ginger.

3. Grill sweet potatoes on rack of an uncovered grill directly over medium coals for 8 to 10 minutes or until tender, turning once halfway through grilling and brushing occasionally with glaze during the last 5 minutes of grilling.

Nutrition Facts per serving: 252 calories, 4 g total fat, 1 mg cholesterol, 58 mg sodium, 53 g carbohydrate, 3 g protein.

2 large sweet potatoes, halved lengthwise
Nonstick cooking spray
¼ cup frozen pineapple-orange juice concentrate, thawed
1 tablespoon snipped fresh parsley
1 tablespoon margarine or butter, melted
1 tablespoon honey
1 teaspoon grated fresh ginger or ¼ teaspoon ground ginger

Vegetable Kabobs

Baby vegetables are perfect for these colorful skewers. However, if the mini vegetables aren't available, just use cut-up sweet peppers, red onions, and zucchini.

Prep: 20 minutes **Grill:** 10 minutes **Makes:** 4 servings

8 tiny new potatoes, quartered

2 tablespoons water

8 baby sunburst squash

4 miniature sweet peppers
   and/or 1 red sweet pepper,
   cut into 1-inch pieces

8 tiny red onions, halved,
   or 2 small red onions,
   each cut into 8 wedges

8 baby zucchini or 1 small
   zucchini, halved lengthwise
   and sliced

¼ cup bottled oil-and-vinegar
   salad dressing

2 teaspoons snipped fresh
   rosemary or ½ teaspoon
   dried rosemary, crushed

   Fresh rosemary stalks
   (optional)*

1. In a 2-quart microwave-safe casserole combine potatoes and the water. Cover and cook in a microwave oven on 100% power (high) for 5 minutes. Gently stir in sunburst squash, sweet peppers, and onions. Microwave, covered, on high for 4 to 6 minutes or until nearly tender. Drain. Cool slightly.

2. On eight 10-inch skewers,* alternately thread the potatoes, sunburst squash, sweet peppers, onions, and zucchini. In a small bowl combine salad dressing and the snipped or dried rosemary; brush over vegetables.

3. Grill kabobs on rack of an uncovered grill directly over medium coals for 10 to 12 minutes or until vegetables are tender and browned, turning and brushing occasionally with dressing mixture. If desired, garnish with rosemary stalks.

Nutrition Facts per serving: **161 calories, 8 g total fat, 0 mg cholesterol, 217 mg sodium, 22 g carbohydrate, 3 g protein.**

Note: Using rosemary skewers will add a special touch to your meal. To use fresh rosemary skewers, first grill the vegetables on regular metal skewers (the rosemary will burn if grilled), then thread grilled vegetables on long stalks of fresh rosemary, removing some of the rosemary leaves for garnish.

Grilled Peppers And Tomatoes

A sprinkling of feta cheese adds a delightful tang.

Prep: 15 minutes   **Grill:** 10 minutes   **Makes:** 6 servings

1. Cut sweet peppers in half lengthwise, leaving stems intact. Remove seeds and membranes.

2. Grill sweet peppers, cut sides down, on rack of an uncovered grill directly over medium-hot coals for 4 minutes; turn. Divide tomatoes among pepper halves; brush with olive oil and sprinkle with garlic salt and black pepper. Grill for 4 minutes more.

3. Sprinkle tomatoes with cheese; grill about 2 minutes more or until cheese is softened. Remove peppers from grill; sprinkle with basil. Serve warm.

Nutrition Facts per serving: **79 calories, 4 g total fat, 4 mg cholesterol, 100 mg sodium, 11 g carbohydrate, 2 g protein.**

- 3 large yellow, green, and/or red sweet peppers
- 3 medium red and/or yellow tomatoes, peeled and quartered, or 12 cherry tomatoes, halved
- 1 tablespoon olive oil
- ¼ teaspoon garlic salt
- ¼ teaspoon freshly ground black pepper
- ¼ cup crumbled feta cheese (1 ounce)
- 2 tablespoons small fresh basil leaves or thinly sliced fresh basil leaves

Hearty Grilled Vegetables

Fresh thyme, basil, oregano, or chives complement the vegetables nicely. For even more flavor, use a mixture of the fresh herbs.

Prep: 10 minutes **Grill:** 6 minutes **Makes:** 4 servings

¼ cup olive oil

¼ cup snipped fresh thyme,
   basil, oregano, or chives

2 fresh portobello mushrooms
   (about 4 inches in
   diameter), halved
   crosswise

8 green onions

2 medium red and/or yellow
   sweet peppers, quartered
   lengthwise

1 medium zucchini, quartered
   lengthwise

   Salt

   Ground black pepper

   Fresh herbs (optional)

1. In a large bowl stir together olive oil and the ¼ cup fresh herbs. Add mushrooms, green onions, sweet peppers, and zucchini. Toss gently to coat vegetables.

2. If desired, place the vegetables on a grilling tray. Place grilling tray or vegetables on rack of an uncovered grill. Grill directly over medium coals for 6 to 10 minutes or until tender, turning vegetables occasionally. Season with salt and black pepper. If desired, garnish with additional fresh herbs.

Nutrition Facts per serving: 159 calories, 14 g total fat, 0 mg cholesterol, 70 mg sodium, 9 g carbohydrate, 0 g protein.

Grilled Peppers And Mushrooms

The size of the giant brown mushrooms called portobellos makes them a great choice for grilling.

Prep: 15 minutes **Grill:** 15 minutes **Makes:** 4 servings

1. Remove stems from mushrooms and discard; cut mushroom caps in half. Brush sweet peppers and mushroom halves with the oil.

2. Grill peppers, skin sides down, and mushroom halves, top sides down, on rack of an uncovered grill directly over medium-low coals about 15 minutes or until peppers are crisp-tender and lightly browned and mushrooms are fork tender, turning once. Slice or quarter mushrooms.

3. Place peppers and mushrooms in a large bowl. Add basil and balsamic vinegar. Toss well to coat. Serve immediately or cool to room temperature.

Nutrition Facts per serving: **82 calories, 4 g total fat, 0 mg cholesterol, 4 mg sodium, 12 g carbohydrate, 2 g protein.**

2 fresh portobello mushrooms
2 green and/or yellow sweet
    peppers, quartered
2 red sweet peppers, quartered
1 tablespoon olive oil
2 tablespoons snipped
    fresh basil
1 tablespoon balsamic vinegar

Honey-Glazed Carrots

Although it may be surprising, the combination of carrots and grapes is definitely delicious.

Prep: 15 minutes **Grill:** 21 minutes **Makes:** 6 servings

¼ cup butter

3 tablespoons honey

2 teaspoons ground ginger

¼ teaspoon ground nutmeg

¼ teaspoon salt

1½ pounds carrots, cut
   diagonally into
   1½-inch-thick slices
   (about 4½ cups)

1½ cups seedless green grapes

2 tablespoons slivered
   almonds or pine nuts,
   toasted

1. Cut up butter and place in a disposable foil pan (about 12×8×2-inches). Place pan on rack of an uncovered grill. Grill directly over medium coals about 1 minute or until butter melts. Remove pan from grill using pot holders; stir in honey, ginger, nutmeg, and salt. Add carrots; toss to coat.

2. Grill for 20 to 25 minutes more or until carrots are lightly golden and just tender and glaze is slightly thickened, stirring occasionally. Remove from heat. Add green grapes; toss to coat.

3. To serve, transfer to a bowl; sprinkle with toasted almonds or pine nuts.

Nutrition Facts per serving: 193 calories, 10 g total fat, 20 mg cholesterol, 237 mg sodium, 28 g carbohydrate, 2 g protein.

Grilled Corn Relish

Save a few of the cornhusks to line the serving bowl.

Prep: 15 minutes **Grill:** 25 minutes **Makes:** 4 servings

1. In medium bowl combine lime juice, oil, and garlic. Brush corn lightly with lime juice mixture. Sprinkle corn with chili powder. Grill corn on the rack of an uncovered grill directly over medium coals for 25 to 30 minutes or until tender, turning occasionally.

2. Meanwhile, add avocado, sweet pepper, cilantro, and salt to remaining lime juice mixture; toss to coat. Cut corn kernels from cobs; stir into avocado mixture.

Nutrition Facts per serving: 159 calories, 12 g total fat, 0 mg cholesterol, 152 mg sodium, 15 g carbohydrate, 3 g protein.

3 tablespoons lime juice
1 tablespoon cooking oil
2 cloves garlic, minced
2 fresh ears of corn, husked and cleaned
1 teaspoon chili powder
1 small avocado, seeded, peeled, and cut up
½ cup chopped red sweet pepper
¼ cup snipped fresh cilantro
¼ teaspoon salt

Grilled Tomato and Mozzarella Salad

Use vine-ripened, yet firm, tomatoes fresh from the garden or a farmer's market.

Prep: 15 minutes **Grill:** 7 minutes **Makes:** 4 servings

Nonstick cooking spray
1 medium yellow summer
   squash, cut lengthwise
   into ¼-inch-thick slices
2 large ripe, yet firm,
   tomatoes, cut into
   ¼-inch-thick slices
1 tablespoon balsamic vinegar
   or red wine vinegar
1 tablespoon olive oil
   or salad oil
1 tablespoon water
⅛ teaspoon salt
⅛ teaspoon pepper
4 ounces part-skim mozzarella
   cheese, thinly sliced and
   cut into triangles
2 tablespoons snipped fresh
   mixed herbs (such as
   oregano, basil, thyme,
   and sage)
Fresh oregano sprigs
   (optional)

1. Coat the unheated grill rack of an uncovered grill with nonstick cooking spray. Place squash on rack. Grill directly over medium coals for 3 minutes. Turn and grill for 2 to 3 minutes more or until crisp-tender. Add tomato slices to rack; grill for 2 to 4 minutes more or until heated through but still slightly firm, turning once. Remove squash and tomato slices as they are done.

2. Meanwhile, for dressing, in a screw-top jar combine vinegar, oil, the water, salt, and pepper. Cover; shake well.

3. Cut squash slices in half. To assemble salad, alternate pieces of tomato, squash, and mozzarella cheese on a shallow plate. Drizzle dressing over vegetables. Sprinkle snipped fresh herbs over the salad. If desired, garnish with fresh oregano sprigs.

Nutrition Facts per serving: **128 calories, 8 g total fat, 16 mg cholesterol, 206 mg sodium, 7 g carbohydrate, 8 g protein.**

Santa Fe Rice and Corn Salad

The Dijon vinaigrette adds just the right tang to this hearty salad.

Prep: 30 minutes **Soak:** 2 to 4 hours **Grill:** 25 minutes **Stand:** 20 minutes
Makes: 6 servings

1. Peel back cornhusks, but do not remove. Remove corn silks. Gently rinse corn. Pull husks back up around corn. Using 100%-cotton kitchen string, tie husks shut. Cover corn with water. Soak for at least 2 hours or up to 4 hours. Drain well.

2. In a medium saucepan bring the 2½ cups water to boiling. Stir in uncooked rice and salt. Return to boiling; reduce heat. Cover; simmer about 15 minutes or until rice is tender. Place in a colander; rinse with cold water. Drain; set aside.

3. Grill corn on rack of an uncovered grill directly over medium-hot coals for 15 minutes. Add sweet pepper and poblano pepper, cut sides up, to grill. Grill about 10 minutes more or until corn kernels are tender and pepper skins are blistered and dark, turning corn frequently.

4. Wrap peppers in foil; let stand for 20 minutes. Cool corn slightly. Remove and discard husks, reserving a few to line serving bowl. Cut kernels from cobs. Remove and discard skins from peppers; chop peppers. In large bowl combine cooked rice, corn, peppers, beans, and cilantro. Add Dijon Vinaigrette; toss gently to coat. Serve at room temperature or chilled.

Dijon Vinaigrette: In screw-top jar combine 3 tablespoons salad oil, 3 tablespoons red wine vinegar, 1½ teaspoons Dijon-style mustard, ½ teaspoon bottled hot pepper sauce (if desired), and ⅛ teaspoon salt. Cover and shake well.

Nutrition Facts per serving: 260 calories, 8 g total fat, 0 mg cholesterol, 310 mg sodium, 45 g carbohydrate, 5 g protein.

- 3 fresh ears of corn (with husks)
- 2½ cups water
- 1¼ cups long grain rice
- ½ teaspoon salt
- 1 medium red sweet pepper, quartered lengthwise
- 1 fresh poblano pepper, halved lengthwise and seeded (see note on page 219)
- ½ cup canned black beans, rinsed and drained
- ⅓ cup snipped fresh cilantro
- 1 recipe Dijon Vinaigrette

Warm Tarragon Potato Salad

For an impressive presentation, serve this gussied-up version of potato salad in artichoke halves.

Prep: 10 minutes **Grill:** 25 minutes **Makes:** 8 servings

¼ cup salad oil

¼ cup vinegar

1 tablespoon sugar (optional)

1 teaspoon snipped fresh
   tarragon or dill or
   ¼ teaspoon dried tarragon,
   crushed, or dried dillweed

½ teaspoon Dijon-style
   mustard

1 pound tiny new potatoes
   and/or small yellow
   potatoes, cut into bite-size
   pieces

2 teaspoons salad oil

1 cup chopped bok choy

½ cup chopped radishes

½ cup thinly sliced green
   onions

2 thin slices Canadian-style
   bacon, chopped (1 ounce)

⅛ teaspoon freshly ground
   black pepper

4 artichokes, cooked, halved
   lengthwise, and chokes
   removed (optional)

1. For dressing, in a small bowl whisk together the ¼ cup oil, the vinegar, sugar (if desired), tarragon, and mustard. Set aside.

2. In a lightly greased 2-quart square disposable foil pan combine potatoes and the 2 teaspoons oil; toss to coat.

3. In a grill with a cover arrange hot coals around edge of grill. Test for medium-hot heat in center of grill (not over coals). Place potatoes in pan in center of grill rack. Cover and grill about 25 minutes or just until potatoes are tender. Cool slightly.

4. In a large bowl combine potatoes, bok choy, radishes, green onions, Canadian-style bacon, and pepper. Add the dressing; toss gently to coat. If desired, spoon the salad into artichoke halves.

Nutrition Facts per serving: 135 calories, 8 g total fat, 2 mg cholesterol, 68 mg sodium, 14 g carbohydrate, 2 g protein.

Bananas Suzette over Grilled Pound Cake

End your cookout with a flair. Heat the banana mixture in a skillet on the grill and serve the sauce over pound cake slices grilled to a golden brown.

Prep: 10 minutes **Grill:** 8 minutes **Makes:** 4 servings

1. Peel bananas; bias-slice each banana into 8 pieces. Preheat a heavy, 8-inch skillet* on the rack of an uncovered grill directly over medium coals for 2 minutes. Add sugar, orange liqueur, orange juice, and butter to skillet. Cook about 1 minute or until butter is melted and sugar begins to dissolve. Add the bananas and cook about 4 minutes more or just until bananas are tender, stirring once. Stir in the ⅛ teaspoon nutmeg. Set skillet to the side of the grill rack. Add pound cake slices to grill rack; grill cake about 1 minute or until golden brown, turning once halfway through grilling.

2. To serve, spoon bananas and sauce over pound cake slices. If desired, garnish with shredded orange peel and additional ground nutmeg.

Nutrition Facts per serving: 292 calories, 12 g total fat, 67 mg cholesterol, 139 mg sodium, 42 g carbohydrate, 3 g protein.

Note: The heat from the grill will blacken the outside of the skillet, so use a cast-iron or old skillet.

2 medium ripe, yet firm, bananas

3 tablespoons sugar

2 tablespoons orange liqueur

2 tablespoons orange juice

1 tablespoon butter

⅛ teaspoon ground nutmeg

½ of a 10¾-ounce package frozen pound cake, thawed and cut into 4 slices

Shredded orange peel (optional)

Ground nutmeg (optional)

Grilled Fruit Crisp

Sweet, juicy peaches star in this cooked-on-the-grill version of an all-time favorite dessert.

Prep: 20 minutes   **Grill:** 50 minutes   **Makes:** 8 servings

4 cups thinly sliced peeled
   peaches
1 8-ounce can pineapple
   tidbits (juice pack)
2 tablespoons brown sugar
1 teaspoon quick-cooking
   tapioca
½ cup quick-cooking oats
¼ cup packed brown sugar
¼ cup all-purpose flour
½ teaspoon ground cinnamon
⅛ teaspoon ground nutmeg
2 tablespoons butter
   Ice cream (optional)
   Fresh mint sprigs (optional)

1. In a medium bowl combine the peaches, pineapple, the 2 tablespoons brown sugar, and the tapioca. Spoon into an 8×8×2-inch metal baking or disposable foil pan; set aside.

2. In a small bowl combine the oats, the ¼ cup brown sugar, the flour, cinnamon, and nutmeg. Using a pastry blender, cut in butter until mixture resembles coarse crumbs; sprinkle over fruit mixture. Cover pan tightly with foil.

3. Place pan on rack of an uncovered grill directly over medium coals; grill about 50 minutes or until mixture is hot and bubbly. Serve warm. If desired, serve with ice cream. If desired, garnish with mint sprigs.

Nutrition Facts per serving: 146 calories, 3 g total fat, 0 mg cholesterol, 37 mg sodium, 29 g carbohydrate, 2 g protein.

Grilled Banana Sundaes

To keep the banana pieces from falling through the grill rack, place them crosswise to the wires and use a long-handled metal spatula or tongs to carefully turn the pieces.

Prep: 15 minutes **Grill:** 4 minutes **Makes:** 4 servings

1. Cut bananas in half lengthwise; cut each piece in half crosswise. (You should have 12 pieces.) In a small bowl stir together butter and 1 teaspoon of the orange juice.

2. Brush butter mixture on all sides of the banana pieces. Grill bananas on the rack of an uncovered grill directly over medium-hot coals for 4 minutes or until heated through, turning once halfway through grilling.

3. Meanwhile, for the sauce, in a heavy, medium skillet or saucepan* combine the caramel topping and the remaining orange juice. Heat the caramel mixture on the grill rack alongside bananas directly over the coals or on a range top until the mixture boils, stirring frequently. Stir in the cinnamon. Add the bananas to the sauce; stir gently to coat.

4. To serve, scoop ice cream into 4 dessert dishes. Spoon sauce and bananas over ice cream. Sprinkle with the toasted coconut and almonds.

Nutrition Facts per serving: **485 calories, 21 g total fat, 53 mg cholesterol, 186 mg sodium, 73 g carbohydrate, 5 g protein.**

Note: The heat from the grill will blacken the outside of the skillet or saucepan, so use a cast-iron skillet or old saucepan if you plan to heat the sauce on the grill.

3 large ripe, yet firm, bananas
1 tablespoon butter, melted
2 teaspoons orange juice
½ cup caramel ice cream
   topping
¼ teaspoon ground cinnamon
1 pint vanilla ice cream
   Toasted coconut
   Toasted sliced almonds

Peanut and Banana Cookie Pizza

Refrigerated chocolate chip cookie dough forms the crust of this sure-to-please dessert.

Prep: 15 minutes **Grill:** 11 minutes **Makes:** 12 servings

1 18-ounce package refrigerated chocolate chip cookie dough

½ cup caramel ice cream topping

1 cup semisweet or milk chocolate pieces and/or miniature candy-coated semisweet baking bits

½ cup chopped dry-roasted peanuts

1 large banana, thinly sliced

2 tablespoons chocolate ice cream topping (optional)

1. Grease a 12-inch metal pizza pan. Press cookie dough evenly into pan. Grill cookie in pan on rack of an uncovered grill directly over medium coals for 10 to 15 minutes or until edges of cookie are lightly golden and top is set but not dry. Remove from grill (cookie may puff and fall at this point).

2. Drizzle caramel topping over cookie. Sprinkle chocolate pieces and/or baking bits and chopped peanuts over caramel topping. Return pan to grill for 1 to 2 minutes more or until chocolate pieces soften. Remove from grill. Cool on a wire rack.

3. To serve, top with sliced bananas. If desired, drizzle with chocolate topping. Cut into wedges.

Nutrition Facts per serving: 334 calories, 16 g total fat, 11 mg cholesterol, 185 mg sodium, 48 g carbohydrate, 4 g protein.

Hot-Off-the-Grill Tropical Treat

Grilled fresh pineapple is a refreshing finale for any cookout.

Prep: 20 minutes   **Grill:** 8 minutes   **Makes:** 6 servings

1. Slice off the bottom and the green top of the pineapple. Stand pineapple on a cut end and slice off the skin in wide strips, from top to bottom. To remove the eyes, cut diagonally around the fruit, following the pattern of the eyes and making narrow, wedge-shaped grooves in the pineapple. Cut pineapple crosswise into 6 slices. Remove core. Set aside.

2. In a small saucepan melt butter or margarine over medium heat. In a small bowl stir together lime peel, lime juice, honey, cornstarch, and ginger. Stir into the melted butter or margarine. Cook and stir until thickened and bubbly. Cook and stir for 2 minutes more. Remove from heat.

3. Grill pineapple slices on rack of an uncovered grill directly over medium coals for 8 to 10 minutes or until heated through, turning once and brushing frequently with butter mixture.

Nutrition Facts per serving: **146 calories, 8 g total fat, 20 mg cholesterol, 79 mg sodium, 20 g carbohydrate, 0 g protein.**

1 large fresh pineapple
   (4 to 5 pounds)
¼ cup butter or margarine
1 teaspoon finely shredded
   lime peel
2 tablespoons lime juice
2 tablespoons honey
1 tablespoon cornstarch
¼ teaspoon ground ginger

Smoke Cooking

The glorious aroma of these beef, pork, poultry,
fish, or seafood delights smoke cooking over wood chips
or chunks is bound to bring everyone flocking to your picnic table.

Memphis-Style Smoked Pork with Bourbon Sauce, page 251

Beer-Sauced Beef Brisket

A savory rub and a beer-vinegar sauce give the beef brisket exceptional flavor.

Prep: 10 minutes **Soak:** 1 hour **Grill:** 2 hours **Makes:** 15 servings

4 cups mesquite or hickory
  wood chips
2 tablespoons sugar
1 tablespoon garlic salt
  or seasoned salt
1 tablespoon paprika
1½ teaspoons chili powder
1½ teaspoons ground black
  pepper
⅛ teaspoon ground red pepper
⅛ teaspoon celery seed
  Dash ground cloves
1 3- to 4-pound fresh
  beef brisket
½ cup beer
1 tablespoon cider vinegar
1 tablespoon olive oil
1 tablespoon Worcestershire
  sauce
1 tablespoon bottled
  barbecue sauce
½ teaspoon seasoned salt
¼ teaspoon celery seed

1. At least 1 hour before grilling, soak wood chips in enough water to cover. Drain before using.

2. For rub, in a small bowl combine sugar, the 1 tablespoon garlic salt or seasoned salt, the paprika, chili powder, black pepper, ground red pepper, the ⅛ teaspoon celery seed, and the cloves. Trim fat from brisket. Sprinkle rub evenly over meat; rub in with your fingers.

3. For mop sauce, in a medium bowl combine beer, vinegar, oil, Worcestershire sauce, barbecue sauce, the ½ teaspoon seasoned salt, and the ¼ teaspoon celery seed. Set aside.

4. In a grill with a cover arrange medium-hot coals around a drip pan. Test for medium heat above pan. Sprinkle the drained wood chips over coals. Place brisket on grill rack over pan. Cover and grill for 2 to 2½ hours or until meat is tender. Add additional coals and wood chips as needed. Brush brisket once or twice with mop sauce during the last hour of grilling. Discard any remaining mop sauce. To serve, thinly slice brisket across the grain.

Nutrition Facts per serving: 262 calories, 20 g total fat, 61 mg cholesterol, 436 mg sodium, 3 g carbohydrate, 16 g protein.

Brisket with 5-Alarm Sauce

Try it and you'll like it—the 5-Alarm Sauce is spicy but not overly hot.

Prep: 15 minutes   **Soak:** 1 hour   **Smoke:** 5 hours   **Makes:** 12 servings

1. At least 1 hour before smoke cooking, soak wood chunks in enough water to cover. Drain before using.

2. For mop sauce, combine wine, Worcestershire sauce, oil, vinegar, garlic, cumin, mustard, and red pepper. Set aside. For rub, combine seasoned salt, paprika, and black pepper. Trim fat from brisket. Sprinkle rub evenly over brisket; rub in.

3. In a smoker arrange preheated coals, half of the wood chunks, and water pan according to manufacturer's directions. Pour water into pan. Place brisket on grill rack over pan. Cover and smoke for 5 to 6 hours or until meat is tender, brushing once or twice with mop sauce during the last hour of smoke cooking. Add additional coals, wood chunks, and water as needed. Discard any remaining mop sauce. To serve, thinly slice meat across the grain. Serve meat with 5-Alarm Sauce.

5-Alarm Sauce: In saucepan combine 1 cup catsup; 1 large tomato, peeled, seeded, and chopped; ½ cup chopped green sweet pepper; 2 tablespoons brown sugar; 2 tablespoons chopped onion; 1 to 2 tablespoons bottled steak sauce; 1 to 2 tablespoons Worcestershire sauce; ½ teaspoon garlic powder; ¼ teaspoon each ground nutmeg, ground cinnamon, and ground cloves; and ⅛ teaspoon each ground ginger and ground black pepper. Bring to boiling; reduce heat. Cover; simmer 5 minutes. Serve warm or at room temperature. To store remaining, cover; refrigerate up to 2 days. Makes about 2½ cups.

- 8 to 10 mesquite or hickory wood chunks
- ¼ cup dry red wine
- 4 teaspoons Worcestershire sauce
- 1 tablespoon cooking oil
- 1 tablespoon red wine vinegar or cider vinegar
- 1 clove garlic, minced
- ½ teaspoon ground cumin
- ½ teaspoon hot-style mustard   Dash ground red pepper
- 2 teaspoons seasoned salt
- 1 teaspoon paprika
- 1 teaspoon ground black pepper
- 1 3- to 3½-pound fresh beef brisket
- 1 recipe 5-Alarm Sauce

Nutrition Facts per serving: 214 calories, 8 g total fat, 66 mg cholesterol, 618 mg sodium, 10 g carbohydrate, 25 g protein.

Lemon-Basil Steaks

Round out the meal with simple serve-alongs, such as crusty bread and a crisp green salad.

Prep: 5 minutes   **Soak:** 1 hour   **Smoke:** 40 minutes   **Makes:** 4 servings

4 hickory, pecan, or oak
    wood chunks
2 teaspoons country-style
    Dijon-style mustard
2 teaspoons balsamic vinegar
1½ teaspoons lemon-pepper
    seasoning
2 cloves garlic, minced
1 teaspoon dried basil,
    crushed
⅛ teaspoon salt
4 boneless beef ribeye steaks,
    cut 1 inch thick (1¾ to
    2 pounds total)

1. At least 1 hour before smoke cooking, soak wood chunks in enough water to cover. Drain before using.

2. For glaze, in a small bowl stir together mustard, balsamic vinegar, lemon-pepper seasoning, garlic, basil, and salt. Brush onto both sides of steaks. Discard any remaining glaze.

3. In a smoker arrange preheated coals, drained wood chunks, and water pan according to the manufacturer's directions. Pour water into water pan. Place steaks on grill rack over pan. Cover and smoke until steaks are desired doneness. [Allow 40 to 50 minutes for medium-rare (145°) or 50 to 60 minutes for medium doneness (160°).]

Nutrition Facts per serving: 307 calories, 12 g total fat, 94 mg cholesterol, 599 mg sodium, 2 g carbohydrate, 44 g protein.

Steady as You Go

Because smoke cooking often involves long, slow grilling, it's important to keep the heat and supply of smoke constant. When using charcoal, you'll need to add briquettes about every hour to keep the fire hot enough so the wood smokes. Adding 10 to 12 briquettes at a time works best—any more and the temperature in the chamber will drop. For even heat distribution, add half of the new briquettes to each side of the burning coals. (If you are using a medium-hot fire, the coals will burn more quickly and you'll need to add a few briquettes about every 30 minutes.) Replenish the soaked wood chips or chunks as often as necessary for a steady stream of smoke. And, to add more water to a pan, use hot water so the temperature in the chamber doesn't fall. Finally, don't peek. Every time you lift the lid to your grill or smoker, you'll add as much as 15 minutes to the smoking time.

Steak Strips with Peanut Sauce

Adjust the heat in the peanut and pineapple sauce by using as little as 1 tablespoon chopped jalapeño pepper or as much as 2 tablespoons.

Prep: 15 minutes **Marinate:** 4 to 24 hours **Soak:** 1 hour **Grill:** 22 minutes
Makes: 8 servings

1. Place steak in a heavy, large self-sealing plastic bag set in a shallow bowl. For marinade, in a small bowl combine the ¼ cup pineapple juice, the oil, lemon juice, the 1 teaspoon ginger, and the mustard. Pour over steak. Seal bag; turn to coat steak. Marinate in the refrigerator for at least 4 hours or up to 24 hours, turning bag occasionally.

2. At least 1 hour before grilling, soak wood chips in enough water to cover. Drain before using.

3. Drain steak, reserving marinade. In a grill with a cover arrange medium-hot coals around a drip pan. Test for medium heat above the pan. Sprinkle wood chips over coals. Place steak on the grill rack over pan. Cover and grill until steak is desired doneness, turning once halfway through grilling and brushing once with reserved marinade after 15 minutes of grilling. [Allow 22 to 26 minutes for medium-rare (145°) or 26 to 30 minutes for medium doneness (160°).] Discard any remaining marinade.

4. Meanwhile, for sauce, in a small saucepan heat peanut butter over low heat just until melted. Gradually stir in the ¼ to ⅓ cup pineapple juice until creamy (mixture may thicken at first but will become creamy as more juice is added). Remove from heat. Stir in jalapeño pepper, chopped green onion, and, if desired, the ½ teaspoon ginger. To serve, thinly slice steak across grain. Serve steak with sauce. If desired, garnish with green onion strips.

Nutrition Facts per serving: 233 calories, 12 g total fat, 69 mg cholesterol, 97 mg sodium, 4 g carbohydrate, 26 g protein.

1 2-pound boneless beef sirloin steak, cut 1 inch thick
¼ cup unsweetened pineapple juice
2 tablespoons cooking oil
1 tablespoon lemon juice
1 teaspoon grated fresh ginger
1 teaspoon Dijon-style mustard
2 cups orange, apple, or cherry wood chips
¼ cup creamy peanut butter
¼ to ⅓ cup unsweetened pineapple juice
1 to 2 tablespoons chopped, seeded fresh jalapeño pepper (see note on page 256)
1 small green onion, chopped
½ teaspoon grated fresh ginger (optional)
Green onion strips (optional)

Ginger-Orange Smoked Beef Ribs

Purchase the beef ribs as a rack or cut into individual pieces. If you grill a rack of ribs, cut into pieces before serving.

Prep: 10 minutes   **Soak:** 1 hour   **Smoke:** 2½ hours   **Makes:** 4 servings

4 to 6 oak or hickory wood
　chunks or 3 to 4 cups oak
　or hickory wood chips
2 teaspoons paprika
1 teaspoon salt
½ teaspoon pepper
3 to 4 pounds beef back ribs
　(about 8 ribs)
½ cup bottled barbecue sauce
¼ cup frozen orange juice
　concentrate, thawed
2 tablespoons soy sauce
1 tablespoon grated
　fresh ginger

1. At least 1 hour before smoke cooking, soak wood chunks or chips in enough water to cover. Drain before using.

2. For rub, in a small bowl combine paprika, salt, and pepper. Sprinkle evenly over both sides of ribs; rub in with your fingers.

3. In a smoker arrange preheated coals, half of the drained wood chunks, and water pan according to manufacturer's directions. Pour water into pan. If desired, place ribs in a rib rack. Place ribs on the grill rack over the water pan. Cover and smoke for 2½ to 3 hours or until tender. Add additional coals, wood chunks, and water as needed.

4. Meanwhile, for sauce, stir together barbecue sauce, juice concentrate, soy sauce, and ginger. Brush ribs with sauce during the last 15 minutes of smoking. Pass any remaining sauce.

Nutrition Facts per serving: 298 calories, 14 g total fat, 65 mg cholesterol, 1,191 mg sodium, 13 g carbohydrate, 30 g protein.

Water Versus Dry Smokers

With all of the smoke cookers available, you may need help sorting things out. Here's an overview of common types.

　Water smokers come in charcoal, electric, and gas models. Most are vertical, cylindrical units with a domed lid. They contain a pan to hold water so moist heat forms as the food grills. This type of smoker uses the heat from the fire to bring the water to boiling while causing soaked wood chunks or chips to smoke. The water particles combine with the smoke and condense on the meat. As a result, the food takes on a sweet smoky flavor, becomes more tender, and stays moist despite a long grilling time. Charcoal water smokers are convenient because they're portable. Electric or gas water smokers have the advantage of maintaining the heat at a constant temperature.

　Dry smokers are horizontal units with an offset firebox that keeps the food away from the heat. They do not use steam and work in the same way as smoking on a regular grill. Dry smokers range in size from small barrels to models designed for hundreds of pounds of meat. Some units have features such as doors that open or trays that pull out so ashes can be removed and vents and dampers to regulate heat and smoke.

Mesquite-Smoked Beef Roast

Leftovers from this juicy roast make great cold sandwiches—especially when you team the beef with sourdough bread and your favorite flavored mayonnaise.

Prep: 10 minutes **Soak:** 1 hour **Smoke:** 3 hours **Stand:** 15 minutes **Makes:** 12 servings

1. At least 1 hour before smoke cooking, soak wood chunks in enough water to cover. Drain before using.

2. Trim fat from beef. Using a long-tined fork, make holes about ¾ inch apart and 1 inch deep on top side of beef; insert a whole peppercorn into each hole. Close holes by rubbing the surface of the meat with the smooth edge of the fork.

3. For rub, in a small bowl combine Worcestershire sauce, seasoned salt, and celery salt. Drizzle mixture evenly over meat; rub in with your fingers. Insert an oven-going meat thermometer into the center of meat.

4. In a smoker arrange preheated coals, half of the drained wood chunks, and water pan according to manufacturer's directions. Pour water into pan. Place beef on the grill rack over the pan. Cover and smoke the beef for 3 to 3½ hours or until medium-rare doneness (140°). Add additional coals, wood chunks, and water as needed.

5. Remove beef from smoker. Cover beef with foil; let stand for 15 minutes before carving (the temperature of the beef will rise 5° during standing).

Nutrition Facts per serving: 226 calories, 9 g total fat, 71 mg cholesterol, 216 mg sodium, 0 g carbohydrate, 33 g protein.

8 to 10 mesquite or hickory wood chunks
1 4-pound boneless beef ribeye roast
Whole black peppercorns
1½ teaspoons Worcestershire sauce
½ teaspoon seasoned salt
½ teaspoon celery salt

Texas-Style Smoky Beef Ribs

Texas and beef are synonymous. These Texas-style beef ribs are grilled over mesquite and slathered with a honey-catsup sauce.

Prep: 10 minutes **Soak:** 1 hour **Grill:** 1 hour **Makes:** 4 servings

---

4 cups mesquite or hickory
    wood chips

1 large onion, finely chopped

½ cup honey

½ cup catsup

1 4-ounce can diced green
    chili peppers, drained

1 tablespoon chili powder

1 clove garlic, minced

½ teaspoon dry mustard

1 teaspoon salt

1 teaspoon ground black
    pepper

3 to 4 pounds beef back ribs
    (about 8 ribs)

1. At least 1 hour before grilling, soak wood chips in enough water to cover. Drain before using.

2. For sauce, in a small saucepan stir together onion, honey, catsup, green chili peppers, chili powder, garlic, and mustard. Cook and stir over low heat for 10 minutes.

3. For rub, combine salt and black pepper. Trim fat from ribs. Sprinkle rub evenly over ribs; rub in with your fingers.

4. In a grill with a cover arrange medium-hot coals around a drip pan. Test for medium heat above the pan. Sprinkle half of the drained wood chips over the coals. Place ribs, bone sides down, on grill rack over pan. (Or place ribs in a rib rack; place on grill rack.) Cover and grill for 1 to 1¼ hours or until ribs are tender, brushing once with sauce during the last 10 minutes of grilling. Add additional coals and remaining wood chips as needed. Pass the remaining sauce with ribs.

Nutrition Facts per serving: 403 calories, 12 g total fat, 79 mg cholesterol, 1125 mg sodium, 49 g carbohydrate, 28 g protein.

Lamb Salad with Roasted Vegetables

Impress guests with this delectable salad featuring spirals of cheese and herb-stuffed lamb.

Prep: 15 minutes **Soak:** 1 hour **Grill:** 1½ hours **Stand:** 15 minutes
Makes: 8 to 10 servings

1. At least 1 hour before grilling, soak wood chips in enough water to cover. Drain before using.

2. Unroll meat; trim off fat. Sprinkle meat with salt and pepper. For filling, in a small bowl combine the Parmesan cheese, parsley, garlic, and lemon peel. Spread filling over meat. Roll up meat; retie securely with 100%-cotton kitchen string. Insert an oven-going meat thermometer into center of meat.

3. In a grill with a cover arrange medium coals around a drip pan. Test for medium-low heat above the pan. Sprinkle half of the wood chips over coals. Place meat on rack over pan. Cover; grill until desired doneness. [Allow 1½ to 2 hours for medium-rare (140°) or 1¾ to 2¼ hours for medium doneness (155°).] Add additional coals and remaining wood chips as needed.

4. Remove meat. Cover with foil; let stand 15 minutes before serving (temperature of meat will rise 5° during standing.)

5. Meanwhile, in a roasting pan toss together corn, potatoes, and onion. Drizzle with oil; sprinkle with salt and pepper. Roast vegetables in a 425° oven for 15 minutes. Add asparagus and/or green beans; toss to combine. Roast about 15 minutes more or until potatoes are tender.

6. To serve, toss roasted vegetables with vinaigrette dressing and dill. Arrange greens on 8 to 10 dinner plates; top with vegetables. Remove strings from meat; slice meat and arrange on the plates. Sprinkle with olives.

Nutrition Facts per serving: 544 calories, 35 g total fat, 114 mg cholesterol, 380 mg sodium, 23 g carbohydrate, 37 g protein.

4 cups oak or hickory wood chips

1 3-pound boneless leg of lamb, rolled and tied
  Salt
  Pepper

3 tablespoons grated Parmesan cheese

2 tablespoons snipped fresh parsley

6 cloves garlic, minced

2 teaspoons finely shredded lemon peel

2 fresh ears of corn, husked, cleaned, and kernels removed, or 2 cups frozen whole kernel corn, thawed

1 pound tiny new potatoes, quartered

1 small red onion, cut into ½-inch-thick wedges

2 tablespoons olive oil

1 pound fresh asparagus, trimmed and cut into 2-inch pieces, and/or small green beans, trimmed

½ cup bottled vinaigrette salad dressing

¼ cup snipped fresh dill

8 cups torn mixed salad greens

¼ cup Greek ripe olives, pitted and halved

Rhubarb-Glazed Pork Roast

For a rosy red sauce, stir in a few drops of red food coloring.

Prep: 10 minutes **Soak:** 1 hour **Grill:** 1¼ hours **Stand:** 15 minutes
Makes: 4 to 6 servings

4 cups apple, cherry,
    or peach wood chips
12 ounces fresh or frozen
    rhubarb, sliced (about
    2 cups)
1 6-ounce can frozen apple
    juice concentrate
    Few drops red food coloring
    (optional)
2 tablespoons honey
1 3-pound pork loin center rib
    roast (backbone loosened)

1. At least 1 hour before grilling, soak wood chips in enough water to cover. Drain before using.

2. For glaze, in a medium saucepan combine rhubarb, apple juice concentrate, and, if desired, red food coloring. Bring to boiling; reduce heat. Cover and simmer for 15 to 20 minutes or until rhubarb is very tender. Strain, pressing liquid out of pulp. Discard pulp. Return liquid to saucepan. Bring to boiling; reduce heat. Simmer, uncovered, about 15 minutes or until liquid is reduced to about ½ cup. Remove from heat. Stir in honey.

3. Meanwhile, insert an oven-going meat thermometer into center of roast, making sure bulb does not touch bone. In a grill with a cover arrange medium coals around a drip pan. Test for medium-low heat above the pan. Sprinkle half of the drained wood chips over the coals. Place meat, bone side down, on the grill rack over drip pan. Cover and grill for 1¼ to 1¾ hours or until meat thermometer registers 155°, brushing once with glaze during the last 15 minutes of cooking. Add additional coals and remaining wood chips as needed.

4. Remove meat from grill. Cover meat with foil; let stand for 15 minutes before carving (the temperature of the meat will rise 5° during standing). Reheat the remaining glaze until bubbly and pass with meat.

Nutrition Facts per serving: 391 calories, 15 g total fat, 102 mg cholesterol, 93 mg sodium, 30 g carbohydrate, 33 g protein.

Memphis-Style Smoked Pork with Bourbon Sauce

A humble pork roast becomes a palate-pleasing main dish for 12 when smoked over hickory chunks and served with a zesty tomato-bourbon sauce.

Prep: 25 minutes **Marinate:** 24 hours **Soak:** 1 hour **Smoke:** 4 hours
Stand: 15 minutes **Makes:** 12 servings

1. For sauce, in a medium saucepan combine tomato sauce, onion, ½ cup of the vinegar, the bourbon or beef broth, Worcestershire sauce, brown sugar, black pepper, and hot pepper sauce. Bring to boiling; reduce heat. Cover and simmer for 15 minutes; cool. Reserve 1 cup of the sauce; cover reserved sauce and refrigerate until ready to serve.

2. Meanwhile, place meat in a heavy, large self-sealing plastic bag set in a shallow bowl. For marinade, in a small bowl combine the remaining sauce and the remaining vinegar. Pour over meat. Seal bag; turn to coat meat. Marinate in the refrigerator for 24 hours, turning bag occasionally.

3. At least 1 hour before smoke cooking, soak wood chunks in enough water to cover. Drain before using.

4. Drain meat, reserving marinade. In a smoker arrange preheated coals, half of the drained wood chunks, and the water pan according to the manufacturer's directions. Pour water into pan. Place meat on rack over pan. Cover; smoke 4 to 5 hours or until tender, basting occasionally with reserved marinade during first 3 hours of smoking. Discard any remaining marinade. Add additional coals, wood chunks, and water as needed.

5. Remove meat from smoker. Cover with foil; let stand for 15 minutes before carving. Meanwhile, reheat chilled sauce until bubbly. Slice meat. Serve meat with warmed sauce.

Nutrition Facts per serving: 324 calories, 17 g total fat, 112 mg cholesterol, 253 mg sodium, 6 g carbohydrate, 30 g protein.

1 8-ounce can tomato sauce
1 cup chopped onion
1 cup vinegar
½ cup bourbon or beef broth
¼ cup Worcestershire sauce
2 tablespoons brown sugar
¼ teaspoon ground black pepper
Dash bottled hot pepper sauce
1 4½- to 5-pound boneless pork shoulder roast
8 to 10 hickory wood chunks

Caribbean Smoked Chops

A refreshing mango sauce tops the smoked-to-perfection pork chops.

Prep: 10 minutes **Soak:** 1 hour **Smoke:** 1¾ hours **Makes:** 4 servings

6 to 8 pecan or cherry wood chunks

2 to 3 teaspoons Jamaican jerk seasoning

4 bone-in or boneless pork loin or rib chops, cut 1½ inches thick (about 3 pounds total)

1 medium mango, peeled, seeded, and finely chopped (about 1 cup)

2 green onions, sliced

2 tablespoons snipped fresh parsley or cilantro

½ teaspoon finely shredded orange peel

2 teaspoons orange juice

¼ teaspoon Jamaican jerk seasoning

Fresh parsley or cilantro sprigs (optional)

1. At least 1 hour before smoke cooking, soak the wood chunks in enough water to cover. Drain before using.

2. Sprinkle the 2 to 3 teaspoons jerk seasoning evenly over chops; rub in with your fingers.

3. In a smoker arrange preheated coals, half of the drained wood chunks, and the water pan according to manufacturer's directions. Pour water into pan. Place chops on grill rack over pan. Cover and smoke for 1¾ to 2¼ hours or until the juices run clear (160°). Add additional coals, wood chunks, and water as needed.

4. Meanwhile, for sauce, in a medium bowl stir together mango, green onions, snipped parsley or cilantro, orange peel, orange juice, and the ¼ teaspoon jerk seasoning. Let stand at room temperature for 15 to 20 minutes to blend flavors. Serve the sauce over chops. If desired, garnish with parsley or cilantro sprigs.

Nutrition Facts per serving: 357 calories, 11 g total fat, 124 mg cholesterol, 188 mg sodium, 11 g carbohydrate, 50 g protein.

Mustard-Rubbed Pork Chops

In the Midwest, thick bone-in pork chops are known as Iowa chops. Throughout the country, the boneless version of this chop is sold as America's cut.

Prep: 10 minutes **Soak:** 1 hour **Grill:** 35 minutes **Makes:** 4 servings

1. At least 1 hour before grilling, soak wood chips in enough water to cover. Drain before using.

2. For rub, in a small bowl stir together dry mustard, salt, paprika, basil, pepper, and garlic powder. Sprinkle the rub evenly over the chops; rub in with your fingers.

3. In a grill with a cover arrange medium-hot coals around a drip pan. Test for medium heat above pan. Sprinkle the drained wood chips over the coals. Place chops on grill rack over pan. Cover; grill for 35 to 40 minutes or until juices run clear (160°).

Nutrition Facts per serving: 356 calories, 14 g total fat, 139 mg cholesterol, 975 mg sodium, 1 g carbohydrate, 52 g protein.

- 2 cups oak or pecan wood chips
- 1 tablespoon dry mustard
- 1½ teaspoons salt
- 1½ teaspoons paprika
- 1½ teaspoons dried basil, crushed
- 1 to 1½ teaspoons freshly ground black pepper
- ½ teaspoon garlic powder
- 4 bone-in or boneless pork loin or rib chops, cut 1¼ inches thick (about 3 pounds total)

Smoke Cook Slow and Sweet

Great-tasting smoked foods come from slow cooking at a low temperature with sweet smoke. What's sweet smoke? It's smoke with a terrific fresh wood aroma. Smoke that's stale or acrid will infuse foods with a strong, bitter taste. There are three keys to keeping smoke sweet. First, maintain a constant heat. Low heat won't create enough smoke, and a fire that's too hot will give foods a burned taste. Second, keep air flowing through the smoker or grill so the smoke keeps forming at a steady rate. And third, use seasoned high-quality wood (see Which Woods Are Best? on page 255 for more information).

Sweet and Spicy Pork Ribs

Slather on your favorite barbecue sauce for the perfect finish to these flavorful ribs.

Prep: 20 minutes **Chill:** 8 to 24 hours **Soak:** 1 hour **Grill:** 1½ hours
Makes: 6 servings

⅓ cup sugar

2 tablespoons paprika

1 tablespoon seasoned salt

1 tablespoon hickory-flavored
    salt

2 teaspoons garlic powder

2 teaspoons pepper

4 pounds pork loin back ribs

4 cups hickory wood chips

1 cup bottled barbecue sauce

1. For rub, in a small bowl combine sugar, paprika, seasoned salt, hickory-flavored salt, garlic powder, and pepper. Remove ¼ cup of the rub. (Store remaining rub in a tightly covered container.)

2. Pull membrane off the back of the ribs; trim fat from ribs. Sprinkle the ¼ cup rub evenly over both sides of ribs; rub in with your fingers. Wrap ribs tightly in plastic wrap; refrigerate for at least 8 hours or up to 24 hours.

3. At least 1 hour before grilling, soak wood chips in enough water to cover. Drain before using.

4. In a grill with a cover arrange medium-hot coals around a drip pan. Test for medium heat above pan. Sprinkle the drained wood chips over the coals. Place ribs, bone sides down, on the grill rack over pan. (Or place ribs in a rib rack; place on grill rack.) Cover and grill for 1½ to 1¾ hours or until ribs are tender. Brush once with barbecue sauce during last 15 minutes of grilling. Heat remaining barbecue sauce until bubbly; pass with ribs.

Nutrition Facts per serving: 365 calories, 19 g total fat, 75 mg cholesterol, 1,014 mg sodium, 10 g carbohydrate, 37 g protein.

Spicy Hoisin-Honey Ribs

Asian hoisin sauce melds with Mexican chipotle peppers for an exotically delicious sauce.

Prep: 30 minutes **Chill:** 1 to 4 hours **Soak:** 1 hour **Smoke:** 3¾ hours **Makes:** 6 to 8 servings

1. For rub, in a small bowl combine paprika, black pepper, and onion salt. Squeeze and rub the cut surfaces of the lime halves over ribs. Sprinkle rub evenly over both sides of ribs; rub in with your fingers. Cover; refrigerate for at least 1 hour or up to 4 hours.

2. At least 1 hour before smoke cooking, soak wood chunks in enough water to cover. Drain before using.

3. In a smoker arrange preheated coals, drained wood chunks, and the water pan according to the manufacturer's directions. Pour water into pan. Place ribs, bone sides down, on the grill rack over the water pan. (Or place ribs in a rib rack; place on grill rack.) Cover and smoke for 3¾ to 4 hours or until tender. Add additional coals, wood chunks, and water as needed.

4. Meanwhile, for sauce, in a small saucepan stir together the chipotle peppers, hoisin sauce, honey, cider vinegar, mustard, and garlic. Cook and stir over low heat until heated through. Just before serving, brush ribs with sauce. Pass remaining sauce.

Nutrition Facts per serving: 626 calories, 41 g total fat, 149 mg cholesterol, 655 mg sodium, 26 g carbohydrate, 31 g protein.

- 1 tablespoon paprika
- ½ teaspoon coarsely ground black pepper
- ¼ teaspoon onion salt
- 1 lime, cut in half
- 4 pounds meaty pork loin back ribs
- 10 to 12 oak or hickory wood chunks
- 1 to 2 tablespoons finely chopped canned chipotle peppers in adobo sauce
- ½ cup hoisin sauce
- ¼ cup honey
- 2 tablespoons cider vinegar
- 2 tablespoons Dijon-style mustard
- 2 cloves garlic, minced

Which Woods Are Best?

The tantalizing flavor of home-smoked foods depends on the wood you use during smoking. The best types are hardwoods such as oak, hickory, pecan, or maple and fruitwoods such as apple, cherry, orange, or peach. Mesquite and alder also are barbecue favorites. Avoid woods from soft needle-bearing trees such as fir or pine because their resin or sap makes foods taste bitter and harsh.

Here are some general pointers to help you decide what wood to use. Hickory is a general-purpose smoking wood that complements just about any food. Mesquite and oak are terrific with beef. Apple, cherry, and pecan are ideal for pork, poultry, or fish. Orange and peach go well with poultry. And delicate alder is perfect with fish.

Country Ribs with Peach Sauce

The sassy sauce gets a double dose of peaches from canned peach slices and peach chutney.

Prep: 10 minutes **Soak:** 1 hour **Grill:** 1½ hours **Makes:** 4 servings

4 cups peach, apple,
    or alder wood chips
1 15- to 16-ounce can peach
    slices, drained
1 medium onion, chopped
¼ cup light-colored corn syrup
    or honey
2 tablespoons bottled steak
    sauce
¼ teaspoon ground cumin
½ cup peach chutney
1 or 2 fresh jalapeño peppers,
    seeded and finely chopped*
2½ to 3 pounds pork
    country-style ribs
    Fresh jalapeño peppers
    (optional)

1. At least 1 hour before grilling, soak wood chips in enough water to cover. Drain before using.

2. For sauce, in a blender container or food processor bowl combine the peach slices, onion, corn syrup or honey, steak sauce, and cumin. Cover and blend or process until nearly smooth. Pour into a small saucepan. Stir in the chutney and finely chopped jalapeño peppers. Cook and stir over low heat until heated through.

3. In a grill with a cover arrange medium-hot coals around a drip pan. Test for medium heat above the pan. Sprinkle half of the drained wood chips over the coals. Place ribs, bone sides down, on the grill rack over pan. (Or place ribs in a rib rack; place on grill rack.) Cover and grill for 1½ to 2 hours or until ribs are tender, brushing once with sauce during the last 15 minutes of grilling. Add additional coals and remaining wood chips as needed.

4. Reheat the remaining sauce until bubbly and pass with ribs. If desired, garnish ribs with additional jalapeño peppers.

Nutrition Facts per serving: **469 calories, 15 g total fat, 69 mg cholesterol, 230 mg sodium, 67 g carbohydrate, 19 g protein.**

Note: Because chile peppers, such as jalapeños, contain volatile oils that can burn your skin and eyes, avoid direct contact with them as much as possible. When working with chile peppers, wear plastic or rubber gloves. If your bare hands do touch the chile peppers, wash your hands and nails well with soap and warm water.

Smoked Gremolata Chicken

Garlic, parsley, and lemon peel—a combination typical of the Italian garnish known as gremolata—are succulent seasonings for smoke-cooked chicken.

Prep: 15 minutes **Soak:** 1 hour **Smoke:** 3¼ hours **Stand:** 15 minutes
Makes: 6 to 8 servings

1. At least 1 hour before smoke cooking, soak wood chunks in enough water to cover. Drain before using.

2. For rub, in a small bowl combine snipped parsley, lemon peel, and pepper. Remove the neck and giblets from chicken. Sprinkle rub evenly over chicken; rub in with your fingers.

3. With a sharp knife, cut off top ½ inch from garlic bulb to expose ends of the individual cloves. Leaving garlic bulb whole, remove any loose, papery outer layers. Place the garlic bulb and lemon wedges from the 1 small lemon in cavity of chicken. Skewer neck skin to back. Twist wing tips under back. Tie legs to tail. Insert an oven-going meat thermometer into the center of an inside thigh muscle, making sure bulb does not touch bone.

4. In a smoker arrange preheated coals, half of the drained wood chunks, and the water pan according to manufacturer's directions. Pour water into pan. Place chicken, breast side up, on the grill rack over pan. Cover and smoke for 3¼ to 4 hours or until thermometer registers 180°. At this time, drumsticks move easily in their sockets and chicken is no longer pink. Add additional coals, wood chunks, and water as needed.

5. Remove chicken from smoker. Cover chicken with foil; let stand 15 minutes before carving. Remove garlic and lemon from cavity. If desired, season chicken with salt. If desired, garnish with parsley sprigs and additional lemon wedges.

Nutrition Facts per serving: 363 calories, 20 g total fat, 162 mg cholesterol, 120 mg sodium, 2 g carbohydrate, 41 g protein.

- **8 to 10 apple or cherry wood chunks**
- **2 to 3 tablespoons snipped fresh flat-leaf parsley**
- **2 teaspoons finely shredded lemon peel**
- **¼ teaspoon coarsely ground black pepper**
- **1 6- to 7-pound whole roasting chicken**
- **1 bulb garlic**
- **1 small lemon, cut into wedges**
  Salt (optional)
  Fresh flat-leaf parsley sprigs (optional)
  Lemon wedges (optional)

Sweet 'n' Sticky Chicken

Finger-lickin' good describes this saucy smoked chicken.

Prep: 10 minutes **Soak:** 1 hour **Smoke:** 1½ hours **Makes:** 6 servings

6 to 8 maple or hickory
    wood chunks
6 chicken legs (thigh-
    drumstick pieces)
1½ teaspoons dried oregano,
    crushed
1½ teaspoons dried thyme,
    crushed
½ teaspoon garlic salt
¼ teaspoon onion powder
¼ teaspoon pepper
1 recipe Sweet 'n' Sticky
    Barbecue Sauce

1. At least 1 hour before smoke cooking, soak wood chunks in enough water to cover. Drain before using.

2. If desired, remove skin from chicken. For rub, in a small bowl combine oregano, thyme, garlic salt, onion powder, and pepper. Sprinkle rub evenly over chicken; rub in with your fingers.

3. In a smoker arrange preheated coals, half of the drained wood chunks, and the water pan according to manufacturer's directions. Pour water into pan. Place chicken on the grill rack over pan. Cover and smoke for 1½ to 2 hours or until chicken is tender and juices run clear. Add additional coals, wood chunks, and water as needed.

4. Remove chicken from smoker. Brush chicken generously with Sweet 'n' Sticky Barbecue Sauce. Pass remaining sauce with chicken.

Sweet 'n' Sticky Barbecue Sauce: In a small saucepan cook ½ cup finely chopped onion and 2 cloves garlic, minced, in 1 tablespoon hot olive oil until onion is tender. Stir in ¾ cup bottled chili sauce, ½ cup unsweetened pineapple juice, ¼ cup honey, 2 tablespoons Worcestershire sauce, and ½ teaspoon dry mustard. Bring to boiling; reduce heat. Simmer, uncovered, for 20 to 25 minutes or until desired consistency. Makes about 1¼ cups.

Nutrition Facts per serving: 535 calories, 29 g total fat, 186 mg cholesterol, 725 mg sodium, 25 g carbohydrate, 43 g protein.

Salt and Pepper Chickens

A simple rub made with four kinds of salt and two kinds of pepper dresses up these grilled birds.

Prep: 20 minutes **Soak:** 1 hour **Chill:** 1 hour **Grill:** 1¼ hours **Stand:** 10 minutes
Makes: 8 servings

1. At least 1 hour before grilling, soak wood chips in enough water to cover. Drain before using.

2. For rub, in a small bowl stir together salt, onion salt, garlic salt, seasoned salt, paprika, black pepper, and, if desired, red pepper. Sprinkle rub evenly over chickens; rub in with your fingers. Skewer neck skin to backs. Tie legs to tails. Twist wing tips under backs. Cover and refrigerate 1 hour.

3. In a grill with a cover arrange medium-hot coals around a drip pan. Test for medium heat above the pan. Sprinkle half of the drained wood chips over the coals. Place chickens, breast sides up, on grill rack over pan. Cover and grill for 1¼ to 1½ hours or until an instant-read thermometer inserted into center of an inside thigh muscle registers 180° (make sure bulb does not touch bone). At this time, drumsticks move easily in their sockets and chicken is no longer pink. Add the remaining drained wood chips halfway through grilling. Add additional coals as necessary.

4. Remove chickens from grill. Cover with foil; let stand 10 minutes before carving. If desired, garnish platter with fresh fruit.

Nutrition Facts per serving: 323 calories, 18 g total fat, 118 mg cholesterol, 911 mg sodium, 0 g carbohydrate, 37 g protein.

**4 cups hickory or mesquite
   wood chips**
1 teaspoon salt
1 teaspoon onion salt
1 teaspoon garlic salt
1 teaspoon seasoned salt
1 teaspoon paprika
**1 teaspoon ground black
   pepper**
**¼ teaspoon ground red pepper
   (optional)**
**2 3- to 3½-pound whole
   broiler-fryer chickens
   Fresh fruit (optional)**

Smoky Chicken Wraps

Serve these hearty sandwiches with sliced tomatoes drizzled with your favorite herb vinaigrette.

Prep: 20 minutes **Soak:** 1 hour **Marinate:** 30 minutes **Grill:** 12 minutes
Makes: 4 servings

---

2 cups mesquite wood chips

12 ounces skinless, boneless chicken breasts

1 tablespoon cooking oil

1 tablespoon Worcestershire sauce

1 teaspoon snipped fresh thyme

¼ teaspoon pepper

½ of an 8-ounce tub plain cream cheese

2 oil-packed dried tomatoes, drained and finely chopped

2 tablespoons chopped pine nuts or almonds (optional)

Salt

Pepper

4 8- or 9-inch tomato tortillas or plain flour tortillas

16 fresh basil leaves, cut into strips

1. At least 1 hour before grilling, soak wood chips in enough water to cover. Drain before using.

2. Place chicken in a shallow dish. For marinade, in a small bowl combine oil, Worcestershire sauce, thyme, and the ¼ teaspoon pepper; pour over chicken. Cover; marinate in the refrigerator for 30 minutes.

3. In a small bowl stir together cream cheese, dried tomatoes, and, if desired, nuts. If necessary, stir in enough water to make a spreading consistency. Season to taste with salt and pepper; set aside. Wrap tortillas in heavy foil.

4. Lightly grease the rack of a grill with a cover. Sprinkle drained wood chips over medium coals. Place chicken breasts on rack directly over medium coals. Cover and grill for 12 to 15 minutes or until chicken is tender and no longer pink, turning chicken once and placing foil packet of tortillas on grill rack halfway through grilling.

5. Transfer chicken breasts to a cutting board; cool slightly and thinly slice. Spread the cream cheese mixture over tortillas; sprinkle with basil. Divide chicken among tortillas; roll up.

Nutrition Facts per serving: **454 calories, 21 g total fat, 77 mg cholesterol, 798 mg sodium, 42 g carbohydrate, 26 g protein.**

Turkey Breast with Apple Stuffing

Heat the savory apple stuffing in a foil packet on the grill.

Prep: 25 minutes **Soak:** 1 hour **Grill:** 1¼ hours **Stand:** 10 minutes **Makes:** 8 servings

1. Thaw turkey, if frozen. At least 1 hour before grilling, soak wood chips in enough water to cover. Drain before using.

2. In a grill with a cover arrange medium-hot coals around edge of grill. Test for medium heat in center of grill (not over coals). Sprinkle about 1 cup of the wood chips onto hot coals. Insert an oven-going meat thermometer into thickest part of turkey breast, making sure bulb does not touch bone.

3. Place turkey breast on a rack in a roasting pan. Place the pan on grill rack in center of grill (not over coals). Cover and grill for 1¼ to 2 hours or until meat thermometer registers 170°. Add additional coals and remaining wood chips as needed.

4. Meanwhile, for stuffing, in a large bowl combine bread, apple, nuts, green onion, juice, melted margarine, and thyme. Tear off a 24×18-inch piece of heavy foil. Spoon stuffing down the center of the foil. Bring up 2 opposite edges of foil; seal with a double fold. Fold in remaining ends to completely enclose the stuffing, leaving space for steam to build. Place foil packet directly over medium-hot coals and grill for the last 20 minutes of turkey grilling or until stuffing is heated through.

5. In small saucepan combine jelly, the 2 tablespoons water, and the ginger. Cook and stir until jelly is melted. Brush jelly mixture on turkey during last 15 minutes of grilling. Remove turkey from grill. Cover with foil; let stand 10 minutes before carving. Serve with stuffing.

Nutrition Facts per serving: 229 calories, 7 g total fat, 41 mg cholesterol, 189 mg sodium, 21 g carbohydrate, 21 g protein

- 1 2- to 2½-pound fresh or frozen bone-in turkey breast half
- 3 cups apple or orange wood chips
- 3 cups dry wheat bread cubes
- 1 large apple, coarsely shredded (about 1 cup)
- ¼ cup chopped almonds or hazelnuts (filberts), toasted
- 3 tablespoons thinly sliced green onion
- ⅓ to ½ cup apple juice, apple cider, or water
- 2 tablespoons margarine or butter, melted
- 1 tablespoon snipped fresh thyme or ¼ teaspoon dried thyme, crushed
- ⅓ cup apple jelly
- 2 tablespoons water
- ¼ teaspoon ground ginger

Chipotle-Rubbed Turkey

Both the wood chips on the coals and the chipotle pepper in the rub contribute to the fantastic smoky flavor of this mouthwatering turkey breast.

Prep: 20 minutes **Soak:** 1 hour **Grill:** 1¼ hours **Stand:** 10 minutes
Makes: 8 to 10 servings

1 2- to 2½-pound fresh or frozen bone-in turkey breast half

3 cups hickory or mesquite wood chips

1 teaspoon ground coriander

½ teaspoon paprika

¼ to ½ teaspoon ground black pepper

1 small dried chipotle pepper, seeded and crushed, or ⅛ to ¼ teaspoon ground red pepper

2 teaspoons cooking oil

Hot cooked rice (optional)*

Fresh parsley or cilantro sprigs (optional)

Fresh chile peppers (optional)

1. Thaw turkey, if frozen. At least 1 hour before grilling, soak wood chips in enough water to cover. Meanwhile, in a small bowl combine coriander, paprika, black pepper, and chipotle pepper. Drain wood chips before using.

2. Remove skin and excess fat from turkey breast. Brush skinned surface of turkey with oil. Sprinkle rub evenly over turkey; rub in with your fingers. Insert an oven-going meat thermometer into the thickest part of the turkey breast, making sure bulb does not touch bone.

3. In a grill with a cover arrange medium-hot coals around the edge of grill. Sprinkle half of the drained wood chips over coals. Test for medium heat above the center of the grill (not over coals). Place turkey, bone side down, in a roasting pan in center of grill rack. Cover and grill for 1¼ to 2 hours or until meat thermometer registers 170°. Add additional coals and remaining wood chips as needed. Remove turkey from grill. Loosely cover with foil. Let stand for 10 minutes before carving. If desired, serve with rice and garnish with parsley or cilantro sprigs and fresh chile peppers.

Nutrition Facts per serving: 105 calories, 3 g total fat, 41 mg cholesterol, 38 mg sodium, 0 g carbohydrate, 18 g protein.

Note: Dress up the hot cooked rice by stirring in some chopped red or green sweet pepper and some snipped fresh parsley or cilantro.

Chili-Mustard Turkey Breast

Spreading an onion-mustard mixture under the skin gives turkey another flavor dimension.

Prep: 20 minutes **Soak:** 1 hour **Grill:** 1¼ hours **Stand:** 10 minutes
Makes: 8 to 10 servings

1. Thaw turkey, if frozen. At least 1 hour before grilling, soak wood chips in enough water to cover. Drain before using.

2. Lightly coat a small skillet with nonstick cooking spray. Preheat over medium heat. Add onion and cook until tender. Stir in brown mustard, brown sugar, chili powder, cumin, and pepper. Cook 1 minute more.

3. Starting at the edge of the turkey breast, slip your fingers between skin and meat, loosening skin to make a pocket. Using your hands or a spoon, spread onion mixture evenly under skin. Insert an oven-going meat thermometer into thickest part of turkey breast, making sure bulb does not touch bone.

4. In a grill with a cover arrange medium-hot coals around edge of grill. Test for medium heat above center of grill (not over the coals). Sprinkle half of the wood chips over coals. Place turkey, bone side down, in a roasting pan in center of grill rack. Cover and grill for 1¼ to 2 hours or until meat thermometer registers 170°. Add additional coals and remaining wood chips as needed. Remove turkey from grill. Loosely cover with foil. Let turkey stand for 10 minutes before carving.

Nutrition Facts per serving: 131 calories, 3 g total fat, 70 mg cholesterol, 89 mg sodium, 1 g carbohydrate, 24 g protein.

1 2- to 2½-pound fresh or frozen bone-in turkey breast half
3 cups hickory or mesquite wood chips (optional)
  Nonstick cooking spray
2 tablespoons chopped onion
2 tablespoons brown mustard
2 teaspoons brown sugar
½ teaspoon chili powder
⅛ teaspoon ground cumin
⅛ teaspoon pepper

Double-Glazed Turkey Breasts

Offer guests a choice yet use only one recipe. Here one of the turkey breast halves gets a five-spice glaze and the other gets a honey-mustard glaze.

Prep: 10 minutes **Soak:** 1 hour **Grill:** 1¼ hours **Stand:** 10 minutes
Makes: 8 to 10 servings

---

2 2- to 2½-pound fresh or frozen bone-in turkey breast halves
4 cups hickory or mesquite wood chips
⅓ cup orange marmalade
1 tablespoon hoisin sauce
¼ teaspoon five-spice powder
¼ teaspoon garlic powder
¼ cup honey
1 tablespoon Dijon-style mustard
1 tablespoon white wine Worcestershire sauce
1 tablespoon margarine or butter, melted
1 tablespoon cooking oil

1. Thaw turkey, if frozen. At least 1 hour before grilling, soak wood chips in enough water to cover. Drain before using.

2. For five-spice glaze, in a small bowl stir together orange marmalade, hoisin sauce, five-spice powder, and garlic powder. Set aside.

3. For honey-mustard glaze, in a small bowl stir together honey, mustard, white wine Worcestershire sauce, and melted margarine or butter. Set aside.

4. Remove bone from each breast half. Brush turkey with oil. Insert an oven-going meat thermometer into the thickest part of 1 of the turkey breasts.

5. In a grill with a cover arrange medium-hot coals around a drip pan. Test for medium heat above the pan. Sprinkle half of the drained wood chips over the coals. Place turkey breasts, side by side, on the grill rack over pan. Cover and grill for 1¼ to 2 hours or until meat thermometer registers 170°, brushing one breast with five-spice glaze and the other breast with honey-mustard glaze once during the last 15 minutes of grilling. Add additional coals and remaining wood chips as needed.

6. Remove turkey breasts from grill. Cover turkey with foil. Let stand for 10 minutes before carving. Heat any of the remaining glazes until bubbly; pass with turkey.

Nutrition Facts per serving with honey-mustard glaze: 422 calories, 18 g total fat, 132 mg cholesterol, 242 mg sodium, 18 g carbohydrate, 45 g protein.
Nutrition Facts per serving with five-spice glaze: 400 calories, 15 g total fat, 132 mg cholesterol, 149 mg sodium, 19 g carbohydrate, 45 g protein.

Smoky Bass with Carambola Salsa

Fruitwood chips—orange, apple, or cherry—give the fish a pleasantly smoky, slightly fruity flavor.

Prep: 10 minutes **Soak:** 1 hour **Grill:** 14 minutes **Makes:** 4 servings

1. Thaw fish, if frozen. At least 1 hour before grilling, soak wood chips in enough water to cover. Drain before using.

2. For salsa, in a dry skillet cook cumin seeds over medium-high heat for 1 to 2 minutes or until toasted, shaking the skillet frequently. Set aside.

3. Slice 1 of the carambola; cover and refrigerate for garnish. Chop the remaining carambola. Finely shred the green part of the lime peel. Set aside. Peel, section, and chop the lime. In a small bowl combine cumin seeds, chopped carambola, chopped lime, poblano pepper, cilantro, and ⅛ teaspoon of the salt. Cover and refrigerate until ready to serve.

4. Rinse fish; pat dry with paper towels. Sprinkle with the finely shredded lime peel, the remaining salt, and the ground red pepper.

5. In a grill with a cover arrange medium-hot coals around a drip pan. Test for medium heat above the pan. Sprinkle the drained wood chips over the coals. Lightly grease grill rack. Place fish on the grill rack over pan. Cover and grill for 14 to 18 minutes or just until fish flakes easily with a fork, turning once halfway through grilling.

6. Serve fish with the salsa. Garnish with the sliced carambola.

Nutrition Facts per serving: **143 calories, 3 g total fat, 47 mg cholesterol, 280 mg sodium, 8 g carbohydrate, 22 g protein.**

- 4 4-ounce fresh or frozen sea bass or red snapper fillets, about 1 inch thick
- 2 cups orange, apple, or cherry wood chips
- ½ to 1 teaspoon cumin seeds
- 3 large carambola (star fruit)
- 1 small lime
- ½ of a small fresh poblano pepper, seeded and finely chopped (see note on page 256)
- 2 tablespoons snipped fresh cilantro
- ½ teaspoon salt
- ¼ teaspoon ground red pepper

Planked Salmon with Cucumber-Dill Sauce

Native Americans in the Pacific Northwest taught early settlers how to place fish on a piece of wood and smoke it over an open fire. Here, a similar technique gives salmon a subtle smokiness.

Prep: 10 minutes **Chill:** 8 to 24 hours **Grill:** 18 minutes **Makes:** 4 to 6 servings

1 1½-pound fresh or frozen
  salmon fillet (with skin),
  about 1 inch thick
1 tablespoon brown sugar
1 teaspoon salt
¼ teaspoon pepper
  Cedar grill plank*
1 recipe Cucumber-Dill Sauce
  Lemon slices, twisted
  (optional)
  Cucumber slices, twisted
  (optional)
  Fresh dill sprigs (optional)

1. Thaw salmon, if frozen. Rinse salmon; pat dry with paper towels. Place salmon, skin side down, in a shallow dish. For rub, in a small bowl stir together brown sugar, salt, and pepper. Sprinkle rub evenly over salmon (not on skin side); rub in with your fingers. Cover and refrigerate for at least 8 hours or up to 24 hours.

2. Wet both sides of cedar grill plank under running water; set aside.

3. In a grill with a cover arrange medium-hot coals around edge of grill. Place salmon, skin side down, on grill plank. Place plank in center of grill rack (not over coals). Cover and grill for 18 to 22 minutes or just until fish flakes easily with a fork.

4. To serve, cut salmon into 4 to 6 pieces. Slide a metal spatula between the fish and skin to release pieces from plank. Serve with Cucumber-Dill Sauce. If desired, garnish with lemon twists, cucumber twists, and dill sprigs.

Cucumber-Dill Sauce: In a small bowl combine ⅓ cup finely chopped cucumber, 3 tablespoons plain yogurt, 2 tablespoons mayonnaise or salad dressing, 2 teaspoons snipped fresh dill, and 2 teaspoons prepared horseradish. Cover and chill until serving time or up to 4 hours. Makes ⅔ cup.

Nutrition Facts per serving: 357 calories, 21 g total fat, 109 mg cholesterol, 715 mg sodium, 3 g carbohydrate, 37 g protein.

Note: Look for a cedar grill plank at a store that specializes in grilling supplies.

Double-Smoked Salmon With Horseradish Cream

With smoked salmon stuffed into pockets in the fresh salmon fillets plus cooking in a smoker, this extraordinary dish really has a double-smoked flavor.

Prep: 15 minutes **Soak:** 1 hour **Smoke:** 30 minutes **Makes:** 4 servings

1. Thaw fish, if frozen. At least 1 hour before smoke cooking, soak wood chunks in enough water to cover. Drain wood chunks before using.

2. Rinse fish; pat dry with paper towels. Make a pocket in each fish fillet by cutting horizontally from 1 side almost through to the other side. Fill pockets with slices of smoked salmon and 2 teaspoons of the dill, folding salmon slices as necessary to fit. Brush fish with lemon juice and top with 2 teaspoons of the dill. Sprinkle with salt and pepper.

3. In a smoker arrange preheated coals, drained wood chunks, and water pan according to the manufacturer's directions. Pour water into pan. Place fish, skin sides down, on grill rack over water pan. Cover and smoke about 30 minutes or just until fish flakes easily when tested with a fork.

4. Meanwhile, for sauce, in a small bowl combine the remaining dill, the sour cream, horseradish, and green onion. Serve fish with the sauce.

Nutrition Facts per serving: **245 calories, 13 g total fat, 48 mg cholesterol, 337 mg sodium, 2 g carbohydrate, 29 g protein.**

- 4 6-ounce fresh or frozen salmon fillets (with skin), about 1 inch thick
- 4 hickory or apple wood chunks
- 4 slices smoked salmon (about 3 ounces)
- 2 tablespoons snipped fresh dill
- 1 tablespoon lemon juice
  Salt
  Pepper
- ½ cup dairy sour cream
- 4 teaspoons prepared horseradish
- 1 green onion, thinly sliced

Tropical Halibut Steaks

A touch of curry powder complements the fruit-studded sauce.

Prep: 15 minutes **Marinate:** 1 hour **Soak:** 1 hour **Smoke:** 45 minutes **Makes:** 4 servings

4 6-ounce fresh or frozen halibut steaks, cut 1 inch thick
4 apple or orange wood chunks
⅓ cup pineapple-orange juice
⅓ cup soy sauce
¼ teaspoon curry powder
1 8-ounce can pineapple chunks (juice-pack)
¼ of a medium cantaloupe or ½ of a papaya
Dash curry powder
Water
2 teaspoons cornstarch
2 tablespoons coconut, toasted

1. Thaw fish, if frozen. At least 1 hour before smoke cooking, soak wood chunks in enough water to cover. Drain before using.

2. Rinse fish; pat dry. Place fish in a heavy, large self-sealing plastic bag set in a shallow bowl. For marinade, in a small bowl combine pineapple-orange juice, soy sauce, and the ¼ teaspoon curry powder. Pour marinade over fish. Seal bag; turn to coat fish. Marinate in refrigerator for 1 hour, turning bag occasionally.

3. Meanwhile, for sauce, drain pineapple chunks, reserving juice. Peel and seed cantaloupe or papaya. Finely chop pineapple and cantaloupe or papaya. In a small saucepan combine the chopped fruit and the dash curry powder. Add enough water to the reserved pineapple juice to measure ½ cup liquid. Stir in cornstarch; add to the fruit mixture. Cook and stir over medium heat until thickened and bubbly. Cook and stir for 2 minutes more. Remove from heat; set aside.

4. Drain fish, reserving marinade. In a smoker arrange preheated coals, drained wood chunks, and water pan according to the manufacturer's directions. Pour water into pan. Grease grill rack. Place fish on rack over water pan. Cover; smoke 45 to 60 minutes or just until fish flakes easily when tested with a fork, brushing once with reserved marinade halfway through smoke cooking. Discard any remaining marinade. To serve, reheat sauce and spoon over fish. Sprinkle fish with toasted coconut.

Nutrition Facts per serving: 262 calories, 5 g total fat, 54 mg cholesterol, 740 mg sodium, 16 g carbohydrate, 38 g protein.

Honey-Bourbon Salmon

This simple yet sophisticated salmon gets distinctive flavor from the bourbon in the marinade.

Prep: 10 minutes **Soak:** 1 hour **Marinate:** 1 hour **Grill:** 14 minutes **Makes:** 4 servings

1. Thaw salmon, if frozen. Rinse salmon and pat dry with paper towels. At least 1 hour before grilling, soak wood chips in enough water to cover. Drain before using.

2. Place salmon in a heavy, large self-sealing plastic bag set in a shallow bowl. In a small bowl stir together the bourbon, brown sugar, honey, soy sauce, ginger, and pepper. Pour over fish in bag. Seal bag; turn to coat fish. Marinate in the refrigerator for 1 hour, turning bag occasionally.

3. Drain fish, reserving marinade. In a grill with a cover arrange medium-hot coals around a drip pan. Test for medium heat above pan. Sprinkle the drained wood chips over the coals. Lightly grease the grill rack. Place fish on rack over pan. Cover and grill for 14 to 18 minutes or just until fish flakes easily when tested with a fork, turning once halfway through grilling.

4. Meanwhile, in a small saucepan heat reserved marinade to boiling; reduce heat. Simmer, uncovered, for 5 to 10 minutes or until slightly thickened. Before serving, brush heated marinade over fish; pass any remaining with fish. If desired, serve with hot cooked rice pilaf.

Nutrition Facts per serving: **402 calories, 15 g total fat, 105 mg cholesterol, 162 mg sodium, 18 g carbohydrate, 36 g protein.**

- **4** **6-ounce fresh or frozen salmon steaks, cut 1 inch thick**
- **2 cups apple or alder wood chips**
- **¾ cup bourbon**
- **½ cup packed brown sugar**
- **2 tablespoons honey**
- **2 teaspoons soy sauce**
- **½ teaspoon ground ginger**
- **¼ teaspoon pepper**
  Hot cooked rice pilaf (optional)

Smoked Salmon with Apple Glaze

Glaze the smoked fish with a drizzle of melted apple jelly.

Prep: 15 minutes **Marinate:** 1 to 2 hours **Soak:** 1 hour **Smoke:** 1¼ hours
Makes: 4 servings

- 2 12-ounce fresh or frozen salmon fillets
- ¾ cup frozen apple juice concentrate, thawed
- 1 tablespoon snipped fresh rosemary or 1 teaspoon dried rosemary, crushed
- ½ teaspoon coarsely ground black pepper
- ¼ teaspoon salt
- 4 to 6 alder or pecan wood chunks
- 2 tablespoons apple jelly, melted
  Steamed beet greens or other fresh greens (optional)

1. Thaw fish, if frozen. Rinse fish; pat dry. Place fish in a shallow nonmetallic dish. For marinade, in a small bowl combine juice concentrate, rosemary, pepper, and salt. Set aside ¼ cup of the marinade. Pour remaining marinade over fish; turn fish to coat. Cover; marinate in refrigerator at least 1 hour or up to 2 hours.

2. At least 1 hour before smoke cooking, soak wood chunks in enough water to cover. Drain before using.

3. Drain fish, discarding marinade. In a smoker arrange preheated coals, drained wood chunks, and water pan according to manufacturer's directions. Pour water into pan. Place fish on grill rack over water pan. Cover and smoke for 1¼ to 1½ hours or just until fish flakes easily with a fork, brushing with the reserved ¼ cup marinade after 1 hour smoke cooking. Add additional coals, wood chunks, and water as needed.

4. Just before serving, drizzle fish with melted apple jelly. If desired, serve with steamed greens.

Nutrition Facts per serving: **311 calories, 6 g total fat, 88 mg cholesterol, 276 mg sodium, 29 g carbohydrate, 34 g protein.**

When Cold Winds Blow

Although smoke cooking is typically a warm weather activity, there's no reason you can't enjoy a smoke-cooked meal when the temperature drops. But you'll need to plan ahead. For most smoke-cooking recipes, the cooking times are based on assumptions that the temperature is above 60° and the winds are calm. If you want to smoke cook on a cold or windy day, make sure to have extra briquettes on hand because it will take more coals to keep the fire up to temperature. Also assume cooking times will be longer than those suggested in the recipe directions.

Raspberry-Shrimp Salad

Succulent shrimp paired with plump fresh raspberries—now that's dining extraordinaire.

Prep: 20 minutes **Soak:** 1 hour **Grill:** 8 minutes **Makes:** 4 servings

1. At least 1 hour before grilling, soak wood chips and wooden skewers in enough water to cover. Drain wood chips and skewers before using.

2. Thaw shrimp, if frozen. Peel and devein shrimp, leaving tails intact. Rinse shrimp; pat dry with paper towels. Loosely thread shrimp onto soaked skewers.

3. For vinaigrette, in a blender container or food processor bowl combine 1 cup raspberries, the oil, vinegar, sugar, orange peel, and mustard. Cover and blend or process until smooth; set aside.

4. Remove tips and strings from pea pods. In a small covered saucepan cook pea pods in a small amount of boiling water for 2 to 4 minutes or until crisp-tender. Drain; set aside.

5. In a grill with a cover arrange medium-hot coals around a drip pan. Test for medium heat above the pan. Sprinkle the drained wood chips over the coals. Lightly grease grill rack. Place skewers on rack over drip pan. Cover and grill for 8 to 10 minutes or until shrimp turn opaque.

6. To serve, arrange the torn lettuce and pea pods on 4 dinner plates. Divide the grilled shrimp among the plates. Top with 1 cup raspberries. Serve with vinaigrette.

Nutrition Facts per serving: 271 calories, 16 g total fat, 129 mg cholesterol, 135 mg sodium, 13 g carbohydrate, 19 g protein.

- **2 cups orange or peach wood chips**
- **8 6- to 8-inch wooden skewers**
- **1 pound fresh or frozen jumbo shrimp in shells**
- **1 cup fresh raspberries**
- **¼ cup olive oil or salad oil**
- **¼ cup white wine vinegar or white vinegar**
- **1 teaspoon sugar**
- **1 teaspoon finely shredded orange peel**
- **¼ teaspoon dry mustard**
- **1 cup fresh pea pods**
- **6 cups torn red-tipped leaf lettuce and/or other leaf lettuce**
- **1 cup fresh raspberries**

Smoked Portobello and Walnut Pasta

Grilling portobello mushrooms, zucchini, and sweet peppers over hickory chips gives the vegetables magnificent flavor.

Prep: 20 minutes **Soak:** 1 hour **Grill:** 30 minutes **Makes:** 6 side-dish servings

4 cups hickory wood chips
3 tablespoons olive oil
2 tablespoons white wine vinegar
1 tablespoon snipped fresh tarragon
1 tablespoon snipped fresh thyme
2 cloves garlic, minced
½ teaspoon ground black pepper
¼ teaspoon salt
8 ounces fresh portobello mushrooms
2 medium zucchini, halved lengthwise
2 medium red sweet peppers, halved lengthwise, or 4 plum tomatoes, halved lengthwise and seeded
¾ cup walnut pieces
2 cups dried bow-tie pasta (about 6 ounces)
½ cup finely shredded Parmesan cheese or 1 cup crumbled feta cheese
¼ cup fresh basil cut into thin strips

1. At least 1 hour before grilling, soak wood chips in enough water to cover. Drain before using.

2. For dressing, in a small bowl combine olive oil, vinegar, tarragon, thyme, garlic, black pepper, and salt; set aside. Cut mushroom stems off even with caps; discard stems. Lightly rinse mushroom caps; gently pat dry with paper towels.

3. In a grill with a cover arrange medium-hot coals around a drip pan. Test for medium heat above the pan. Sprinkle drained wood chips over coals. Place mushrooms, zucchini, and sweet peppers or tomatoes on grill rack over pan; brush with some of the dressing. Place walnuts on a piece of heavy foil; place on grill rack. Cover and grill for 15 minutes. Remove walnuts from grill. Turn vegetables; brush with remaining dressing. Cover and grill about 15 minutes more or until peppers are crisp-tender and mushrooms are tender.

4. Meanwhile, cook pasta according to package directions; drain. Return pasta to hot pan. Cut vegetables into bite-size pieces. Add grilled vegetables, walnuts, cheese, and basil to cooked pasta; toss to combine. Serve immediately.

Nutrition Facts per serving: **316 calories, 20 g total fat, 31 mg cholesterol, 205 mg sodium, 27 g carbohydrate, 11 g protein.**

Smoky Gazpacho

Grilling the sweet peppers, tomatoes, onions, and jalapeño peppers over wood chips adds a delightfully different dimension to this classic chilled soup.

Prep: 40 minutes **Soak:** 1 hour **Grill:** 40 minutes **Chill:** 2 to 24 hours **Makes:** 8 side-dish servings

1. At least 1 hour before grilling, soak wood chips in enough water to cover. Drain before using.

2. Brush sweet peppers, tomatoes, onion, and jalapeño peppers with olive oil.

3. In a grill with a cover sprinkle wood chips over medium-low coals. Place vegetables on grill rack directly over coals. Cover and grill until vegetables are tender, turning once halfway through grilling. (Allow about 40 minutes for onion, 30 minutes for sweet peppers, and 20 minutes for tomatoes and jalapeño peppers.) Remove vegetables from grill as they are done.

4. Wrap sweet peppers and jalapeño peppers in foil; let stand for 20 minutes. Remove and discard pepper skins. Place about half of each of the grilled vegetables and half of the garlic in a blender container or food processor bowl. Cover and blend or process until smooth. Transfer to a large storage container. Repeat with the remaining grilled vegetables and the remaining garlic. Add to storage container. Stir in chicken broth, cucumber, cilantro, lime juice, salt, and black pepper. Cover and chill for at least 2 hours or up to 24 hours.

5. To serve, ladle into chilled bowls or mugs. If desired, garnish with lime slices.

Nutrition Facts per serving: **78 calories, 4 g total fat, 0 mg cholesterol, 240 mg sodium, 9 g carbohydrate, 3 g protein.**

2 cups hickory wood chips
5 medium red sweet peppers, quartered lengthwise
4 large tomatoes, halved lengthwise and seeded
1 medium onion, cut into ½-inch-thick slices
3 or 4 fresh jalapeño peppers, halved lengthwise and seeded (see note on page 256)
2 tablespoons olive oil
2 cloves garlic, minced
1 14-ounce can chicken broth
¾ cup chopped, seeded cucumber
1 tablespoon snipped fresh cilantro
1 tablespoon lime juice
¼ teaspoon salt
¼ teaspoon ground black pepper
Lime slices (optional)

Grill-Smoked Mushrooms

Enhance grilled steaks or chicken breasts by topping them with these flavorful mushrooms.

Prep: 5 minutes **Soak:** 1 hour **Grill:** 45 minutes **Makes:** 4 to 6 side-dish servings

---

2 cups hickory or oak wood
   chips
4 cups thickly sliced or halved
   fresh mushrooms
¼ cup butter or margarine,
   cut up
1 teaspoon instant chicken
   bouillon granules

1. At least 1 hour before grilling, soak wood chips in enough water to cover. Drain before using.

2. In an 8×8×2-inch or 9×9×2-inch baking pan or disposable foil pan combine the mushrooms, butter, and bouillon granules.

3. In a grill with a cover arrange medium-hot coals around edge of grill. Test for medium heat above center of grill. Sprinkle wood chips over coals. Place mushrooms in pan on the grill rack over center of grill. Cover and grill for 45 to 60 minutes or until mushrooms are tender, stirring once halfway through grilling.

Nutrition Facts per serving: **136 calories, 14 g total fat, 33 mg cholesterol, 344 mg sodium, 3 g carbohydrate, 3 g protein.**

Raising the Flavor Ante

While smoke cooking makes grilled foods irresistible, you can boost their flavor even more by adding a seasoning to the smoker pan. Liquids such as wine, fruit juice, or a marinade are all excellent options, as are herbs and spices—such as dill, rosemary, tarragon, cinnamon, and cardamom—added to the water. As the seasonings steam, the flavor particles combine with the smoke and condense on whatever is being grilled. Another way to add a pleasingly unique note is to drop a couple of cloves of garlic, several bay leaves, or a few strips of orange or lemon peel into the water.

Grilling Charts

Grilling is a versatile cooking technique that works well for many foods. The charts below and on the next few pages show you at a glance how long to cook everything from a spur-of-the-moment steak to the holiday bird to corn on the cob.

Direct-Grilling Poultry

If desired, remove skin from poultry. For a charcoal grill, place poultry on grill rack, bone side up, directly over medium coals. Grill, uncovered, for the time given below or until the proper temperature is reached and meat is no longer pink, turning once halfway through grilling. (For a gas grill, preheat grill. Reduce heat to medium. Place poultry on grill rack, bone side down, over heat. Cover and grill as above.)

Test for doneness using a meat thermometer (use an instant-read thermometer to test smaller portions). Thermometer should register 180°, except in breast meat when thermometer should register 170°. Poultry should be tender and no longer pink. If desired, during last 5 to 10 minutes of grilling, brush often with a sauce.

Type of Bird	Weight	Grilling Temperature	Approximate Direct-Grilling Time	Doneness
Chicken				
Chicken, broiler-fryer, half or quarters	1½- to 1¾-pound half or 12- to 14-ounce quarters	Medium	40 to 50 minutes	180°
Chicken breast half, skinned and boned	4 to 5 ounces	Medium	12 to 15 minutes	170°
Chicken thigh, skinned and boned	4 to 5 ounces	Medium	12 to 15 minutes	180°
Meaty chicken pieces (breast halves, thighs, and drumsticks)	2½ to 3 pounds total	Medium	35 to 45 minutes	180°
Turkey				
Turkey breast tenderloin steak	4 to 6 ounces	Medium	12 to 15 minutes	170°

All cooking times are based on poultry removed directly from refrigerator.

Indirect-Grilling Poultry

If desired, remove skin from poultry. Rinse whole birds; pat dry. For a charcoal grill, arrange medium-hot coals around a drip pan. Test for medium heat above the pan. Place unstuffed poultry, breast side up, on grill rack over drip pan. Cover and grill for the time given below or until the proper temperature is reached and meat is no longer pink, adding more charcoal to maintain heat as necessary. (For a gas grill, preheat grill. Adjust for indirect cooking over medium heat. Place unstuffed poultry, breast side up, over unlit burner. Cover and grill as above.) For large poultry cuts and whole birds, we suggest placing the poultry on a rack in a roasting pan and omitting the drip pan.

Test for doneness using a meat thermometer (use an instant-read thermometer to test smaller portions). For whole birds, insert thermometer into the center of an inside thigh muscle, not touching bone. Thermometer should register 180°, except in breast meat when thermometer should register 170°. Poultry should be tender and no longer pink. (Note: Birds vary in size and shape. Use these times as general guides.)

Type of Bird	Weight	Grilling Temperature	Approximate Indirect-Grilling Time	Doneness
Chicken				
Chicken, whole	2½ to 3 pounds 3½ to 4 pounds 4½ to 5 pounds	Medium Medium Medium	1 to 1¼ hours 1¼ to 1¾ hours 1¾ to 2 hours	180° 180° 180°
Chicken breast half, skinned and boned	4 to 5 ounces	Medium	15 to 18 minutes	170°
Chicken, broiler-fryer, half	1½ to 1¾ pounds	Medium	1 to 1¼ hours	180°
Chicken, broiler-fryer, quarters	12 to 14 ounces each	Medium	50 to 60 minutes	180°
Chicken thigh, skinned and boned	4 to 5 ounces	Medium	15 to 18 minutes	180°
Meaty chicken pieces (breast halves, thighs, and drumsticks)	2½ to 3 pounds total	Medium	50 to 60 minutes	180°
Game				
Cornish game hen, whole	1¼ to 1½ pounds	Medium	50 to 60 minutes	180°
Pheasant, whole	2 to 3 pounds	Medium	1 to 1½ hours	180°
Quail, semiboneless	3 to 4 ounces	Medium	15 to 20 minutes	180°
Squab	12 to 16 ounces	Medium	¾ to 1 hour	180°
Turkey				
Turkey, whole	6 to 8 pounds 8 to 12 pounds 12 to 16 pounds	Medium Medium Medium	1¾ to 2½ hours 2½ to 3½ hours 3 to 4 hours	180° 180° 180°
Turkey breast, half	2 to 2½ pounds	Medium	1½ to 2 hours	170°
Turkey breast, whole	4 to 6 pounds 6 to 8 pounds	Medium Medium	1¾ to 2¼ hours 2½ to 3½ hours	170° 170°
Turkey breast tenderloin steak	4 to 6 ounces	Medium	15 to 18 minutes	170°
Turkey drumstick	½ to 1 pound	Medium	¾ to 1¼ hours	180°
Turkey tenderloin	8 to 10 ounces (¾ to 1 inch thick)	Medium	25 to 30 minutes	170°
Turkey thigh	1 to 1½ pounds	Medium	50 to 60 minutes	180°

All cooking times are based on poultry removed directly from refrigerator.

Direct-Grilling Meat

For a charcoal grill, place meat on grill rack directly over medium coals. Grill, uncovered, for the time given below or to desired doneness, turning once halfway through grilling. (For a gas grill, preheat grill. Reduce heat to medium. Place meat on grill rack over heat. Cover and grill as above.) Test for doneness using a meat thermometer.

Cut	Thickness or Weight	Grilling Temperature	Approximate Direct-Grilling Time	Doneness
Beef				
Boneless steak (ribeye, tenderloin, top loin)	1 inch	Medium	11 to 15 minutes	145° medium rare
			14 to 18 minutes	160° medium
	1½ inches	Medium	15 to 19 minutes	145° medium rare
			18 to 23 minutes	160° medium
Boneless top sirloin steak	1 inch	Medium	14 to 18 minutes	145° medium rare
			18 to 22 minutes	160° medium
	1½ inches	Medium	20 to 24 minutes	145° medium rare
			24 to 28 minutes	160° medium
Boneless tri-tip steak (bottom sirloin)	¾ inch	Medium	9 to 11 minutes	145° medium rare
			11 to 13 minutes	160° medium
	1 inch	Medium	13 to 15 minutes	145° medium rare
			15 to 17 minutes	160° medium
Flank steak	1¼ to 1¾ pounds	Medium	17 to 21 minutes	160° medium
Steak with bone (porterhouse, rib, T-bone)	1 inch	Medium	11 to 14 minutes	145° medium rare
			13 to 16 minutes	160° medium
	1½ inches	Medium	18 to 21 minutes	145° medium rare
			22 to 25 minutes	160° medium
Ground Meat				
Patties (beef, lamb, pork, or veal)	½ inch	Medium	10 to 13 minutes	160° medium
	¾ inch	Medium	14 to 18 minutes	160° medium
Lamb				
Chop (loin or rib)	1 inch	Medium	12 to 14 minutes	145° medium rare
			15 to 17 minutes	160° medium
Chop (sirloin)	¾ to 1 inch	Medium	14 to 17 minutes	160° medium
Pork				
Chop with bone (loin or rib)	¾ to 1 inch	Medium	11 to 14 minutes	160° medium
	1¼ to 1½ inches	Medium	18 to 22 minutes	160° medium
Chop (boneless top loin)	¾ to 1 inch	Medium	12 to 15 minutes	160° medium
	1¼ to 1½ inches	Medium	17 to 21 minutes	160° medium
Sausages, cooked (frankfurters, smoked bratwurst, etc.)		Medium	3 to 7 minutes	Heated through
Veal				
Chop (loin or rib)	1 inch	Medium	12 to 15 minutes	160° medium

All cooking times are based on meat removed directly from refrigerator.

Indirect-Grilling Meat

For a charcoal grill, arrange medium-hot coals around a drip pan. Test for medium heat above pan, unless chart says otherwise. Place meat, fat side up, on grill rack over drip pan. Cover and grill for the time given below or to desired temperature, adding more charcoal to maintain heat as necessary. (For a gas grill, preheat grill. Adjust for indirect cooking over medium heat. Place meat, fat side up, over unlit burner. Cover and grill as above.)

To test for doneness, insert a meat thermometer, using an instant-read thermometer to test smaller portions. Thermometer should register the "final grilling temperature." Remove meat from grill. For larger cuts, such as roasts, cover with foil and let stand 15 minutes before carving. The meat's temperature will rise 5° to 10° during the time it stands (thermometer should register "final doneness temperature"). Thinner cuts, such as steaks, do not have to stand.

Cut	Thickness or Weight	Approximate Indirect-Grilling Time	Final Grilling Temperature (when to remove from grill)	Final Doneness Temperature (after 15 minutes standing)
Beef				
Boneless top sirloin steak	1 inch	22 to 26 minutes	145° medium rare	No standing time
		26 to 30 minutes	160° medium	No standing time
	1½ inches	32 to 36 minutes	145° medium rare	No standing time
		36 to 40 minutes	160° medium	No standing time
Boneless tri-tip roast (bottom sirloin)	1½ to 2 pounds	35 to 40 minutes	140°	145° medium rare
		40 to 45 minutes	155°	160° medium
Flank steak	1¼ to 1¾ pounds	23 to 28 minutes	160° medium	No standing time
Ribeye roast (medium-low heat)	4 to 6 pounds	1¼ to 1¾ hours	135°	145° medium rare
		1½ to 2¼ hours	150°	160° medium
Rib roast (chine bone removed) (medium-low heat)	4 to 6 pounds	2 to 2¾ hours	135°	145° medium rare
		2½ to 3¼ hours	150°	160° medium
Steak (porterhouse, rib, ribeye, T-bone, tenderloin, top loin)	1 inch	16 to 20 minutes	145° medium rare	No standing time
		20 to 24 minutes	160° medium	No standing time
	1½ inches	22 to 25 minutes	145° medium rare	No standing time
		25 to 28 minutes	160° medium	No standing time
Tenderloin roast (medium-high heat)	2 to 3 pounds	¾ to 1¼ hours	135°	145° medium rare
	4 to 5 pounds	1¼ to 1½ hours	135°	145° medium rare
Ground Meat				
Patties (beef, lamb, pork, or veal)	½ inch	15 to 18 minutes	160° medium	No standing time
	¾ inch	20 to 24 minutes	160° medium	No standing time
Lamb				
Boneless leg roast (medium-low heat)	3 to 4 pounds	1½ to 2¼ hours	140°	145° medium rare
		1¾ to 2½ hours	155°	160° medium
	4 to 6 pounds	1¾ to 2½ hours	140°	145° medium rare
		2 to 2¾ hours	155°	160° medium
Boneless sirloin roast (medium-low heat)	1½ to 2 pounds	1 to 1¼ hours	140°	145° medium rare
		1¼ to 1½ hours	155°	160° medium

All cooking times are based on meat removed directly from refrigerator.

Cut	Thickness or Weight	Approximate Indirect-Grilling Time	Final Grilling Temperature (when to remove from grill)	Final Doneness Temperature (after 15 minutes standing)
Lamb (continued)				
Chop (loin or rib)	1 inch 1 inch	16 to 18 minutes 18 to 20 minutes	145° medium rare 160° medium	No standing time No standing time
Leg of lamb (with bone) (medium-low heat)	5 to 7 pounds	1¾ to 2¼ hours 2¼ to 2¾ hours	140° 155°	145° medium rare 160° medium
Pork				
Boneless sirloin roast (medium-low heat)	1½ to 2 pounds	1 to 1½ hours	155°	160° medium
Boneless top loin roast (medium-low heat)	2 to 3 pounds (single loin) 3 to 5 pounds (double loin, tied)	1 to 1½ hours 1½ to 2¼ hours	155° 155°	160° medium 160° medium
Chop (boneless top loin)	¾ to 1 inch 1¼ to 1½ inches	20 to 24 minutes 30 to 35 minutes	160° medium 160° medium	No standing time No standing time
Chop (loin or rib)	¾ to 1 inch 1¼ to 1½ inches	22 to 25 minutes 35 to 40 minutes	160° medium 160° medium	No standing time No standing time
Country-style ribs		1½ to 2 hours	Tender	No standing time
Ham, cooked (boneless) (medium-low heat)	3 to 5 pounds 6 to 8 pounds	1½ to 2 hours 2 to 2¾ hours	140° 140°	No standing time No standing time
Ham, cooked (slice) (medium-high heat)	1 inch	20 to 24 minutes	140°	No standing time
Loin back ribs or spareribs		1½ to 1¾ hours	Tender	No standing time
Loin center rib roast (backbone loosened) (medium-low heat)	3 to 4 pounds 4 to 6 pounds	1¼ to 2 hours 2 to 2¾ hours	155° 155°	160° medium 160° medium
Sausages, uncooked (bratwurst, Polish, or Italian sausage links)	about 4 per pound	20 to 30 minutes	160° medium	No standing time
Smoked shoulder picnic (with bone), cooked (medium-low heat)	4 to 6 pounds	1½ to 2¼ hours	140°	No standing time
Tenderloin (medium-high heat)	¾ to 1 pound	40 to 50 minutes	160° medium	No standing time
Veal				
Chop (loin or rib)	1 inch	19 to 23 minutes	160° medium	No standing time

All cooking times are based on meat removed directly from refrigerator.

Direct-Grilling Fish and Seafood

Thaw fish or seafood, if frozen. Place fish fillets in a well-greased grill basket. For fish steaks and whole fish, grease grill rack. Thread scallops or shrimp on skewers, leaving about ¼ inch of space between pieces. For a charcoal grill, place fish on grill rack directly over medium coals. Grill, uncovered, for the time given below or until fish flakes easily when tested with a fork (seafood should look opaque), turning once halfway through grilling. (For a gas grill, preheat grill. Reduce heat to medium. Place fish on grill rack over heat. Cover and grill as above.) If desired, brush fish once with melted butter or margarine halfway through grilling.

Form of Fish	Thickness, Weight, or Size	Grilling Temperature	Approximate Direct-Grilling Time	Doneness
Dressed whole fish	½ to 1½ pounds	Medium	6 to 9 minutes per 8 ounces	Flakes
Fillets, steaks, cubes (for kabobs)	½ to 1 inch thick	Medium	4 to 6 minutes per ½-inch thickness	Flakes
Lobster tails	6 ounces 8 ounces	Medium Medium	6 to 10 minutes 12 to 15 minutes	Opaque Opaque
Sea scallops (for kabobs)	12 to 15 per pound	Medium	5 to 8 minutes	Opaque
Shrimp (for kabobs)	Medium (20 per pound) Jumbo (12 to 15 per pound)	Medium Medium	5 to 8 minutes 7 to 9 minutes	Opaque Opaque

All cooking times are based on fish or seafood removed directly from refrigerator.

Indirect-Grilling Fish and Seafood

Thaw fish or seafood, if frozen. Place fish fillets in a well-greased grill basket. For fish steaks and whole fish, grease grill rack. Thread scallops or shrimp on skewers, leaving a ¼-inch space between pieces. For a charcoal grill, arrange medium-hot coals around a drip pan. Test for medium heat above the pan. Place fish on grill rack over drip pan. Cover and grill for the time given below or until fish flakes easily when tested with a fork (seafood should look opaque), turning once halfway through grilling, if desired. (For a gas grill, preheat grill. Adjust for indirect cooking over medium heat. Place fish on grill rack over unlit burner. Cover and grill as above.) If desired, brush once with melted butter or margarine halfway through grilling.

Form of Fish	Thickness, Weight, or Size	Grilling Temperature	Approximate Indirect-Grilling Time	Doneness
Dressed fish	½ to 1½ pounds	Medium	15 to 20 minutes per 8 ounces	Flakes
Fillets, steaks, cubes (for kabobs)	½ to 1 inch thick	Medium	7 to 9 minutes per ½-inch thickness	Flakes
Sea scallops (for kabobs)	12 to 15 per pound	Medium	11 to 14 minutes	Opaque
Shrimp (for kabobs)	Medium (20 per pound) Jumbo (12 to 15 per pound)	Medium Medium	8 to 10 minutes 9 to 11 minutes	Opaque Opaque

All cooking times are based on fish or seafood removed directly from refrigerator.

Direct-Grilling Vegetables

Before grilling, rinse, trim, cut up, and precook vegetables as directed below. To precook vegetables, bring a small amount of water to boiling in a saucepan; add desired vegetable and simmer, covered, for the time specified in the chart. Drain well. Generously brush vegetables with olive oil, butter, or margarine before grilling to prevent vegetables from sticking to the grill rack. Place vegetables on a piece of heavy foil or directly on grill rack. (If putting vegetables directly on grill rack, lay them perpendicular to wires of the rack so they won't fall into the coals.) For a charcoal grill, place vegetables directly over medium coals. Grill, uncovered, for the time given below or until crisp-tender, turning occasionally. (For a gas grill, preheat grill. Reduce heat to medium. Place vegetables on grill rack directly over heat. Cover and grill as above.) Monitor grilling closely so vegetables don't char.

Vegetable	Preparation	Precooking Time	Approximate Direct-Grilling Time
Asparagus	Snap off and discard tough bases of stems. Precook, then tie asparagus in bundles with strips of cooked green onion tops.	3 minutes	3 to 5 minutes
Baby carrots, fresh	Cut off carrot tops. Wash and peel carrots.	3 to 5 minutes	3 to 5 minutes
Corn on the cob	Peel back corn husks, but do not remove. Remove corn silks. Rinse corn; pat dry. Fold husks back around cobs. Tie husk tops with 100%-cotton kitchen string.	Do not precook	25 to 30 minutes
Eggplant	Cut off top and blossom ends; cut crosswise into 1-inch-thick slices.	Do not precook	8 minutes
Fennel	Snip off feathery leaves; cut off stems.	10 minutes; then cut into 6 to 8 wedges	8 minutes
Leeks	Cut off green tops; trim bulb roots and remove 1 or 2 layers of white skin.	10 minutes or until almost tender; halve lengthwise	5 minutes
New potatoes	Halve potatoes.	10 minutes or until almost tender	10 to 12 minutes
Potatoes	Scrub potatoes; prick with a fork. Wrap individually in a double thickness of foil.	Do not precook	1 to 2 hours
Sweet peppers	Remove stems. Halve peppers lengthwise; remove seeds and membranes. Cut into 1-inch-wide strips.	Do not precook	8 to 10 minutes
Tomatoes	Remove cores; cut in half crosswise.	Do not precook	5 minutes
Zucchini or yellow summer squash	Wash; cut off ends. Quarter lengthwise.	Do not precook	5 to 6 minutes

Index

Metric Information

The charts on this page provide a guide for converting measurements from the U.S. customary system, which is used throughout this book, to the metric system.

Product Differences

Most of the ingredients called for in the recipes in this book are available in most countries. However, some are known by different names. Here are some common American ingredients and their possible counterparts:

- Sugar (white) is granulated, fine granulated, or castor sugar.
- Powdered sugar is icing sugar.
- All-purpose flour is enriched, bleached or unbleached, white household flour. When self-rising flour is used in place of all-purpose flour in a recipe that calls for leavening, omit the leavening agent (baking soda or baking powder) and salt.
- Light-colored corn syrup is golden syrup.
- Cornstarch is cornflour.
- Baking soda is bicarbonate of soda.
- Vanilla or vanilla extract is vanilla essence.
- Green, red, or yellow sweet peppers are capsicums or bell peppers.
- Golden raisins are sultanas.

Volume and Weight

The United States traditionally uses cup measures for liquid and solid ingredients. The chart below shows the approximate imperial and metric equivalents. If you are accustomed to weighing solid ingredients, the following approximate equivalents will be helpful.

- 1 cup butter, castor sugar, or rice = 8 ounces = ½ pound = 250 grams
- 1 cup flour = 4 ounces = ¼ pound = 125 grams
- 1 cup icing sugar = 5 ounces = 150 grams

Canadian and U.S. volume for a cup measure is 8 fluid ounces (237 ml), but the standard metric equivalent is 250 ml.

1 British imperial cup is 10 fluid ounces.

In Australia, 1 tablespoon equals 20 ml, and there are 4 teaspoons in the Australian tablespoon.

Spoon measures are used for smaller amounts of ingredients. Although the size of the tablespoon varies slightly in different countries, for practical purposes and for recipes in this book, a straight substitution is all that's necessary. Measurements made using cups or spoons always should be level unless stated otherwise.

Common Weight Range Replacements

Imperial / U.S.	Metric
½ ounce	15 g
1 ounce	25 g or 30 g
4 ounces (¼ pound)	115 g or 125 g
8 ounces (½ pound)	225 g or 250 g
16 ounces (1 pound)	450 g or 500 g
1¼ pounds	625 g
1½ pounds	750 g
2 pounds or 2¼ pounds	1,000 g or 1 Kg

Oven Temperature Equivalents

Fahrenheit Setting	Celsius Setting*	Gas Setting
300°F	150°C	Gas Mark 2 (very low)
325°F	160°C	Gas Mark 3 (low)
350°F	180°C	Gas Mark 4 (moderate)
375°F	190°C	Gas Mark 5 (moderate)
400°F	200°C	Gas Mark 6 (hot)
425°F	220°C	Gas Mark 7 (hot)
450°F	230°C	Gas Mark 8 (very hot)
475°F	240°C	Gas Mark 9 (very hot)
500°F	260°C	Gas Mark 10 (extremely hot)
Broil	Broil	Grill

*Electric and gas ovens may be calibrated using celsius. However, for an electric oven, increase celsius setting 10 to 20 degrees when cooking above 160°C. For convection or forced air ovens (gas or electric), lower the temperature setting 25°F/10°C when cooking at all heat levels.

Baking Pan Sizes

Imperial / U.S.	Metric
9×1½-inch round cake pan	22- or 23×4-cm (1.5 L)
9×1½-inch pie plate	22- or 23×4-cm (1 L)
8×8×2-inch square cake pan	20×5-cm (2 L)
9×9×2-inch square cake pan	22- or 23×4.5-cm (2.5 L)
11×7×1½-inch baking pan	28×17×4-cm (2 L)
2-quart rectangular baking pan	30×19×4.5-cm (3 L)
13×9×2-inch baking pan	34×22×4.5-cm (3.5 L)
15×10×1-inch jelly roll pan	40×25×2-cm
9×5×3-inch loaf pan	23×13×8-cm (2 L)
2-quart casserole	2 L

U.S./Standard Metric Equivalents

⅛ teaspoon	= 0.5 ml
¼ teaspoon	= 1 ml
½ teaspoon	= 2 ml
1 teaspoon	= 5 ml
1 tablespoon	= 15 ml
2 tablespoons	= 25 ml
¼ cup = 2 fluid ounces	= 50 ml
⅓ cup = 3 fluid ounces	= 75 ml
½ cup = 4 fluid ounces	= 125 ml
⅔ cup = 5 fluid ounces	= 150 ml
¾ cup = 6 fluid ounces	= 175 ml
1 cup = 8 fluid ounces	= 250 ml
2 cups = 1 pint	= 500 ml
1 quart	= 1 litre